SHEET M

A Price Gu

By Debbie Dillon

Published by

L-W BOOK SALES

P.O. Box 69
Gas City, IN 46953

ISBN#: 0-89145-284-2

All sheet music titles are listed alphabetically in this price guide to enable quick reference. In most cases a title that begins with the word "The" will be listed in the section beginning with the letter T. However, there may be a few cases where the word "The" has been left off and you will find it listed under the first letter of the second word of the title.

PRICING INFORMATION

All prices in this book are for sheet music in fine condition.

GRADING

FINE: No tears, no writing, no stains on the cover or inside. In other words (near mint). The prices in this book are for sheet music in fine condition.

GOOD: Some wear, maybe a smudge or small stain, inside complete, small tears less than 3/4 inch. (Approximately 25% off listed price).

FAIR: Some stains, tears and smudges etc. (Approx. 50% off listed price).

POOR: Large tears, stains, generally "beat-up". (Approx. 90% off listed price).

A Bag of Rags, MacKanlass, 1912 .... 6.00
A Beautiful Girl, 1947 .... 2.00
A Bicycle Built for Two, Dacre, 1941 .... 3.00
A Bird From O'er the Sea, White, 1880 .... 30.00
A Bird in a Gilded Cage, Lamb, 1900 .... 15.00
A Boy in Khaki - A Girl in Blue, 1942 .... 3.00
A Bundle of Old Love Letters, 1929 .... 3.00
A Bundle of Southern Sunshine, 1951 .... 2.00
A Daisy a Day, Strunk/Pic, 1972 .... 3.00
A Darn Fool Woman Like Me, Dubin/Burke, 1929 .... 7.00
A Day Without You, 1933 .... 3.00
A Dear John Letter, Barton/Talley/Owen, 1953 .... 5.00
A Dream of Love, Petrosemolo 2.00
A Dream of the South, Lincoln, 1909 .... 10.00
A Feeling in Your Heart, Cohan, 1927 .... 6.00
A Fella With an Umbrella, Garland/Berlin, 1947 .... 5.00
A Fellow on a Furlough, 1943 .... 3.00
A Fine Romance, Kern/Fields, 1936 .... 6.00
A Fool There Was, 1913 .... 3.00
A Full Time Job, Teifer/Arnold, 1952 .... 2.00
A Gal in Calico, 1946 .... 3.00
A Girlie was Just Made to Love, Goodwin, 1911 .... 8.00
A Gypsy Told Me, Pokrass/Yellen, 1938 .... 6.00
A Hot Coon, Mills, 1897 .... 25.00
A Hot Time in the Old Town, Metz, 1896 .... 6.00
A Hundred & 60 Acres, Kapp, 1948 .... 3.00
A Hundred Years From Now, 1914 .... 3.00
A Hymm of Faith, Metcalf, 1902 .... 3.00
A Journey to a Star, 1943 .... 3.00
A Kiss to Build a Dream On, 1951 .... 3.00
A Latin Tune, A Manhattan Moon & You, Dubin/McHugh, 1940 .. 8.00
A Letter to His Dad, 1891 .... 5.00
A Little Birch Canoe and You, Roberts, 1918 .... 3.00
A Little Bit of Heaven, Ball, 1914 .... 3.00
A Little Bit of Honey, Bond, 1917 .... 8.00
A Little Boy Called Taps, Madden/Morse, 1904 .... 8.00
A Little Bunch of Shamrocks, Tilzer, 1913 .... 8.00
A Little Bungalow, Berlin, 1925 .... 6.00
A Little Love, Ross/Silseu, 1912 .... 3.00
A Little More Pepper, Linoln, 1914 .... 15.00
A Little Street Where Old Friends Meet, 1932 .... 3.00
A Lonesome Boy's Letter Back Home, 1926 .... 5.00
A Long, Long Way From Home, 1914 .... 3.00
A Love Tale of Alsace Lorraine, 1928 .... 3.00
A Lovely Way to Spend an Evening, 1943 .... 3.00

A Lover's Lullaby, 1940 .... 2.00
A Man Has Gotta Sing, 1954 .... 2.00
A Man, A Maid, A Moon, A Boat, 1908 .... 5.00
A Marshmallow World, 1949 .... 2.00
A Mid Summer Night's Dream, 1915 .... 2.00
A Midnight Romance, Stewart, 1919 .... 5.00
A Million Dreams, 1932 .... 3.00
A Mother's Prayer, Holt, 1945 .... 3.00
A New Kind of Man, Manning, 1924 .... 6.00
A Night of Kisses, Prival/Farnum, 1919 .... 7.00
A Night on the Pike, Heinzman, 1904 .... 5.00
A Penny a Kiss-A Penny a Hug, 1950 .... 5.00
A Perfect Day, Bond, 1910 .... 3.00
A Picture of Dear Old Ireland, Costello, 1916 .... 10.00
A Plantation Medley, Snow, 1905 .... 15.00
A Pretty Girl is Like a Melody, Berlin, 1919 .... 5.00
A Regular Guy, Sissle/Blake, 1922 .... 6.00
A Rose with a Broken Stem, Evans, 1937 .... 2.00
A Rural Festival, Losey, 1908 .... 7.00
A Sailor's Not A Sailor, Berlin, 1954 .... 15.00
A Signal From Mars, Paull, 1901 .... 35.00
A Sinner Kissed an Angel, 1941 .... 3.00
A Song of Old Kilkenny, Baer 2.00
A Song of the Hills, Bond, 1915 .... 7.00
A Song of the Oak, 1906 .... 3.00
A Southern Jamboree, 1898 .... 18.00
A Story of the Shamrock, 1890 .... 4.00
A Summer's Night Out on the Blue, 1906 .... 4.00
A Sweetheart of a Boy in Blue, 1906 .... 5.00
A Touch of Texas, Loesser/McHugh, 1942 .... 3.00
A Trip to Niagra, Cornish, 1904 .... 20.00
A Twentieth Century Woman, 1910 .... 3.00
A Wandering Minstrel, From Mikado, 1910 .... 2.00
A Warm Proposition, Rosenfeld, 1899 .... 20.00
A Warm Reception, Anthony, 1899 .... 20.00
A Warmin' Up in Dixie, Paull, 1899 .... 35.00
A Wedding Day Alphabet, Toy, 1907 .... 5.00
A Yankee Cutup, McHugh, 1907 .... 8.00
Aaraby, Berlin, 1915 .... 15.00
Aba Daba Honeymoon, Fields/Donovan, 1914 .... 2.00
Abdul the Bulbul Ameer, 1935 .... 2.00
Abide With Me, Liddle, 1896 .... 5.00
About a Quarter to Nine, Warren/Dublin, 1935 .... 3.00
Above the Moon, Tardiff/Lessard, 1920 .... 3.00
Ac-Cent-Tchu-Ate the Positive, 1946 .... 3.00

Accent on Youth, 1935 .... 2.00
Across the Continent, Marvin, 1910 .... 12.00
Across the Wide Missouri, Shirl/Drake, 1951 .... 2.00
Actor's Lonely Grave, 1888 .... 8.00
Adam and Eve Had a Wonderful Time, 1913 .... 7.00
Adele, Briquet/Philipp, 1913 .... 3.00
Adios Muchachos, 1942 .... 2.00
Adorable, 1933 .... 3.00
Afraid to Dream, Gordon/Revel, 1937 .... 3.00
Africa, 1924 .... 2.00
Africana, Berliner, 1903 .... 15.00
After All I've Been to You, Drislane/Smith, 1912 .... 3.00
After All, Callahan, 1919 .... 5.00
After Sundown, 1933 .... 3.00
After the Ball, Harris, 1892 .... 10.00
After the Battle, Dresser, 1905 .... 15.00
After the First of July, Allen, 1919 .... 5.00
After the Roses, 1914 .... 2.00
After the War is Over, 1917 .... 20.00
After We Kiss, 1927 .... 2.00
After You're Gone, Waldron, 1926 .... 5.00
After You've Gone, Layton, 1918 .... 10.00
Again, Abbott/Stults, 1904 .... 3.00
Again, Sweetheart, Again, 1908 .... 3.00
Ah-Ha!, Clare, 1925 .... 8.00
Ain't She Sweet, 1927 .... 4.00
Ain't We Got Fun, 1921 .... 2.00
Ain't You Ashamed, Simons, 1923 .... 2.00
Ain't You Coming Back to Dixieland, Jolson, 1917 .... 15.00
Alabama Jubilee, Cobb, 1915 .... 15.00
Alabamy Bound, 1925 .... 5.00
Alagazam, Holzman, 1902 .... 15.00
Alamo Rag, Dealy/Wenrich, 1910 .... 12.00
Alexander's Back From Dixie, 1917 .... 15.00
Alexander's Ragtime Band, Berlin, 1911 .... 22.00
Alexander, Don't You Love Your Baby No More, 1904 .... 10.00
Algeria, Herbert, 1908 .... 10.00
All Aboard For Blanket Bay, Tilzer, 1910 .... 3.00
All Aboard For Chinatown, Davis, 1915 .... 6.00
All Alone, 1924 .... 3.00
All Ashore, Hill, 1938 .... 2.00
All By Myself, 1921 .... 3.00
All Dressed Up, With a Broken Heart, 1946 .... 2.00
All I Do Is Dream of You, 1934 .... 2.00
All Full of Talk, Wodehouse/Kern, 1916 .... 15.00

5

**Pictured above is a small selection of
Sheet Music Covers that are listed within this book.**

All I Need is a Girl Like You, Burkhart/Olman, 1917 .... 3.00
All I Want in This World Is You, Phillips, 1912 .... 2.00
All I Want Is a Cottage, Some Roses & You, 1916 .... 5.00
All I Want Is One Loving Smile From You-Oo-Oo 3.00
All My Love, Jolson, 1942 .... 10.00
All Night Long, Brooks/Wilson, 1912 .... 3.00
All of a Sudden, 1932 .... 2.00
All Over Nothing at All, Rule, 1922 .... 5.00
All She'd Say Was Umh-Hum, Emery, 1920 .... 2.00
All That I Want, 1923 .... 2.00
All the Things You Are, 1939 .... 2.00
All the Way, Cahn/Van Huesen, 1957 .... 3.00
All the World Will Be Jealous of Me, 1917 .... 3.00
All the Wrongs You've Done To Me, 1924 .... 6.00
All Through the Day 3.00
Allegiance, Smith, 1918 .... 2.00
Aloha Oe-Lilvokalani, 1915 .... 3.00
Aloha Soldier Boy, 1918 .... 3.00
Alone, 1935 .... 10.00
Alone With Memory, 1931 .... 3.00
Alone With My Sorrows, 1932 .... 5.00
Alone, Brown/Freed, 1935 .... 6.00
Along Came Ruth, Berlin, 1914 .... 15.00
Along the Navajo Trail, 1942 .... 3.00
Along the Road to Singapore, 1915 .... 3.00
Along the Rocky Road to Dublin, 1915 .... 8.00
Along the Santa Fe Trail, 1940 .... 3.00
Along the Way to Waikiki, Jolson, 1917 .... 15.00
Alpine Hut, Lang, 1907 .... 3.00
Alsacian Railroad Gallops, Guignard, 1845 .... 65.00
Always and Always, 1937 .... 6.00
Always in the Way, Harris, 1903 .... 5.00
Always Remember Mother, 1909 .... 3.00
Always Take a Girl Named Daisy, 1913 .... 4.00
Always Take Mother's Advice, 1894 .... 8.00
Always the Same Sweet Pal, 1928 .... 2.00
Always Think of Mother, Haller/Stafford, 1908 .... 3.00
Always, Berlin, 1925 .... 6.00
Am I Blue, 1929 .... 3.00
Am I in Love, 1937 .... 2.00
Am I That Easy to Forget, 1958 .... 2.00
Am I Wasting My Time on You, Johnson, 1926 .... 2.00
Am I Wasting My Time, 1931 .... 3.00
Ambolena Show, Bodine & Maywood, 1897 .... 8.00
Amelia Earhart's Last Flight, McEnery, 1939 .... 40.00

America Forever March, Paull, 1898 .... 30.00
America Here's My Boy, Sterling/Lang, 1917.............................. 15.00
America I Love You, Leslie, 1915 .... 25.00
America Needs You Like a Mother, Schwartz, 1917 .... 5.00
America Prepare, Day, 1916... 3.00
American Beauty Rose, 1950 .... 2.00
American Beauty, Pragg, 1917 .... 3.00
American Guard, Pratt, 1897 .... 10.00
American Marsailliase, Michel, 1898 .... 25.00
American Patrol, 1942 .... 3.00
Americana's Boys, 1917.. 3.00
Americans Come, Foster, 1918... 3.00
Among the Whispering Pines, 1928 .... 5.00
An Afterthought, Henneman, 1905... 5.00
An American in Paris, Gershwin, 1929 .... 8.00
An Apple for the Teacher, 1939 .... 3.00
An Earful of Music, Kahn/Donaldson, 1934.............................. 3.00
An Echo of Her Smile, 1918 .... 4.00
An Egyptian Love Dance, Pryer, 1907... 5.00
An Old Fashioned Home in New Hampshire, 1931 .... 3.00
An Old Grand Army Man, DeCosta, 1918................................... 8.00
An Old Horse that Knows His Name, 1917 .... 3.00
An Old Virginia, Gustin, 1899... 15.00
An Old-Fashioned Wife, 1917.. 3.00
An Operatic Nightmare, Arndt, 1916.. 5.00
Anastasia, 1956... 8.00
Anchored, Watson.. 12.00
And A Little Child Shall Lead Them, 1906 .... 3.00
And God Shall Wipe Away All the Tears, 1901 .... 3.00
And He'd Say Oo-La-Wee-Wee, Ruby/Jessell, 1919.................... 3.00
And Her Tears Flowed Like Wine, 1944 .... 3.00
And It Still Goes, 1949... 2.00
And Still I Care, 1931 .... 2.00
And That Ain't All, 1919... 4.00
And Then I Forget, 1926 .... 3.00
And Then Your Lips Met Mine, 1930 .... 4.00
And Then, Bryan/Paley, 1913 .... 8.00
And There You Are, 1945 .... 3.00
And They Call It Dixieland, 1916... 15.00
And Yet, Bowles/Hathaway, 1917 .... 2.00
And You'll Be Home, Burke/Van Heusen, 1950 .... 10.00
Angel Child, 1922 .... 3.00
Angel Eyes, Bryan/Paley, 1909 .... 5.00
Angela Mia, 1928 .... 15.00
Angels of Mercy, Berlin, 1941 .... 6.00

Angry, Mecum, 1925.. 3.00
Annie Doesn't Live Here Anymore, 1933 .... 6.00
Annie Laurie, 1935 .... 4.00
Anniversary Song, 1946 .... 3.00
Another Rag, Morse/Esrom, 1911 .... 7.00
Answer, Robyn, 1908 .... 3.00
Any Little Girl's a Nice Little Girl...., 1910 .... 3.00
Any Rags, Allen, 1902 .... 15.00
Any Time, Lawson, 1921 .... 3.00
Appassionata, Jones, 1916 .... 3.00
Apple Blossoms and Chapel Bells, 1939 .... 3.00
Apple Tree and the Bumble Bee, Berlin, 1913 .... 10.00
April Showers, Jolson, 1921 .... 8.00
Arabella, I'll Be Your Fella, Hotchkiss, 1921 .... 5.00
Araby, Berlin, 1915 .... 7.00
Are You Sincere, Herbert, 1917 .... 6.00
Are you From Dixie, Yellen/Cobb, 1915 .... 15.00
Are you From Heaven, 1917 .... 3.00
Aren't You Glad You're Here, 1945 .... 3.00
Arizona, Smith/Paull, 1903 .... 25.00
Arkansas Traveler, Weybright, 1948 .... 3.00
Arkansas, 1943 .... 3.00
Army and Navy, Branham, 1911 .... 6.00
Army Bonds Today, Berlin, 1941 .... 15.00
Arrah Go On I'm Gonna Go Back to Oregon, 1916 .... 3.00
Art Song, Herbert, 1917 .... 6.00
As in Days of Old, Stauffer-Conley, 1908 .... 5.00
As Long as I Live, 1944 .... 6.00
As The Lusitania Went Down, Pfeiffer, 1913 .... 15.00
As the Petals Fall, Allison/Kellog, 1913 .... 3.00
As Time Goes By, 1931 .... 6.00
Ask My Heart, 1949 .... 2.00
Asthmore, Bingham/Trotere, 1893 .... 5.00
At a Georgia Campmeeting, Mills, 1897 .... 15.00
At An Ole Virginia Wedding, 1899 .... 40.00
At Last, 1942 .... 6.00
At Peace With the World, Berlin, 1926 .... 3.00
At Sundown, Donaldson, 1927...................................... 5.00
At That Bully Wooly Wild West Show, 1913 .... 15.00
At the Devil's Ball, Berlin, 1913 .... 15.00
At the End of a Beautiful Day, Perrins, 1916 .... 3.00
At the End of the Road, MacDonald, 1924 .... 3.00
At the Flying "W", 1948... 3.00
At the Gate of the Palace of Dreams, 1912........................ 3.00
At the Midnight Masquerade, 1913 .... 3.00

At the Mississippi Cabaret, Gumble, 1914 .... 15.00
At the Rag Time Ball, Lewis/Monaco, 1911 .... 10.00
At the Shim-Me-Sha-Wabbler's Ball, Lewis, 1918 .... 15.00
Au Revoir, But Not Good Bye, Von Tilzer, 1917 .... 6.00
Auf Wiedersehn, Romberg, 1915 .... 3.00
Aunt Jemima's Picnic Day, 1914 .... 25.00
Aunt Mandy's Wedding March, 1899 .... 30.00
Auto Race, Wenrich, 1908 .... 25.00
Automobile Honeymoon, Norris, 1902 .... 15.00
Automobiling, Parker, 1905 .... 15.00
Autumn Leaves, Ellis, 1905 .... 5.00
Avalon, Jolson, 1920 .... 7.00
Babalu, Lecuona, 1939 .... 8.00
Babes in the Woods, 1915 .... 2.00
Babes in Toyland, 1903 .... 3.00
Baby It's Cold Outside, 1949, "Neptune's Daughter" 5.00
Baby Shoes, Goodwin/Piantadosi, 1916 .... 5.00
Baby Won't You Please Come Home, 1919 .... 3.00
Baby's Birthday Party, Ronell, 1930 .... 2.00
Baby, I Found Out All About You, Mason, 1947 .... 2.00
Baby, MacDonald & Mallinson, 1901 .... 5.00
Bachelor Days, Buck/Hirsch, 1916 .... 3.00
Back Among the Old Folks Once Again, 1893 .... 4.00
Back Back Back to Indiana, 1914 .... 3.00
Back Home for Keeps, 1945 .... 2.00
Back Home in Tennessee, Donaldson, 1915 .... 12.00
Back in Your Own Backyard, Jolson, 1928 .... 15.00
Back To Dixieland, Yellen, 1914 .... 12.00
Back to Hawaii and Me, 1917 .... 3.00
Back to Mother, 1917 .... 2.00
Back to the Carolina You Love, 1914 .... 2.00
Bagpipe Dance, Sawyer, 1919 .... 3.00
Balck Eyed Susan Brown, 1933 .... 2.00
Bali Ha'i, 1949 .... 2.00
Ballad of Davy Crockett, 1954 .... 2.00
Ballin' the Jack, Burris/Smith, 1913 .... 8.00
Bambalina, 1923 .... 2.00
Bamboola, Wenrich, 1920 .... 2.00
Band Played On, 1926 .... 3.00
Bar Room Polka, 1949 .... 2.00
Barbara Polka, 1940 .... 2.00
Bartels Purity March, Walkingshaw, 1909 .... 15.00
Battle Cry Of Freedom, 1862 .... 60.00
Battle in the Sky, Luxton, 1915 .... 35.00
Battle of the Nations, Paull, 1915 .... 20.00

**Pictured above is a small selection of
Sheet Music Covers that are listed within this book.**

Battle Song, Harry Ruby, 1916 .... 12.00
Battlefields of France, P. J. O'Neill, 1918 .... 10.00
Be Careful It's My Heart, Berlin, 1942 .... 8.00
Be My Little Baby Bumble Bee, Murphy/Marshall, 1912 .... 3.00
Be My Love, 1949 .... 2.00
Beale Street Mama, 1923 .... 10.00
Beatrice Fairfax Tell Me What To Do, 1915 .... 4.00
Beautiful Annabell Lee, Meyer, 1920 .... 2.00
Beautiful Faces, Berlin, 1920 .... 6.00
Beautiful Girl of Somewhere, 1918 .... 3.00
Beautiful Isle of Somewhere, Fearis, 1901 .... 10.00
Beautiful Land of Somewhere, Haywood, 1918 .... 2.00
Beautiful Ohio, 1918 .... 3.00
Beautiful Shells, 1886 .... 20.00
Beautiful Thoughts of Love, Heller, 1910 .... 2.00
Beautiful Wisconsin, 1949 .... 2.00
Bebe, 1923 .... 8.00
Because He Loves His Mother, 1899 .... 10.00
Because I Love You Truly, 1915 .... 3.00
Because I Love You, Berlin, 1926 .... 6.00
Because of You, 1898 .... 6.00
Because of You, Briggs, 1903 .... 3.00
Because You Love Me, Payne, 1950 .... 2.00
Because, 1902 .... 3.00
Becky From Babylon, 1920 .... 3.00
Becky Joined A Musical Show, Berlin, 1912 .... 10.00
Bedelia, 1903 .... 3.00
Beeswax Rag, 1911 .... 20.00
Before We Say Goodbye, Stillman/Lewis, 1969 .... 8.00
Begin the Beguine, Porter, 1935 .... 3.00
Behind These Gray Walls, 1926 .... 2.00
Belgian Rose, Benoit/Levenson/Garton, 1918 .... 10.00
Belgian Rose, Hart/Nelson, 1917 .... 8.00
Believe Me If All Those Endearing Young Charms, 1912 .... 3.00
Belle Of the Cakewalk, O'Connor, 1897 .... 20.00
Bells of St. Mary's, Adams 2.00
Bells of Trinity, Arnold/Brown, 1913 .... 2.00
Bells, Berlin, 1920 .... 10.00
Belly Up to the Bar, Boys, 1960 .... 5.00
Beloved, Kahn, 1928 .... 2.00
Benzine Buggy Man, Kramer, 1908 .... 20.00
Best Place of All, 1910 .... 3.00
Beta Tau Sigman Song, 1918 .... 2.00
Betrothed, 1905 .... 3.00
Betty, Black, 1919 .... 2.00

Between Sweetie and Me, 1925 .... 2.00
Bibbidi-Bobbidi-Boo, 1949 .... 15.00
Big Boy, Yellen, 1924 .... 6.00
Big Brown Bear, 1919 .... 10.00
Big Chief Battle-Axe, Allen, 1907 .... 10.00
Big Four Two-Step, Bernard, 1897 .... 25.00
Big Indian Chief, 1904 .... 7.00
Big Noise From Winnetka, Crosby, 1940 .... 8.00
Big Red Motor & the Little Blue Limousine, Whiting, 1913 .... 20.00
Big Rock Candy Mountain, 1935 .... 3.00
Bill Bailey, Won't You Please Come Home, Cannon, 1965 .... 2.00
Billet Doux, 1900 .... 3.00
Billie's Big Bank Girl, 1914 .... 5.00
Billie-Joe, Goodwin/Kendis/Paley, 1911 .... 5.00
Billy Dear, 1907 .... 3.00
Billy-Billy Bounce Your Baby Doll, McCarthy, 1912 .... 2.00
Bimini Bay, 1921 .... 2.00
Bird on Nellie's Hat, 1906 .... 10.00
Birth of Passion, 1910 .... 3.00
Black Bottom, 1926 .... 2.00
Black Diamond Express, Alexander, 1897 .... 35.00
Black Eyed Blues, 1922 .... 8.00
Black Hawk, Walsh, 1908 .... 3.00
Black Sheep Loves You Best of All, 1897 .... 15.00
Blacksmith Rag, Rednip, 1920 .... 12.00
Bless Em All, 1950 .... 2.00
Bless My Swanee River Home, 1919 .... 3.00
Blossoms on Broadway, 1937 .... 2.00
Blow the Smoke Away, 1906 .... 3.00
Blue and Gold, 1907 .... 5.00
Blue and the Grey, 1900 .... 15.00
Blue Baby, 1927 .... 2.00
Blue Bell, 1924 .... 2.00
Blue Bells of Scotland, 1882 .... 35.00
Blue Bird, Graff/Grant, 1917 .... 2.00
Blue Danube Blues, 1921 .... 4.00
Blue Diamonds, 1920 .... 2.00
Blue Evening Blues, 1924 .... 4.00
Blue Feather, Mahoney, 1909 .... 5.00
Blue For A Boy, Davies/Purcell, 1950 .... 8.00
Blue Hawaii, Robin/Rainger, 1937 .... 8.00
Blue Hoosier Blues, 1923 .... 3.00
Blue Kentucky Moon, 1931 .... 2.00
Blue Line Galop, Stephens, 1867 .... 60.00
Blue Moon, 1921 .... 3.00

Blue of the Night, 1931 .... 2.00
Blue Orchids, 1939 .... 2.00
Blue Over You, Davis, 1928 .... 2.00
Blue Pacific Moonlight, 1930 .... 2.00
Blue Ridge Sweetheart, 1929 .... 3.00
Blue River, Meyer, 1927 .... 2.00
Blue Velvet, 1951 .... 2.00
Blue, 1922 .... 2.00
Blue, Handman, 1922 .... 2.00
Blue-Just Blue, Bafunno, 1916 .... 5.00
Blues in the Night, 1941 .... 2.00
Blues in the Night, 1941 .... 2.00
Blues My Naughty Sweetie Gives to Me, Swanstone, 1919 .... 8.00
Blues, 1919 .... 2.00
Bo-Peep, Cooke, 1916 .... 5.00
Bobbin' Up and Down, Esrom, 1913 .... 15.00
Bombay, Jardon, 1907 .... 6.00
Bon Voyage and Return, 1918 .... 3.00
Boo Boo Boo, 1894 .... 6.00
Boo-Hoo-Hoo, 1922 .... 3.00
Boogie Woogie Bugle Boy, 1941 .... 4.00
Boom Our State, Verge, 1921 .... 2.00
Born and Bred in Brooklyn, Cohan, 1923 .... 10.00
Born at Sea and a Sailor, Graham, 1898 .... 20.00
Born to Lose, 1943 .... 2.00
Botch-A Me, 1941 .... 2.00
Boulevard March, Hussar, 1912 .... 3.00
Boulevard of Nightingales, 1954 .... 2.00
Bounding Billows, Elliot, 1827 .... 35.00
Bouquet of Roses, 1949 .... 2.00
Bow Wow Blues, 1921 .... 3.00
Boys in Blue Are Turning Gray, 1895 .... 25.00
Brave Jennie Creek, Newkirk, 1895 .... 30.00
Bravest Heart of All, Egan/Whiting, 1917 .... 10.00
Break the News to Mother, Harris, 1897 .... 20.00
Breezin' Along with the Breeze, 1926 .... 15.00
Bride and Groom Polka, 1948 .... 2.00
Bright Mohawk Valley, 1935 .... 3.00
Bring Back My Golden Dreams, 1911 .... 2.00
Broadway Baby Dolls, 1929 .... 6.00
Broadway Blues, Sherman, 1915 .... 3.00
Broadway Melody, 1929 .... 6.00
Broadway Rose, 1920 .... 2.00
Broadway's Gone Hawaii, 1937 .... 3.00
Broadway, Brown/Paley, 1913 .... 3.00

Broken Blossoms, 1919 .... 3.00
Broken Vows, 1947 .... 2.00
Broken-Down, Merry-Go-Round, 1950 .... 2.00
Broncho Buster, Madden/Jordon, 1907 .... 5.00
Broncho Sal, 1909 .... 5.00
Brother Can You Spare A Dime, 1932 .... 2.00
Buddy, 1920 .... 2.00
Bugle Blasts, Wayne, 1906 .... 3.00
Bugle Call Rag, 1923 .... 4.00
Build a Little Home, 1933 .... 4.00
Bumming Around, Graves, 1953 .... 3.00
Bump, Bump, Bump in Your Automobile, Tilzer, 1912 .... 25.00
Bunker Hill Quickstep, Prentice, 1836 .... 50.00
Burlington Bertie from Bow, Hargraves, 1915 .... 10.00
Burning Love, 1912 .... 4.00
Burning of Rome, Paull, 1908 .... 25.00
Burning Sands, 1922 .... 4.00
Bury Me Out ion the Prairie, Manoloff, 1935 .... 3.00
Busybody, 1952 .... 2.00
Buttons and Bows, 1948 .... 8.00
Buy A Liberty Bond For the Baby, Moran/Tilzer, 1917 .... 12.00
Buzzin' the Bee, Wells, 1917 .... 6.00
By All the Stars Above You, 1930 .... 3.00
By and By, Burleigh, 1917 .... 8.00
By Heck, Henry, 1914 .... 12.00
By the Beautiful Sea, Pfeiffer, 1914 .... 14.00
By the Light of the Jungle Moon, Ford, 1911 .... 3.00
By the Old Cathedral Door, Lamb/Solman, 1912 .... 3.00
By the Old Mill Where Waterlillies Grow, Morgan, 1912 .... 15.00
By the Watermelon Vine, Allen, 1904 .... 10.00
Bye Baby Bye, Powell, 1889 .... 10.00
Bye Bye Blackbird, 1926 .... 3.00
Byrd (You're the Bird of Them All), 1935 .... 30.00
C'est Magnifique, Porter, 1953 .... 3.00
Cairo Blues, Perillo/Rossman, 1919 .... 6.00
Cairo, 1909 .... 3.00
Cake Walk Neath the Dixie Moon, Allan 22.00
Calcutta, 1958 .... 2.00
California and You, Leslie, 1912 .... 5.00
Call Me Back Again, 1884, ... 4.00
Call Me Back Pal of Mine, Rossiter, 1910 .... 5.00
Call Me Irresponsible, 1963 .... 5.00
Call Me Up Some Rainy Afternoon, Berlin, 1910 .... 8.00
Call of the Canyon, Hill, 1940 .... 2.00
Campin' On De Ole Su Wanee, Smith 10.00

**Pictured above is a small selection of
Sheet Music Covers that are listed within this book.**

Campus Rag, Richmond, 1911 .... 20.00
Can You Blame the Woman After All, 1916 .... 3.00
Can You Guess ?, Drake, 1943 .... 6.00
Can't Help Lovin Dat Man, 1927 .... 7.00
Can't We Be Friends, 1929 .... 2.00
Can't You Love Me Like You Do in Dreams, Weeks, 1918 .... 3.00
Can't You Understand, Osterman/Young, 1929 .... 8.00
Canadian Capers, 1921 .... 2.00
Candlelight and Wine, 1943 .... 2.00
Candy, 1944 .... 5.00
Caprice De Concert, Hoffman, 1860 .... 18.00
Captain Baby Bunting, 1906 .... 8.00
Captive, Hawthorne, 1909 .... 5.00
Caravan, 1937 .... 2.00
Careless, Quadling, 1939 .... 2.00
Carioca, 1933 .... 6.00
Carnation, Noonan, 1907 .... 4.00
Carolina Mammy, 1923 .... 25.00
Carolina Rolling Stone, 1922 .... 2.00
Carolina Sunshine, Hirsch, 1919 .... 6.00
Carolina Town, 1937 .... 2.00
Carry Me Back to Old Virginny, Bland, 1906 .... 10.00
Carry Me Back to the Lone Prairie, Robison, 1934 .... 4.00
Casey Jones Went Down on the Robert E. Lee, 1912 .... 10.00
Casey Jones, Newton, 1909 .... 25.00
Castillian Dreams, 1914 .... 3.00
Castle Rock, Sears 2.00
Castles of Dreams, 1919 .... 3.00
Cat Tails, Crayton, 1927 .... 23.00
Catalina, Gay, 1921 .... 2.00
Cause I Feel Low-Down, 1928 .... 2.00
Cavalier Rustican, Williams/VanAlstyne, 1910 .... 10.00
Cazneau's Quick Step, Thayer, 1842 .... 35.00
Cecile, McKee, 1914 .... 2.00
Celistia, 1915 .... 4.00
Chant of the Jungle, 1929 .... 5.00
Chante Moi, 1950 .... 2.00
Chantilly Lace, Richardson, 1958 .... 6.00
Chapel Chimes, Greenwald, 1913 .... 3.00
Chapel in the Forest, Jungman, 1914 .... 3.00
Charge of the Light Brigade, Paull, 1896 .... 25.00
Charge of the Uhland, Bohm, 1912 .... 20.00
Chariot Race, Paull, 1894 .... 30.00
Charity, 1904 .... 4.00
Charmaine, Rapee, 1926 .... 15.00

Charming, Grey, 1929 .... 2.00
Chattanooga Choo Choo, Gordon, 1941 .... 9.00
Chatterbox, 1939 .... 2.00
Che Faro Senza Euridice, Millard 3.00
Cheatin' on Me, Yellen, 1925 .... 3.00
Cheating Muchachita, 1935 .... 8.00
Checkers, 1919 .... 3.00
Cheek to Cheek, Berlin, 1935 .... 9.00
Cheer Up Father Cheer Up Mother, 1918 .... 6.00
Cheer Up Mary, Bryan/Pauley, 1906 .... 4.00
Cheerful Little Earful, 1930 .... 2.00
Cherie, I Love You, Goodman, 1926 .... 2.00
Cherry Blossom Time, 1951 .... 2.00
Cherry Pink and Apple Blossom White, Russell, 1951 .... 8.00
Chew Tobacco Rag, Briggs, 1951 .... 10.00
Chi-Nee, Cravello, 1921 .... 2.00
Chicago, Fisher, 1922 .... 34.00
Chicken Chowder, Giblin, 1910 .... 15.00
Chicken Reel, 1910 .... 9.00
Childhood, Bryan, 1908 .... 10.00
Chili Bean, 1920 .... 6.00
Chili Sauce Rag, Fischer, 1910 .... 15.00
Chimes of Normandy, Wells, 1918 .... 6.00
China Girl, 1924 .... 3.00
China Moon, 1920 .... 3.00
Chinatown, My Chinatown, Jerome/Schwartz, 1910 .... 4.00
Chinese Blues, Moorc, 1915 .... 6.00
Chinese Lullaby, Bowers, 1919 .... 2.00
Chinese Temple Garden, 1923 .... 2.00
Ching A Ling's Jazz Bazaar, Johnson, 1920 .... 15.00
Ching Chong, Callahan/Roberts, 1917 .... 7.00
Chiquita, Wayne, 1928 .... 2.00
Cho Cho San, 1921 .... 2.00
Choc'late Ice Cream Cone, 1943 .... 2.00
Chocolate Creams, Burke 30.00
Chong-Weeks, 1919 .... 6.00
Choo Choo Ch'Boogie, 1945 .... 2.00
Christ in Flanders, 1919 .... 3.00
Christmas Alphabet, 1954 .... 2.00
Christopher Robin Is Saving His Prayers, 1924 .... 8.00
Chrsitmas, Carson, 1949 .... 2.00
Cincinnati Dancing Pig, Lewis, 1950 .... 2.00
Cinderella, Powell, 1906 .... 2.00
Circus Day in Dixie, 1915 .... 4.00
Ciribiribin, Pestalooza, 1909 .... 8.00

City of Dreams, 1918 .... 2.00
Cla-wench (Don't Tweat Me So Wuff), Manuel, 1923 .... 12.00
Clap My Hands, Riley/Farley 2.00
Clarinet Polka, 1940 .... 2.00
Clayton's Grant March, Blake, 1905 .... 10.00
Cleanin' My Rifle, Wrubel, 1943 .... 4.00
Cleopatra Had a Jazz Band, Morgan, 1917 .... 15.00
Clicquot, Reser, 1926 .... 3.00
Climbing Up the Golden Stairs, 1935 .... 2.00
Close As Pages in a Book, 1944 .... 2.00
Close to My Heart, Sterling, 1915 .... 8.00
Close to You, 1936 .... 2.00
Close to Your Heart, Tilzer, 1920 .... 3.00
Clouds Will Soon Roll By, 1932 .... 2.00
Coal Black Mammy, Cliff, 1921 .... 15.00
Coax Me a Little Bit, 1946 .... 2.00
Cobble Stones, 1927 .... 2.00
Cock-A doodle Doo, Friend, 1922 .... 2.00
Cocktails for Two, 1934 .... 6.00
Cold, Cold Heart, Williams, 1951 .... 3.00
Colleen Bawn, 1906 .... 3.00
Colonial Love, Grooms, 1913 .... 3.00
Colorado Sunset, 1938 .... 2.00
Colorado, 1924 .... 2.00
Colored Aristocracy Cake Walk, Bernard, 1899 .... 3.00
Columbia the Gem Of the Ocean, 1843 .... 30.00
Columbia's Call, Wyman, 1917 .... 12.00
Come Along Boys, Jefford, 1917 .... 20.00
Come Along With Me, Porter, 1953 .... 6.00
Come Back Any Old Time, 1913 .... 3.00
Come Back Home to Old Kentucky, Reisner, 1915 .... 3.00
Come Back to Arizona, Bryan, 1916 .... 3.00
Come Back to Erin, Claribel, 1909 .... 8.00
Come Back to Your Little Grey Home, Freema, 1915 .... 3.00
Come Back, Dixie, 1915 .... 5.00
Come Back, Harris, 1916 .... 3.00
Come Easy, Go Easy Sweetheart, 1926 .... 2.00
Come Josephine in My Flying Machine, Fischer, 1910 .... 30.00
Come On and Play Wiz Me, Kalmar, 1919 .... 8.00
Come On For A Jolly Good Time, Flanders, 1916 .... 25.00
Come on Down to Cincinnati Town, Yellen/Cobb, 1916 .... 3.00
Come on Over Mary to Old Father John, Lyons, 1917 .... 3.00
Come on Papa, Ruby, 1918 .... 12.00
Come Out of the Kitchen Mary Ann, 1915 .... 6.00
Come Over to Dover, 1914 .... 3.00

Come to Baby Do, 1945	5.00
Come to Bohemia, 1916	3.00
Come to Me Love, Merrill & Dinsmore, 1913	3.00
Come to Me Now When I Need You, 1916	3.00
Come to the Moon, Gershwin, 1919	10.00
Come Ye Lofty, Come Ye Lowly, Warren, 1897	15.00
Comical Eyes, 1909	7.00
Comin' in on A Wing and A Prayer, 1943	3.00
Comin' Thru the Rye, Burns, 1938	2.00
Comrades in France, 1919	4.00
Concerto for Two, 1941	2.00
Congo Love Song, 1903	4.00
Connecticut March, Nassann, 1921	5.00
Conover March, Arnold, 1893	22.00
Constantly, 1942	4.00
Consternation, 1949	2.00
Contrary Mary Clary, 1915	3.00
Convent Bells, Ludovic, 1902	3.00
Coo-Se-Coo, 1942	2.00
Cool Water, 1936	2.00
Coon, Coon, Coon, Jefferson, 1901	30.00
Coons In the Canebrake, Clayson, 1900	25.00
Copenhagen, 1924	2.00
Coquette, Berlin, 1928	7.00
Corn Flower Waltz, Coote, 1912	3.00
Corn Huskin', Corin, 1908	15.00
Corns for My Country, 1944	3.00
Cossack Love Song, Gershwin, 1926	3.00
Cottage By the Moon, 1936	2.00
Cotton Pickers, Tarbox, 1899	25.00
Cotton Time, 1910	10.00
Could Be, Donaldson, 1938	2.00
Could the Dreams of a Dreamer Come True, 1915	4.00
Could You Ever Learn to Love Me, 1918	3.00
Countin' Sheep, Fortner, 1952	2.00
Countin' the Days, 1927	3.00
Covered Wagon, 1923	2.00
Cow Cow Boogie, 1942	10.00
Cowboy Jack, 1935	2.00
Cowboy Songs, 1935	4.00
Cowboy Yodel, 1932	2.00
Cranky Old Yank, Carmichael, 1942	3.00
Crazy Bone Rag, Johnson, 1913	15.00
Crazy People, 1932	2.00
Crinoline Days, Berlin, 1922	7.00

**Pictured above is a small selection of
Sheet Music Covers that are listed within this book.**

Croon a Little Lullaby, 1925 .... 3.00
Crooning, Caesar, 1921 .... 2.00
Cross the Great Divide, Lewis, 1913 .... 8.00
Cross the Mason Dixon Line, 1913 .... 10.00
Cross Your Fingers, 1929 .... 2.00
Cross Your Heart, 1926 .... 2.00
Crossing on the Ferry, Newcomb, 1869 .... 25.00
Cruising Down the River, Beadell/Tollerton, 1945 .... 3.00
Cry, Kohlman, 1951 .... 2.00
Cryin for the Carolines, 1930 .... 6.00
Cryin' for the Moon, Conley, 1926 .... 2.00
Cuckoo Waltz, 1948 .... 2.00
Cuckoo's Call, Selden, 1885 .... 25.00
Cuddle Up a Little Closer, 1908 .... 7.00
Cupid's Awakening Waltzes, Paull, 1896 .... 40.00
Cupid's Private Code, 1906 .... 6.00
Cupids Patrol, Moret, 1910 .... 4.00
Curfew, Hatton, 1869 .... 25.00
Curley Head, Lewis/Meyer, 1913 .... 3.00
Curse of an Aching Heart, Fink, 1913 .... 3.00
Cutey, 1910 .... 3.00
D.O.A., Rutledge/Hill/Grundy/Taylor/Pickens/Cobb, 1970 .... 5.00
Da Dee Dum Dum, Elbel, 1927 .... 2.00
Daddy Found You Down Beside the Garden Wall, 1917 .... 3.00
Daddy of the Honor Roll, Lehman, 1919 .... 2.00
Daddy Won't You Please Come Home, Coslow, 1929 .... 10.00
Daddy's Lullaby, De Voll, 1929 .... 2.00
Daddy's Prayer, Freeman, 1918 .... 3.00
Daddy, 1907 .... 3.00
Daddy, Lemon, 1882 .... 15.00
Dainty Little Ingenue, Luders, 1904 .... 3.00
Daisies Won't Tell, Owen, 1908 .... 3.00
Daisy Bell (Bicycle Built for Two), 1892 .... 20.00
Daisy Petal Pickin', McCormack/Jordan/Thames, 1964 .... 3.00
Dallas Blues, Wand, 1912 .... 25.00
Dan Patch Two-Step, Trautvetter, 1901 .... 25.00
Dance Away the Night, Thompson/Stamper, 1929 .... 6.00
Dance Me Loose, Howard, 1951 .... 2.00
Dance of Dew Drops, Mann, 1914 .... 5.00
Dance of the Butterflies, Wise, 1911 .... 5.00
Dance of the Lunatics, Allen, 1912 .... 5.00
Dance of the Paper Dolls, Tucker/Schuster/Siras, 1928 .... 3.00
Dance of the Stars, Richmond, 1905 .... 5.00
Dance of the Wild Flowers, Wenrich, 1905 .... 6.00
Dancin' on a Rainbow, Freed/Brown, 1933 .... 9.00

Dancing Around, McCarthy, 1913 .... 3.00
Dancing in Blue, Trent/Clifford/Moret, 1933 .... 7.00
Dancing in the Dark, Dietz/Schwartz, 1931 .... 6.00
Dancing on the Levee, Wilkes, 1921 .... 14.00
Dancing the Jelly Roll, Paley, 1915 .... 3.00
Dancing Under the Stars, Owens, 1937 .... 2.00
Dancing with Tears in My Eyes, Burke, 1930 .... 2.00
Danger! Heartbreak Ahead, Stutz, 1954 .... 2.00
Danger! Love at Work, Gordon/Revel, 1937 .... 12.00
Danny Boy, Weatherly, 1913 .... 2.00
Dansero, Hayman, 1953 .... 2.00
Dark Eyed Cora, Webster, 1872 .... 20.00
Dark Eyes, Raven, 1929 .... 12.00
Dark Night, Grey/Stothart/Cugat, 1930 .... 6.00
Darkness on the Delta, 1932 .... 2.00
Darktown Strutter's Ball, Brooks, 1917 .... 30.00
Darlin', Frost, 1916 .... 2.00
Darling Boy Is Dead - -, 1865 .... 20.00
Darling Je Vous Aime Beaucoup, Sosenko, 1935 .... 5.00
Darling Nellie Gray, Hanby, 1898 .... 10.00
Darling Sue, Sterling/Tilzer, 1907 .... 6.00
Darling, Jackson/Schonberg, 1920 .... 5.00
Darling, Not Without You, Silver, 1936 .... 2.00
Darn that Dream, 1939 .... 2.00
Daughter of Rosie O'Grady, Brice, 1918 .... 3.00
Davis Jimmie, 1936 .... 6.00
Dawn of the Century, Paull, 1900 .... 25.00
Dawn, 1925 .... 2.00
Day After Day, 1938 .... 2.00
Day and Night, Johnson, 1933 .... 3.00
Day by Day (She Watches and Waits for Him), 1900 .... 14.00
Day by Day, Cahn, 1945 .... 2.00
Day You Came Along, Johnston, 1933 .... 2.00
Daydreams Come True at Night, Jurgens, 1940 .... 5.00
Daylight Katy, Lightfoot, 1978 .... 5.00
De Bad Man Will Ketch Yo, Ruhlman, 1898 .... 7.00
De Blin' Man Stood on De Road An' Cried, Burleigh, 1928 .... 12.00
De Gospel Train, Burleigh, 1921 .... 12.00
De Ol' Ark's a Moverin', Guion, 1918 .... 9.00
De Stories Uncle Remus Tells, 1899 .... 25.00
De Wes' Wind Blows From De Wes', Johnson, 1924 .... 7.00
Dead Actress, Bley, 1888 .... 6.00
Dead On the Battlefield, Beckel, 1862 .... 30.00
Dear Heart, Mancini, 1964 .... 2.00
Dear Hearts and Gentle People, Hilliard, 1949 .... 3.00

Dear Little Buddy of Mine, Bernard, 1920 .... 3.00
Dear Little Girl, Whittier, 1920 .... 3.00
Dear Lonely Hearts, Halley/Anton, 1962 .... 6.00
Dear Mom, Harris, 1941 .... 5.00
Dear Old Daddy Long Legs, 1919 .... 10.00
Dear Old Fashioned Mother, Friedman, 1920 .... 2.00
Dear Old Germany, Ascher 2.00
Dear Old Girl, Bick/Morse, 1903 .... 5.00
Dear Old Hartford, Conn., Ross, 1928 .... 6.00
Dear Old Hudson, Flynn, 1897 .... 10.00
Dear Old Ma, Frost, 1915 .... 2.00
Dear Old Moonlight, Creamer, 1909 .... 5.00
Dear Old Pal of Mine, Rice, 1918 .... 6.00
Dear Old Songs of Long Ago, Force, 1913 .... 5.00
Dear Rose Marie, Havez/Barron, 1913 .... 5.00
Dearie (I Still Love You), Young/Naylor/Squires, 1924 .... 5.00
Dearie, Kummer, 1905 .... 3.00
Dearly Beloved, Kern, 1942 .... 5.00
Deenah My Argentine Rose, Dubin/Scharf, 1920 .... 6.00
Deep Henderson, 1926 .... 5.00
Deep in My Heart Dear, Donnelly, 1924 .... 2.00
Deep in the Heart of Texas, Hershey, 1941 .... 2.00
Deep Purple, Parish/Rose, 1934 .... 2.00
Deep River, Burleigh, 1917 .... 5.00
Defend America, Stickney, 1917 .... 3.00
Delaware, Smolev/McDaniel, 1921 .... 5.00
Delilah, Rose/Fisher, 1926 .... 3.00
Delishious, Gershwin, 1921 .... 6.00
Derry Down Dilly, Mercer/Green, 1952 .... 8.00
Desperados Waiting for a Train, Clark, 1973 .... 5.00
Destiny, Bryan/Spencer, 1919 .... 6.00
Diamonds are a Girl's Best Friend, 1949 .... 3.00
Diana, Kummer, 1907 .... 5.00
Did I Remember, 1936 .... 5.00
Did You Ever See A Dream Walking, Gordon/Revel, 1933 .... 3.00
Did You Mean It, Baker, 1927 .... 2.00
Did You Think to Pray, Johnson/Pride, 1971 .... 6.00
Didn't We, Webb, 1966 .... 6.00
Dill Pickels, Johnson, 1906 .... 15.00
Dinah Green, Emerson, 1899 .... 8.00
Dippy Doodlums, Brown, 1919 .... 2.00
Dirty Hands Dirty Face, Jolson, 1923 .... 5.00
Divorce Me C. O. D., Travis, 1946 .... 2.00
Dixie Darlings, Wenrich, 1909 .... 7.00
Dixie Highway, Kahn/Donaldson, 1922 .... 5.00

Dixie Land, Emmett, 1909 .... 3.00
Dixie Lullaby, Dixon, 1919 .... 6.00
Do Buy Me That, Mamma Dear, Arnold, 1894 .... 5.00
Do Do Do, Gershwin, 1926 .... 6.00
Do I Love You, Porter, 1939 .... 2.00
Do I Worry, Cowan/Worth, 1941 .... 6.00
Do It Again, Gershwin, 1922 .... 6.00
Do It Again, Wilson/Love, 1968 .... 8.00
Do It, Diamond, 1970 .... 5.00
Do Something, Green, 1929 .... 5.00
Do What Your Mother Did, Dillon, 1916 .... 3.00
Do Ya Love Me, Gillespie/Wayne, 1929 .... 2.00
Do You Believe in Love at First Sight, Kahn/Fiorito, 1931 .... 3.00
Do You Ever Dream of Me?, Goldye, 1925 .... 2.00
Do You Remember, Carroll, 1914 .... 3.00
Do You Take This Woman for Your Lawful Wife, 1913 .... 2.00
Do You, Don't You, Will You, Won't You, 1923 .... 2.00
Doctor, Lawyer, Indian Chief, 1945 .... 5.00
Dodge Brothers March, Herbert, 1920 .... 20.00
Doin' the New Low-Down, Fields, 1928 .... 2.00
Doin' the Suzi-Qu, Davis, 1936 .... 2.00
Doin' the Uptown Lowdown, 1933 .... 3.00
Doing What Comes Naturally, Berlin, 1946 .... 5.00
Dolce Far Niente, Wilson, 1960 .... 3.00
Dolly Dimples, Alter, 1928 .... 7.00
Domage Domage (Too Bad), Pockriss/Vance, 1966 .... 5.00
Domino, 1950 .... 2.00
Don't Ask Me Not to Sing, Kern/Harbach, 1931 .... 7.00
Don't Be a Stranger, Weasner/O'Hara, 1924 .... 6.00
Don't Be Afraid to Dream, Ziehler/Hays/Capano, 1947 .... 5.00
Don't Be Sad, Manning, 1919 .... 7.00
Don't Be That Way, Goodman, 1935 .... 2.00
Don't Be Too Sure, Billings/Cohen, 1922 .... 6.00
Don't Believe Everthing You Dream,Adamson/McHugh,1943 ...... 3.00
Don't Bite the Hand That's Feeding You, Hoier, 1915 .... 10.00
Don't Blame It All On Broadway, Williams, 1913 .... 3.00
Don't Blame It All on Me, Terriss/Wood/Morse, 1924 .... 6.00
Don't Blame Me for What Happens in the Moonlight, 1915 .... 5.00
Don't Bother Me, Munn/Rupp, 1925 .... 3.00
Don't Call It Love, 1947 .... 2.00
Don't Call It Love, Snow/Pitchford, 1980 .... 5.00
Don't Call My Name, 1953 .... 2.00
Don't Come Cryin' to Me, Drake/Mizzy, 1956 .... 6.00
Don't Cry Baby, Kahn/Fiorito, 1928 .... 5.00
Don't Cry Frenchy, Lewis, 1919 .... 3.00

**Pictured above is a small selection of
Sheet Music Covers that are listed within this book.**

Don't Ever Leave Me, 1929 .... 4.00
Don't Fence Me In, 1944 .... 4.00
Don't Forget the Boys, Jolson, 1919 .... 15.00
Don't Get Around Much Anymore, 1942 .... 2.00
Don't Give Up the Ship, Warren/Dubin, 1934 .... 5.00
Don't Give Up, Hatch/Trent, 1968 .... 5.00
Don't Hang Your Dreams on a Rainbow, Gorney, 1929 .... 2.00
Don't Hold Everything, 1928 .... 2.00
Don't Keep It a Secret, Larkin/Simpson, 1955 .... 5.00
Don't Leave Me Daddy, Verges, 1916 .... 2.00
Don't Let 'Em Take It Way, Sour/Wayne, 1952 .... 8.00
Don't Let It Bother You, Gordon, 1934 .... 3.00
Don't Let It Get You Down, Harburg/Lane, 1940 .... 9.00
Don't Let It Happen Again, 1934 .... 2.00
Don't Let that Moon Get Away, Monaco, 1938 .... 3.00
Don't Let the Good Life Pass You By, Rucker, 1971 .... 10.00
Don't Let the Stars Get In Your Eyes, 1952 .... 2.00
Don't Let Your Foot Slip, Gregg, 1917 .... 5.00
Don't Let Your Love Go Wrong, 1934 .... 6.00
Don't Look Now, Clinton, 1939 .... 2.00
Don't Look Now, Slate/Silbar, 1981 .... 5.00
Don't Make Me Cry Over You, Webster/Trautman, 1922 .... 5.00
Don't Marry That Girl!!, Capp/Stept, 1946 .... 14.00
Don't Play That Song (You Lied), Ertegun/Nelson, 1962 .... 7.00
Don't Pull Your Love, Lambert/Potter, 1970 .... 5.00
Don't Say Good Night, Dubin/Warren, 1934 .... 8.00
Don't Say Goodbye, Friedland, 1922 .... 5.00
Don't Sing Aloha When I Go, 1926 .... 5.00
Don't Take Advantage, Monaco, 1919 .... 10.00
Don't Take Away Those Blues, McKiernan, 1920 .... 2.00
Don't Take My Darling Boy Away, Tilzer, 1915 .... 10.00
Don't Tell a Bluebird, Lewis/Young/Little, 1927 .... 5.00
Don't Tell Me Goodbye, Butcher, 1951 .... 2.00
Don't Tell the Folks You Saw Me, Allen & Daly, 1915 .... 3.00
Don't Try to Steal the Sweetheart of a Soldier, 1917 .... 8.00
Don't Wait Till the Night Before Christmas, Lewis, 1928 .... 2.00
Don't Wait Too Long, Berlin, 1925 .... 6.00
Don't Wake Me Up, I'm Dreaming, Whitson/Ingraham, 1910 .... 3.00
Don't Worry 'Bout Me, Koehler/Bloom, 1939 .... 6.00
Don't Worry, Styne/Gannon, 1943 .... 6.00
Don't You Go and Worry Mary, 1918 .... 15.00
Don't You Know I Care, David, 1944 .... 5.00
Don't You Know?, Worth, 1958 .... 6.00
Don't You Love Your Baby No More, Frost, 1915 .... 3.00
Don't You Remember Sally,Hirsch/Grossman/Samuels,1928 ...... 5.00

Done Too Soon, Diamond, 1970 .... 5.00
Doo Dah Blues, Rose/White, 1922 .... 3.00
Doodle Doo Doo, Kassel/Stitzel, 1924 .... 3.00
Dormi-Dormi-Dormi, Cahn, 1948 .... 3.00
Dorothy, Robinson, 1922 .... 6.00
Dorothy, Rodenbeck, 1914 .... 5.00
Dorothy, Smith, 1907 .... 3.00
Down a Carolina Lane, 1933 .... 2.00
Down Among the Sheltering Palms, Brockman, 1915 .... 6.00
Down Among the Sugar Cane, 1929 .... 5.00
Down Argentina Way, 1940 .... 3.00
Down Around the 'Sip 'Sip 'Sippy Shore, Young/Lewis, 1921 .... 6.00
Down Beside the Sea (Hawaiian Dreamerie), Wings, 1922 .... 5.00
Down By the Gas House, Tracey/Piantadosi, 1926 .... 6.00
Down By the Millside Alongside the Hillside, Brown, 1918 .... 2.00
Down By the O-Hi-O, Yellen, 1920 .... 2.00
Down By the Old Apple Tree, Wilson, 1922 .... 2.00
Down By the Old Mill Stream, Taylor, 1910 .... 2.00
Down By the River's End, Hanna, 1933 .... 2.00
Down By the Toll Gate Jennie, Rosenfield, 1909 .... 3.00
Down Hearted Blues, Hunter, 1923 .... 3.00
Down Home Rag, Lewis/Sweatman, 1913 .... 20.00
Down Honolulu Way, Dempsey, 1916 .... 5.00
Down In Arkansas, Cobble/Carleton, 1949 .... 2.00
Down In Bom-Bombay, Jolson, 1915 .... 15.00
Down In Borneo Isle, Creamer/Layton, 1917 .... 3.00
Down In Chattanooga, Berlin, 1913 .... 7.00
Down In Dixie Feelin' Hangin' Round Me, Perkins, 1921 .... 3.00
Down In Honky Tonk Town, McCarron/Smith, 1916 .... 6.00
Down In Jungle Town, Madden Morse, 1908 .... 18.00
Down In Old Havana Bay, Madden/Phillips, 1911 .... 3.00
Down In Old Nantucket, Ryan, 1913 .... 12.00
Down In Shady Lane, Ballard/Kelly, 1910 .... 3.00
Down In the Deep, Let Me Sleep When I Die, Titus, 1900 .... 20.00
Down In the Old Apple Orchard, Garton/Clay, 1917 .... 3.00
Down Linger Longer Lane, 1939 .... 2.00
Down on 33rd and 3rd, Ryan, 1926 .... 6.00
Down on De Levee, Cobb, 1912 .... 14.00
Down on the Farm, 1923 .... 2.00
Down Souf In Alabama, Janssen 30.00
Down South, Spaeth, 1901 .... 5.00
Down South, Vincent/Paley, 1917 .... 13.00
Down the Lane and Home Again, Leslie, 1919 .... 2.00
Down the Trail to Home Sweet Home, Ball, 1920 .... 2.00
Down Virginoa Way, Davis/Conley, 1926 .... 5.00

Down Went McGinty, Flynn, 1889 .... 20.00
Down Where the Breezes Blow, Moss, 1903 .... 12.00
Down Where the Passion Flower Blooms Beside the Sea, 1907 ... 3.00
Down Where the Silv'ry Mohawk Flows, Rosenfield, 1904 .... 10.00
Down Where the Swanee River Flows, Jolson, 1916 .... 12.00
Down Where the Yellow Corn Is Waving, Barnes/White, 1905 ..... 6.00
Down with Love, Harburg/Arlen, 1937 .... 9.00
Down Yonder, Gilbert, 1921 .... 2.00
Downhearted, 1932 .... 2.00
Draggin' My Heart Around, Hill, 1930 .... 2.00
Dragnet, 1953 .... 2.00
Dream Daddy, Herscher, 1923 .... 5.00
Dream Days, Johnson, 1913 .... 5.00
Dream Days, Vision of Bliss, Reinhardt/Smith, 1909 .... 3.00
Dream Face, Allison, 1915 .... 2.00
Dream Girl, Livingston/Evans, 1948 .... 12.00
Dream House, Cowan, 1926 .... 2.00
Dream I Had Last Night, Caddigan, 1915 .... 3.00
Dream Kisses, Yellen/Pic/Tucker, 1927 .... 5.00
Dream Lover, Schertzinger, 1929 .... 3.00
Dream of a Soldier Boy, Dubin/Monaco, 1917 .... 6.00
Dream of Paradise, Johnston, 1902 .... 3.00
Dream On Dear Heart Dream On, Buck/Morse, 1907 .... 5.00
Dream River, Hill, 1928 .... 3.00
Dream Shadows, Silver/Sherman/Lewis, 1936 .... 6.00
Dream Smoke, Wimperis/Finck, 1922 .... 8.00
Dream Train, Newman, 1928 .... 5.00
Dream Waltz, 1914 .... 3.00
Dreamer Dreamer!, Caesar/Straus, 1945 .... 7.00
Dreamer of Dreams, Fiorito, 1924 .... 2.00
Dreamin' Out Loud, Coslow, 1940 .... 10.00
Dreamin' Time, Strickland, 1921 .... 2.00
Dreaming A Dream, Bert/Lee/Waller/Tunbridge, 1934 .... 8.00
Dreaming My Dreams Alone, 1931 .... 2.00
Dreaming of Home Sweet Home, 1918 .... 2.00
Dreaming of Love of You, Harris, 1905 .... 2.00
Dreaming of My Southern Home, Corless, 1917 .... 2.00
Dreaming of Tomorrow, Davis/Sanders, 1925 .... 6.00
Dreaming That's All, Moseley, 1901 .... 8.00
Dreaming, Joyce, 1911 .... 3.00
Dreams Are a Dime a Dozen, 1946 .... 2.00
Dreams of India, Wenrich, 1923 .... 6.00
Dreams of Long Ago, Carroll, 1912 .... 3.00
Dreams of Mother, Caddigan, 1913 .... 2.00
Dreams, Denison/Dusenberry, 1911 .... 2.00

Dreams, Just Dreams, Berlin, 1909 .... 15.00
Dreamy Alabama, Earl, 1919 .... 3.00
Dreamy Amazon, 1927 .... 3.00
Dreamy Argentina, 1925 .... 4.00
Dreamy Delaware, Violinsky/Donaldson, 1924 .... 5.00
Dreamy Melody, 1922 .... 5.00
Dreamy Moon, Smith, 1917 .... 2.00
Dreamy Oriental Melody, Paull, 1920 .... 25.00
Dreamy Weather, 1924 .... 2.00
Drifting, Polla, 1920 .... 2.00
Drifting, Siegel, 1930 .... 2.00
Drinking Song, Donnelly, 1925 .... 3.00
Drowsy Head, Berlin, 1920 .... 8.00
Drowsy Waters, Ailau/Howard, 1917 .... 3.00
Drug Store Cowboys, Murray/Dilworth, 1924 .... 12.00
Drum Major March, Ellis, 1921 .... 6.00
Dry Bones, Burleigh, 1930 .... 5.00
Dublin Saunter, Maquire, 1953 .... 6.00
Duel in the Sun, Tiomkin/Adams/Judell, 1947 .... 7.00
Dumb Dora, Coslow/Silver, 1924 .... 2.00
Dumbell, Confrey, 1922 .... 2.00
Dusty, Aufderheide, 1908 .... 15.00
E Bob O Lee Bop, Dixon, 1946 .... 5.00
E-A-S-T-E-R, Rodgers/Estes, 1950 .... 2.00
Each Step of the Way, Harper, 1952 .... 2.00
East of the Sun, 1935 .... 2.00
Easter Parade, Berlin, 1933 .... 10.00
Easter Sunday with You, Reid/Tobias, 1944 .... 2.00
Eastside of Heaven, Burke/Monaco, 1939 .... 5.00
Easy Come Easy go, Heyman/Gree, 1934 .... 2.00
Easy Goin', Trent/De Rose, 1928 .... 2.00
Easy Street, Browne/Penn, 1905 .... 8.00
Easy to Love, 1936 .... 3.00
Ebb Tide, Sigman/Maxwell, 1953 .... 3.00
Echoes from My Old Plantation Home, Bernard/Garber 5.00
Eddie Cantor's "Automobile Horn" Song, Gaskill, 1929 .... 20.00
Eeny Meeny Miny Mo, Fitzgibbons, 1906 .... 6.00
Egypt, Kummer, 1903 .... 5.00
Egyptian Nights, Flynn/Siragusa, 1919 .... 5.00
Eh, Cumpari, 1953 .... 2.00
Eight Little Letters, Donaldson/Manning, 1931 .... 27.00
Eighteen Seventy Five, Anderson, 1942 .... 6.00
Eisenhower March, 1952 .... 6.00
Either It's Love or It Isn't, Roberts/Fisher, 1946 .... 3.00
El Rancho Grande, Moral/Costello/Uranga, 1934 .... 5.00

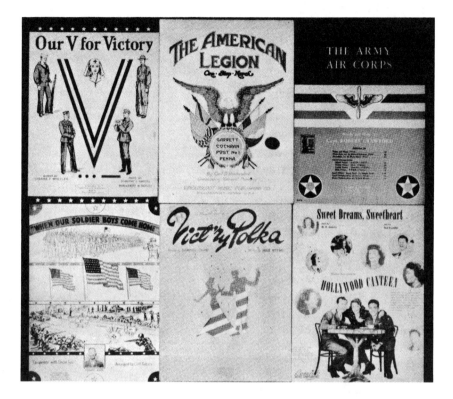

**Pictured above is a small selection of
Sheet Music Covers that are listed within this book.**

Eleanor, McCarthy/Hanley, 1930 .... 3.00
Eleventh Hour Melody, 1956 .... 2.00
Elmer's Tune, 1941 .... 2.00
Emma Lee, Bren, 1919 .... 2.00
Empty Saddles, 1936 .... 3.00
En Ballon, D'Orso, 1880 .... 25.00
Endlessly, Gannon/Kent, 1945 .... 3.00
Endlessly, Otis/Benton, 1963 .... 6.00
Enjoy Yourself, 1948 .... 2.00
Envy, London/Gussin, 1949 .... 2.00
Ephasafa Dill, Sterling/Costello/VonTilzer, 1940 .... 15.00
Eskimo, Perry/Castello, 1909 .... 3.00
Eternally, Chaplin/Parsons, 1953 .... 3.00
Ethiopian National Anthem, 1914 .... 2.00
Etiquette Blues, Grubb/Marvin, 1928 .... 6.00
Eugenie, Simpson, 1906 .... 3.00
Ev'ery Ship Will Find a Harbor, 1906 .... 8.00
Ev'rthing Is Hotsy Totsy Now, 1925 .... 2.00
Ev'ry Day I Hear My Daddy Say, Randall,1924 .... 5.00
Ev'ry Little Bit Helps, Whiting/Fischer, 1904 .... 6.00
Ev'ry Little Flower Has a Sweetheart, 1911 .... 2.00
Ev'ry Night About this Time, 1942 .... 2.00
Ev'ry Step Toward Killarney, Evans, 1925 .... 3.00
Ev'rything You Do, Hirsch/Olman, 1924 .... 2.00
Evangeline, Jolson, 1929 .... 12.00
Eve Wasn't Modest Till She Ate That Apple, McCarron, 1917 .... 8.00
Evening Bringing Dreams of You, Abel, 1925 .... 2.00
Evening Brings Memories of You, Miller/Brooks, 1918 .... 3.00
Evening Chimes, Liebich, 1869 .... 20.00
Evening Chimes, Marazian, 1913 .... 2.00
Evening Glow, McKanlass, 1912 .... 3.00
Evening in Erin, Clerken, 1920 .... 2.00
Evening Star, Liszt, 1927 .... 2.00
Evening, Ronald, 1901 .... 3.00
Everglades, Leslie/Fenstock, 1935 .... 6.00
Every Day Is Mother's Day to Mother, Gerber, 1942 .... 2.00
Every Day, Howard, 1923 .... 6.00
Every Day, Jackson, 1922 .... 2.00
Every Day, Williams/Brooks, 1918 .... 3.00
Every Evening (I miss you), Rose/McHugh, 1927 .... 6.00
Every Hour, Every Day, Frost, 1916 .... 2.00
Every Little Bit of Me Loves You, Bryan/Gumble, 1928 .... 5.00
Every Little Movement, 1910 .... 3.00
Every Mother's Son, Gregg, 1917 .... 8.00
Every Road Leads Back to You, 1920 .... 2.00

Every Star Falls In Love With Its Mate, 1907 .... 8.00
Every Tear Is a Smile in An Irishman's Heart, 1919 .... 2.00
Everybody Calls Me Honey, Lyons/Straight, 1919 .... 8.00
Everybody Knows I Love You, 1930 .... 2.00
Everybody Loves a Chicken, Jones, 1912 .... 3.00
Everybody Loves a College Girl, Mills, 1911 .... 3.00
Everybody Loves Me But the One I Love, Edwards, 1908 .... 10.00
Everybody Loves My Girl, 1927 .... 2.00
Everybody Rag With Me, Kahn/LeBoy, 1914 .... 10.00
Everybody Shimmies Now, West/Gold, 1918 .... 10.00
Everybody Step, Berlin, 1921 .... 7.00
Everybody Turned and Looked at Me, O'Brien, 1908 .... 6.00
Everybody Two-Step, Jones/Herzer, 1912 .... 10.00
Everybody Wants a Key to My Cellar, 1919 .... 5.00
Everybody Wish, Evans/Jonson/Powell, 1931 .... 6.00
Everybody Works But Father, Havez, 1905 .... 6.00
Everybody's Darling, Ruby/Jerome, 1929 .... 6.00
Everybody's Doin' It Now, Berlin, 1911 .... 15.00
Everybody's Got the Right to Love, 1970 .... 10.00
Everybody's Happy Now, Kendis, 1918 .... 3.00
Everybody's Pining for a Home in Royal Pines, 1925 .... 5.00
Everybody's Rag, Goldsmith/Sharp, 1909 .... 10.00
Everyone is in Slumberland But You and Me,1905 .... 5.00
Everything I Love, Porter, 1941 .... 2.00
Everything Is Rosie Now for Rosie, Berlin, 1919 .... 15.00
Everything is K.O. in K-Y, Egan/Whiting, 1923 .... 3.00
Everything is Ticketty-Boo, Mercer/Chaplin, 1958 .... 8.00
Everything's In Rhythm With My Heart, 1929 .... 3.00
F. D. R. Jones, Rome, 1938 .... 2.00
Fair Co-Ed, Bryan/Axt, 1927 .... 3.00
Fairland of Mine, Guest/Holmes, 1931 .... 3.00
Fairy Footsteps, Statham, 1892 .... 15.00
Fairy Kisses, Johnson, 1908 .... 3.00
Fairy Of Wildwood, Brown, 1866 .... 15.00
Fairy Tales, Hanlon/Morrissey, 1911 .... 3.00
Fairy Wedding, Turner, 1902 .... 3.00
Faithful Forever, 1939 .... 7.00
Fall In! U.S.A., Kraft, 1917 .... 6.00
Fallen Idols, Bryan/Kellette, 1919 .... 5.00
Fallen, Harris, 1892 .... 8.00
Falling Waters, Truax, 1905 .... 3.00
Fancy Free, 1950 .... 8.00
Fare Thee Honey Fare Thee Well, Queen/Wilson, 1901 .... 20.00
Fare Thee Well Annabelle, Dixon/Wrubel, 1937 .... 3.00
Fare Thee Well to Harlem, Mercer/Hanighen, 1934 .... 10.00

Farewell Blues, Schoebel/Ehrlich/Robbolo,1923 .... 10.00
Farewell Daisy Bell, Mabon/Fry, 1905 .... 3.00
Farewell Dear Home, Farewell, Solman, 1900 .... 3.00
Farewell My Little Sunbeam, Anderson/Conrad, 1906 .... 3.00
Farewell to Arms, Wrubel/Silver, 1933 .... 3.00
Farewell, Liliuokalani, 1918 .... 7.00
Fascination, Powell, 1906 .... 5.00
Fascino Infranto, Gioe, 1927 .... 2.00
Fast Line Gallop, Beck, 1853 .... 100.00
Fate, Gay/Lewis, 1923 .... 3.00
Father of the Land We Love, Cohan, 1931 .... 5.00
Father Was a Grand Old Man, Cahill/Henry, 1909 .... 6.00
Fawn Eyes, 1908 .... 3.00
Ferdinand the Bull, Morey/Malotte, 1936 .... 10.00
Feelin' Good, Ager/Murphy, 1928 .... 2.00
Feelin' Sorry, 1950 .... 2.00
Feeling I'm Falling, Gershwin, 1928 .... 13.00
Fellow on a Furlough, Worth/Russell, 1943 .... 2.00
Festival Time and Apple Blossoms, Lynn, 1948 .... 6.00
Feudin' and Fightin' Lane, Hillbillies Warring, 1947 .... 3.00
Fiddle and I, Goodeve 2.00
Fiddle Dee Dee, 1949 .... 3.00
Fifteen Kisses on a Gallon of Gas, David, 1939 .... 6.00
Fighting Tommies, Boulton, 1918 .... 7.00
Fire Drill March, Lincoln, 1909 .... 12.00
First Last and Always (I love you), Davis/Akst, 1923 .... 6.00
Five Foot Two, Eyes of Blue, 1925 .... 2.00
Five O'Clock Whistle, 1940 .... 2.00
Five Pound Box of Money, Barker/Bailey, 1959 .... 10.00
Five Salted Peanuts, Abbott/Pastor, 1945 .... 2.00
Five Women to Every Man, Hersher/Downing/Burke, 1908 .... 7.00
Flag of Our Country Long May Thou Wave, Snow, 1918 .... 10.00
Flim Flam Man (hands off the man), Nyro, 1966 .... 7.00
Flirtation Walk, Dixon/Wrubel, 1939 .... 3.00
Flo, Stewart/Monroe, 1904 .... 3.00
Floating Down the River, White, 1913 .... 8.00
Floating, Sheridan/McCarthy, 1911 .... 2.00
Floradora, Hall/Stuart, 1903 .... 3.00
Floreine, Schuster, 1908 .... 3.00
Floretta, 1903 .... 2.00
Flow Along River Tennessee, 1912 .... 2.00
Flower Garden Blues, Graham/White, 1919 .... 7.00
Flower of France, Levenson, 1919 .... 3.00
Flower of Love, 1928 .... 4.00
Flower Song, Lang, 1915 .... 3.00

Fluffy Ruffles, 1919 .... 4.00
Fly Little Children, Fly, Ballou, 1891 .... 3.00
Flying Spray Boat Song, Adamson, 1903 .... 5.00
Flying Trapeze Waltz, Richter, 1855 .... 20.00
Follow Me, Deutsch, 1953 .... 15.00
Follow the Crowd, Berlin, 1914 .... 17.00
Following the Sun Around, Tierney/McCarthy, 1926 .... 2.00
Foolin, Craig, 1946 .... 2.00
Foolish, 1940 .... 2.00
Fools Rush In, Mercer, 1940 .... 2.00
Footprints On the Snow, Murphy, 1866 .... 20.00
For Days and Days, Kalmar/Puck, 1913 .... 3.00
For Dixie And Uncle Sam, Brennan, 1916 .... 15.00
For Every Boy Who's on the Level, 1920 .... 3.00
For Every Boy Whose Lonely, Hauerbach/Hoschna, 1911 .... 4.00
For Every Man There's a Woman, 1948 .... 3.00
For Every Tear You've Shed, Lawrence/Bard, 1919 .... 2.00
For God and For Country and to the Auxiliary, 1938 .... 6.00
For His Mothers Sake, Nathan, 1904 .... 15.00
For Instance, Denniker/Osborne, 1930 .... 2.00
For Johnnie and Me, Brown/VonTilzer, 1919 .... 10.00
For Killarney and You, Walsh/Teasdale, 1910 .... 5.00
For Me and My Gal, Meyer, 1917 .... 6.00
For My Baby, Kahal/Wheeler/Snyder, 1927 .... 5.00
For the Freedom of the World, 1917 .... 8.00
For the Glory of Yankee Land, Dutcher, 1917 .... 5.00
For the Sake of Auld Lang Syne, 1922 .... 3.00
For the Sake of You, Dear Mother, 1909 .... 5.00
For the Two of Us, Leslie/Ruby, 1918 .... 2.00
For You a Rose, Cobb/Edwards, 1917 .... 3.00
For You and the Grand Old Flag, Coleman, 1910 .... 10.00
For You Bright Eyes, Hauerbach/Hoschna, 1909 .... 3.00
For You, For Me, For Evermore, 1941 .... 3.00
For Your Boy & My Boy, Van Alstyne, 1918 .... 20.00
For-Get-Me-Not, Schultz, 1915 .... 2.00
Ford's Grand March, Dunn, 1925 .... 7.00
Ford, Zickel, 1908 .... 20.00
Forever Amber, Mercer/Raksin, 1947 .... 10.00
Forevermore, Callahan/Smith, 1912 .... 5.00
Forget Me Not, Tully, 1912 .... 2.00
Forget, Mack/Aldens, 1905 .... 5.00
Forgive Me, 1920 .... 2.00
Forgotten, Coweles/Ditson, 1895 .... 7.00
Forgotten, Denison/Dusenberry, 1913 .... 2.00
Forty-Nine Songs in This Album, 1938 .... 7.00

**Pictured above is a small selection of
Sheet Music Covers that are listed within this book.**

Fountain Fay, Reinhardt/Smith, 1909 .... 3.00
Fountain Waltzes, De Micheles, 1910 .... 2.00
Four and Twenty Little, Hall/Stuart. 1901 .... 3.00
Four Buddies, Cunningham/Whitcup, 1943 .... 2.00
Four Jacks March, Losch, 1907 .... 3.00
Four Leaf Clover, Brownell, 1897 .... 15.00
Four Little Blackberries, O'Conner, 1907 .... 20.00
Four Thousand Years Ago, Manoloff/Long, 1935 .... 2.00
Four Walls, Jolson, 1927 .... 7.00
Four Walls, Moore/Campbell, 1957 .... 2.00
Fox Trail March, Zamecnik, 1917 .... 2.00
Frankie and Johnny, 1935 .... 2.00
Frat March, Barth, 1910 .... 3.00
Freed Man's Lament, Murphy, 1868 .... 20.00
Freedom For All Forever, Hilliam, 1918 .... 2.00
Freshie, Greer/Berg, 1925 .... 3.00
Friendly Persuasion, 1956 .... 5.00
Friendly Star, Garland/Kelly 7.00
Friends, Johnson/Santly/Meyer, 1919 .... 3.00
Frolic of the Imps, Lincoln, 1939 .... 5.00
From Here to Eternity, 1953 .... 3.00
From Here to Shanghi, Berlin, 1917 .... 15.00
From Me to Mandy Lee, Grossman/Lange, 1917 .... 3.00
From Me to You, 1933 .... 2.00
From Sunrise to Sunset, McLaughlin/Miller, 1929 .... 2.00
From the North, South, East and West, Lauder, 1918 .... 3.00
From the Top of Your Head to the Tip of Your Toes, 1935 .... 2.00
From the Vine Came the Grape, 1949 .... 2.00
From This Day Foward, Greene/Harline, 1946 .... 11.00
Frosty the Snow Man, Nelson/Rollins, 1950 .... 2.00
Fuddy Duddy Watchmaker, Loesser/McHugh, 1943 .... 3.00
Funny Moon, McCarthy, 1910 .... 5.00
Furs and Frills, Clark/Hein, 1917 .... 2.00
Fuss & Feathers, Moreland, 1904 .... 2.00
G. I. Jive, Mercer, 1943 .... 3.00
Gambella (the gamblin' lady), Gilkyson, 1951 .... 5.00
Gang Awa' Bonnie Lassie, Ellis/Gibson, 1916 .... 2.00
Garden of Dreams, Lincoln, 1909 .... 3.00
Garden of Flowers, Vandersloot, 1916 .... 3.00
Garden of Love, Rolfe, 1909 .... 3.00
Garden of My Dreams, Buck/Stamper, 1918 .... 3.00
Garden of Roses, Dempsey/Schmidt, 1909 .... 3.00
Garden of the Moon, Warren/Dubin/Mercer, 1938 .... 6.00
Gasoline Gus and His Jitney Bus, Gay, 1915 .... 25.00
Gather Lip Rouge While You May, 1933 .... 3.00

Gathering Shells From the Sea Shore, Thompson, 1875 .... 15.00
Gay Chauffeur, Valentine, 1907 .... 15.00
Gee Dear I'm lonesome, Baldwin, 1931 .... 13.00
Gee Whiz, Losch, 1919 .... 3.00
Gee, But I'm Lonesome and Blue, Forest, 1932 .... 6.00
Gee, But I's Like to Make You Happy, 1930 .... 3.00
Gee, But It's Good to Get Home, Griswold/Draper, 1916 .... 3.00
Gee, But It's Great to Meet a Friend From Yur Home Town 3.00
Geezer of Geck "Mother Pin a Rose on Me", 1905........................ 4.00
General Pershing, Vandersloot, 1918... 6.00
General Von Stueben, Engles, 1925 .... 7.00
Genevieve, Cooper/Tucker, 1902 .... 3.00
Georgette, Brown, 1922 .... 6.00
Georgia I Love You, Wilkie, 1922 .... 8.00
Georgia Moon, Barron, 1914 .... 6.00
Georgia, Donaldson, 1922.. 6.00
Geraldine Loves Awakening, Jordan, 1895 .... 7.00
Get 'Em in a Rumble Seat, Marshall, 1927 .... 12.00
Get An Automobile, Watts, 1906 .... 20.00
Get Married the Same As Me, Collin/Murray, 1909 .... 3.00
Get Out of Town, Porter, 1938... 2.00
Get Yourself a Broom and Sweep Your Troubles Away, 1924 .... 6.00
Gettin' Sentimental, Kahn/Malneck, 1931 .... 6.00
Giannina Mia, 1912 .... 3.00
Gigi, 1957 .... 7.00
Gin Gin Ginny Shore, Berlin, 1922 .... 10.00
Gipsy Trail, 1897 .... 15.00
Girl Friend of the Whirling Dervish, 1938 .... 3.00
Girl I Loved in Sunny Tenn., 1899 .... 6.00
Girl on the Automobile, Nathan, 1905 .... 25.00
Girl Shy, Merrill/Harris, 1923... 11.00
Girl That I Marry, Berlin, 1946... 7.00
Girl Who Threw Me Down, Burt/Gumble, 1907 .... 3.00
Girl Wtih a Brogue, 1909 .... 3.00
Git a Horse, Reed, 1902 .... 25.00
Give a Little Credit to the Navy, Grumble, 1918......................... 6.00
Give Back the Kiss I Gave You, Jones/Moret, 1911 .... 2.00
Give Me a Heart To Sing To, Washington/Young, 1934 .... 3.00
Give Me a Little Bit More Than You Gave, Reilly, 1917 .... 6.00
Give Me a Moment Please, Robin/Whiting, 1930 .... 8.00
Give Me a Spin in Your Mitchell, Bill/Gilson, 1909 .... 20.00
Give Me Jesus, Burleigh, 1926.. 3.00
Give Me Liberty or Give Me Love, Robin/Rainger, 1933.............. 3.00
Give Me the Moonlight, Brown, 1917... 3.00
Give Me the Right to Love You, Bard/Glatt, 1917 .... 3.00

Give Me the Simple Life, Ruby/Bloom, 1945 .... 3.00
Give Me Your Heart for Christmas, Goodman, 1954 .... 3.00
Give Me Your Tired & Poor, Berlin, 1949 .... 7.00
Glad Rag Doll, Yellen/Ager, 1929 .... 5.00
Glimpses of the Moon, Cook/Johnstone, 1922 .... 3.00
Glory of Love, Hill, 1936 .... 2.00
Glow Worm, Lincke, 1902 .... 5.00
Go Down Moses, Burleigh, 1917 .... 15.00
Go Fly a Kite, 1939 .... 3.00
Go to Bed, Dubin/Burke, 1929 .... 3.00
Go to Sleep My Little Greole Babe, 1902 .... 3.00
Go to Sleep, Curley Head, 1908 .... 2.00
God Be With Our Boys Tonight, Bowles/Sanderson, 1917 .... 2.00
God Bless America, Berlin, 1939 .... 6.00
God's Country, Harburg/Arlen, 1938 .... 23.00
God's Little Candles, Kennedy/Boyd, 1952 .... 2.00
God, Please Protect America, Osborne, 1950 .... 2.00
Goin' Steady, Young, 1952 .... 3.00
Goin' to Shout, Manney, 1922 .... 3.00
Goin' to the County Fair, Gordon/Warren, 1943 .... 3.00
Going Back H-O-M-E, Clark, 1914 .... 3.00
Going My Way, Burke/Van Heusen, 1944 .... 2.00
Gold, Foster, 1890 .... 6.00
Golden Girl (Indian Love Song), 1903 .... 3.00
Goldenrod Two-Step, Chadwick, 1896 .... 20.00
Gondolier, Powell, 1903 .... 6.00
Gone, Rogers/Husky, 1952 .... 2.00
Good Bye Broadway, Hello France, Reisner/Davis, 1917 .... 5.00
Good Bye Dearest One Goodbye, 1907 .... 3.00
Good Bye Ma, Good Bye Pa, Good Bye Mule, 1917 .... 10.00
Good Bye Mamie, Drislane/Morse, 1907 .... 3.00
Good Bye Mother Hello Uncle Sam, 1917 .... 12.00
Good Bye My Love Good Bye, Graff/Ball, 1911 .... 2.00
Good Bye Sweet Marie, Cobb/Mills, 1905 .... 3.00
Good Bye Virginia, Clarke/Schwartz, 1915 .... 3.00
Good Bye, Tosti, 1907 .... 3.00
Good Evening Caroline, Norworth,/Tilzer, 1908 .... 6.00
Good Gracious Annabelle, 1919 .... 3.00
Good Gravy Rag, Belding, 1913 .... 7.00
Good Mornin', Coslow, 1937 .... 3.00
Good Morning Dixieland, Marshall, 1916 .... 8.00
Good Morning Glory, Gordon/Revel, 1933 .... 3.00
Good Morning Mr. Zip-Zip-Zip, Lloyd, 1918 .... 5.00
Good Morning, 1939 .... 3.00
Good Morning, Brohers Sunshine, Lehman 2.00

Good Night Angel, 1937 .... 3.00
Good Night Germany, 1918 .... 3.00
Good Night Little Girl, Good Night, Macy, 1898 .... 10.00
Good Night Lovely Little Lady, Gordon/Revel, 1934 .... 3.00
Good Night Mr. Moon, Dawson/Tilzer, 1911 .... 5.00
Good Night Nurse, Walker/Gray, 1912 .... 3.00
Good Night Vienna, 1932 .... 3.00
Good Night, Sweet Dreams, Bischoff, 1887 .... 10.00
Good Night-Good Night, Gardiner/Ball, 1913 .... 3.00
Good Old Winter Time, Fyfe/Cheney, 1912 .... 5.00
Good Ship Mary Ann, Kahn/Boy, 1914 .... 5.00
Good-By, But Come Again, Thomas, 1867 .... 25.00
Good-By-Boys, Jolson, 1918 .... 14.00
Good-Bye Everybody, Gilbert/Hough,1912 .... 2.00
Good-Bye Good Luck, God Bless You, Ball/Brennan, 1916 .... 3.00
Good-Bye Little Girl of My Dreams, Howard/Phillips, 1913 .... 3.00
Good-Bye Little Girl, Good Bye, Cobb/Edwards, 1904 .... 3.00
Good-Bye Mister Greenback, Allen, 1906 .... 20.00
Good-Bye My Lady Love, Howard, 1904 .... 5.00
Good-Bye My Little Lady, Goodwin/Hanley, 1917 .... 3.00
Good-Bye My Soldier Boy, Gregg, 1917 .... 10.00
Good-Bye Rose, Ingraham/Burkart, 1910 .... 3.00
Good-Bye Sally, Habelow, 1919 .... 5.00
Good-Bye Summer, So Long Fall, Hello Winter, 1913 .... 5.00
Good-Bye, Good Luck, God Bless You, Ball/Brennan, 1916 .... 6.00
Good-Bye, May/Fitzpatrick, 1917 .... 10.00
Good-Bye, Sears, 1920 .... 2.00
Goodbye Dear, I'll Be Back in a Year, Kay, 1940 .... 3.00
Goodbye France, Berlin, 1918 .... 12.00
Goodbye Girls, I'm Through, 1914 .... 2.00
Goodbye Pal, Hauerbach/Hoschins, 1906 .... 3.00
Goodbye Sweetheart, Lamb/Tilzer, 1905 .... 3.00
Goodbye, My Lady Love, 1904 .... 3.00
Goodnight Beloved, Goodnight, Fay/Oliver, 1902 .... 3.00
Goodnight My Love, 1936 .... 12.00
Goody Goody, Mercer/Malneck, 1935 .... 2.00
Goody, Goody, Goody, Goody, Good, Berlin, 1912 .... 10.00
Got a Gal in Californ-i-a, Robin/Rainger, 1935 .... 6.00
Got to Have my Daddy Blues (Lonesome Lovesick), 1921 .... 10.00
Gotta Big Date With a Little Girl, Tobias, 1928 .... 5.00
Gotta Feelin' for You, Trent/Alter, 1929 .... 3.00
Gotta Get Me Somebody to Love, Wrubel, 1946 .... 3.00
Gotterdamerung, Wagner, 1913 .... 5.00
Grand Truck Waltzes, D'Albert, 1854 .... 40.00
Grange Song, Reynolds, 1904 .... 10.00

**Pictured above is a small selection of
Sheet Music Covers that are listed within this book.**

Great Rock Island Route, Roff, 1880 .... 35.00
Green River, Fogerty, 1969 .... 7.00
Green River, Van/Schenck/Cantor, 1920 .... 6.00
Grieving for You, Gibson, 1920 .... 6.00
Grieving, Shields/Conlin, 1911 .... 3.00
Guild Polka Militaire, Fox, 1876 .... 15.00
Gum Shoe Fox Trot, Stark, 1917 .... 3.00
Gunner Jim, Daly/Cool, 1918 .... 6.00
Gypsy Blues, 1921 .... 3.00
Gypsy Song, Smith/Jacobi, 1917 .... 3.00
Ha-Cha-Cha, 1934 .... 3.00
Hail America, Medorn, 1896 .... 12.00
Hail Columbia, 1836 .... 35.00
Hail To the Chief, Sanderson, 1942 .... 2.00
Hail! All Hail, Holland/Arthur, 1918 .... 5.00
Hail, Hail, The Gang's All Here, Esrom/Sullivan, 1917 .... 10.00
Half a Moon, Dowling/Hanley, 1926 .... 2.00
Half a Photograph, Russell/Stanley, 1953 .... 3.00
Hallelujah I'm a Bum, Manoloff, 1935 .... 2.00
Hallelujah, 1927 .... 2.00
Hammock Love Song, Herbert/KeKoven, 1909 .... 3.00
Hands That Rocked the Cradle, 1943 .... 2.00
Hang Your Hat In Detroit, McKenna, 1910 .... 18.00
Happiness Is A Thing Called Joe, Harburg/Arlen, 1943 .... 10.00
Happy Days Are Here Again, Yellen/Ager, 1929 .... 3.00
Happy Days in Dixie, 1897 .... 15.00
Happy Darkies, Godfrey, 1892 .... 20.00
Happy Holligans Reception, 1902 .... 10.00
Happy Hours in Coontown, Brown, 1899 .... 25.00
Happy Little Country Girl, Berlin, 1913 .... 20.00
Happy School Days, Sudds, 1881 .... 15.00
Happy Tom O'Day, Gary, 1915 .... 10.00
Harbor of Love, 1911 .... 5.00
Hard to Get, Meyer/Bryan, 1929 .... 3.00
Hard Trails, Burleigh, 1919 .... 3.00
Hardtimes Come Again No More, Foster, 1882 .... 15.00
Harlem Lullaby, Robison, 1932 .... 12.00
Harmony Bay, Walsh/Sherman, 1914 .... 2.00
Harnden's Express Line Gallopade and Trio, 1841 .... 50.00
Harry Fox Trot, Pollock, 1918 .... 5.00
Has Anybody Here Seen Kelly?, Murphy, 1909 .... 6.00
Hath No Need of the Sun, Whittington 2.00
Haunted Heart, 1948 .... 2.00
Have a Little Faith in Me, 1930 .... 2.00
Have I Stayed Away Too Long, 1943 .... 3.00

Have You Forgotten, Denison/Dusenberry, 1912 .... 3.00
Have You Got Any Castles, Baby?, 1937 .... 3.00
Have You Seen Him In France, 1918 .... 3.00
Hawaiian Butterfly, Little/Baskette/Santly, 1917 .... 3.00
Hawaiian Dreams, Maple, 1916 .... 3.00
Hawaiian Lullaby, 1919 .... 4.00
Hawaiian Twilight, Maple, 1918 .... 3.00
He Cannot Talk at All, Flynn, 1895 .... 10.00
He Likes the Girlies, Solek, 1948.. 2.00
He May Be Old, But He's Got Young Ideas, 1916 .... 3.00
He Never Came Back, Jerome, 1891 .... 5.00
He Played It on His Fid, Fid Fiddle Dee-Dee, Berlin, 1912 .... 16.00
He Wears a Pair of Silver Wings, 1941 .... 2.00
He Went in Like a Lion and Came Out Like a Lamb, 1920 .... 6.00
He'd Have to Get Under-Get Out and Get Under, 1913 .... 20.00
He's a College Boy, Mahoney/Morse, 1909 .... 6.00
He's a Cousin of Mine, 1906 .... 3.00
He's a Devil in His Own Home Town, Berlin, 1914 .... 20.00
He's a Good Man to Have Around, 1929 .... 8.00
He's a Rag Picker, Berlin, 1914 .... 20.00
He's Coming Home on the 8 O'Clock Train, Kendall, 1912 .... 25.00
He's Had No Lovin' For a Long Long Time, 1919 .... 2.00
He's My Uncle, 1940 .... 2.00
He's on a Boat That Sailed Last Wednesday, Goodwin, 1913 .... 6.00
He's the Last Word, Kahn/Donaldson, 1927 .... 2.00
Headin' Home, Hall, 1927 .... 2.00
Heart and Soul, Loesser/Carmichael, 1938 .... 5.00
Heart O'Mine, Rose/Silvers, 1928 .... 5.00
Heart of a Clown, 1952 .... 2.00
Hearts & Flowers, Tobani, 1899 .... 5.00
Hearts of Stone, Ray/Jackson, 1954 .... 5.00
Heat Wave, Berlin, 1933 .... 6.00
Heaven Born Banner, Hoffman, 1906.. 3.00
Heaven Help This Heart of Mine, 1937 .... 2.00
Heavenly Night, 1930.. 3.00
Heavens Artillery, Lincoln, 1904 .... 15.00
Heidelberg, 1908 .... 4.00
Heigh Ho the Gang's All Here, Adamson/Lane, 1933 .... 5.00
Heigh-Ho, 1938 .... 12.00
Helen, Ellis/Wilson, 1908 .... 3.00
Helen-Polka, 1947 .... 2.00
Helen of Troy, Wimperis/Darewski, 1920 .... 8.00
Heliotrope Rag, Braham, 1906 .... 15.00
Hello Central! Give Me No Man's Land, Lewis, 1918 .... 10.00
Hello Daddy, I Knew That Was Your Car, Browne, 1896.............. 35.00

Hello Dolly, 1963 .... 2.00
Hello Montreal, 1928 .... 2.00
Hello My Dearie, Stamper, 1917 .... 2.00
Hello Stranger, Leslie/Muir, 1911 .... 5.00
Hello Swanee Hello, Coslow, 1927 .... 8.00
Hello! I've Been Looking for You, 1916 .... 2.00
Hello, Aloha, Hello, 1917 .... 3.00
Hello, Angel Face, Bob White, 1909 .... 5.00
Hello, My Sweetheart I Love You, Heath/James, 1916 .... 3.00
Henry's Made a Lady Out of Lizzie, O'Keefe, 1928 .... 15.00
Here Comes Cookie, Gordon, 1935 .... 3.00
Here Comes Heaven Again, 1945 .... 2.00
Here Comes My Daddy Now, Gilbert/Muir, 1912 .... 5.00
Here Comes Santa Claus, 1947 .... 3.00
Here Comes the Groom, 1916 .... 3.00
Here Comes the Navy, Oakes, 1934 .... 2.00
Here Lies Love, Robin/Rainger, 1932 .... 3.00
Here's a Rose for You, Dubin, 1914 .... 3.00
Here's Love In Your Eye, Robin/Rainger, 1936 .... 3.00
Here's To Love, Rubens, 1913 .... 3.00
Hernando's Hideaway, 1954 .... 2.00
Hero of the Isthmus, Lampg, 1912 .... 3.00
Herself and Meself, Gaul, 1926 .... 2.00
Hesitation Blues, Middleton/Smythe, 1915 .... 15.00
Hesitation Waltz, Klickman, 1913 .... 3.00
Hesitation, Shaw, 1913 .... 5.00
Hey There, 1954 .... 2.00
Hey! Jealous Lover, 1956 .... 2.00
Hey, Babe, Hey, Porter, 1936 .... 5.00
Hey, Look Me Over, 1960 .... 2.00
Hi Lola, 1958 .... 2.00
Hi Neighbor, 1941 .... 3.00
Hiawatha's Melody of Love, Bryan, 1920 .... 15.00
Hiawatha, 1901 .... 10.00
Hidden, 1936 .... 28.00
High and the Mighty, 1954 .... 2.00
High Cost of Loving, Meyer 1919 .... 3.00
High Noon, 1952 .... 4.00
Highland Grand March, Bailey, 1877 .... 35.00
Hindustan, Wallace/Weeks, 1918 .... 5.00
Hiram, Burt, 1915 .... 3.00
His Buttons Are Marked U.S., 1902 .... 15.00
His Rocking Horse Ran Away, 1944 .... 3.00
Hit the Grit, Wilson, 1911 .... 3.00
Hitchy Koo, Gilbert/Muir, Abrahams, 1912 .... 3.00

Hobson Of the Merrimac, Jewell, 1898 .... 20.00
Hold Me, Hicam, 1920 .... 3.00
Hold My Hand, 1950 .... 2.00
Holding Hands, 1906 .... 3.00
Home Again Blues, Berlin, 1921 .... 12.00
Home Again, Weston, 1918 .... 5.00
Home Coming, Paull, 1908 .... 20.00
Home in Maine, 1949 .... 2.00
Home in San Antone, Jenkins, 1943 .... 2.00
Home on the Range, Manoloff, 1935 .... 5.00
Home Sweet Home Polka, Mason/Berman, 1948 .... 2.00
Home Sweet Home, Presser, 1914 .... 3.00
Homes in Pasadena, 1923 .... 2.00
Homesick, Berlin, 1922 .... 8.00
Homeward Bound, Johnson/Goetz/Meyer, 1917 .... 10.00
Honest and Truly, Rose, 1952 .... 2.00
Honey Babe, Webster/Steiner, 1954 .... 3.00
Honey Behave, 1913 .... 3.00
Honey Boy, 1907 .... 2.00
Honey Bunch 'N' Me, 1924 .... 2.00
Honey Man, McCarthy/Piantadosi, 1911 .... 5.00
Honey Rose, McCarthy/Goodwin/Smith, 1912 .... 3.00
Honey Smile for Me, Mack, 1913 .... 2.00
Honey, 1928 .... 3.00
Honey, Dat's All, Van Alstyne, 1921 .... 7.00
Honey, Odoms/Raybould, 1913 .... 3.00
Honeycomb, Merrill, 1954 .... 3.00
Honeymoon Hotel, Dubin/Warren, 1933 .... 5.00
Honeymoon Lane, 1931 .... 3.00
Honeymoon Love, Brown/Ayer, 1911 .... 5.00
Honeymoon, 1932 .... 2.00
Hong Kong, 1916 .... 3.00
Honky Tonk Sweetheart, 1952 .... 2.00
Honky Tonky, McCarron/Smith, 1916 .... 4.00
Honolulu America Loves You, 1916 .... 3.00
Honolulu Eyes, 1920 .... 3.00
Honolulu, 1939 .... 3.00
Hoo-oo, Ingraham, 1907 .... 6.00
Hooray For Love, Robin/Arlen, 1948 .... 3.00
Hoosier Hop, 1929 .... 3.00
Hop a Jitney With Me, Donovan, 1915 .... 15.00
Hop Scotch Polka, 1949 .... 2.00
Hot Diggity, Hoffman/Manning, 1956 .... 2.00
Hot Hands, Straight, 1916 .... 7.00
Hot Lips, 1922 .... 10.00

**Pictured above is a small selection of
Sheet Music Covers that are listed within this book.**

Hot Time in the Old Town, Hayden/Metz, 1896 .... 20.00
Hot Time in the Town of Berlin, 1943 .... 3.00
Hot Toddy, 1953 .... 2.00
Hotshoe, Stevens, 1953 .... 13.00
Hotsy Totsy Town, 1923 .... 2.00
How About Me, Berlin, 1928 .... 3.00
How Am I to Know, 1919 .... 4.00
How Are Things in Glocca Morra, 1946 .... 2.00
How Blue the Night, Adamson/McHugh, 1944 .... 3.00
How Could I Ever Forget You, Leopold/Carus, 1919 .... 2.00
How Deep Is the Ocean, Berlin, 1932 .... 6.00
How Did I Know, 1954 .... 2.00
How Do I Know It's Real, 1941 .... 2.00
How Do I Know It's Sunday, Kahal/Fain, 1934 .... 3.00
How Do You Miss Josephine, Mccree/Vontilzer, 1909 .... 10.00
How Easy It Is to Remember, Allen/Daly, 1914 .... 3.00
How Late Can You Stay Out Tonight, 1913 .... 4.00
How Many Times, Berlin, 1939 .... 6.00
How Sweet You Are, Loesser/Schwartz, 1943 .... 3.00
How the Money Rolls In, Havez/Barron, 1913 .... 3.00
How Ya Gonna Keep Them Down on the Farm, 1919 .... 4.00
How'd ja Like to Love Me, Loesser/Lane, 1938 .... 3.00
How's Ev'ry Little Thing In Dixie, Yellen/Gumble, 1916 .... 2.00
Howdy Do, Mis' Springtime, Guion/Gordon, 1924 .... 3.00
Howdy, 1918 .... 3.00
Huckelberry Finn, Lewis-Hess/Young, 1917 .... 10.00
Huckleberry Finn Cake Walk, Brennan, 1900 .... 12.00
Humoreske, Dvorak, 1911 .... 3.00
Humpty Dumpty Heart, Burke/Van Huesen, 1941 .... 3.00
Hundred Years From Now, Caddigan/Brennan/Story, 1914 .... 3.00
Hungarian Rag, Lenzberg, 1913 .... 7.00
Hunk-a-Tin, Levy, 1918 .... 20.00
Hunky Dory, Holzmann, 1900 .... 15.00
Hurrah! For the Liberty Boys, Hurrah!, Paull, 1918 .... 20.00
Hush A Bye, Baby Mine, Bertrand, 1920 .... 2.00
Hush a Bye Island, 1946 .... 3.00
Hush a Bye Ma Baby, 1914 .... 4.00
Hush a Bye, Koehler/Jerome, 1947 .... 3.00
I Adore You, 1936 .... 3.00
I Ain't 'en Got'en No Time To Have the Blues, Tilzer, 1919 .... 20.00
I Ain't Goin' Ter Work No Mo, 1900 .... 20.00
I Ain't Gonna Give Nobody None O'This Jelly Roll, 1919 .... 7.00
I Ain't Got No Use For Sleep, Bickwell, 1903 .... 8.00
I Ain't Got Nobody Much, Williams/Graham, 1916 .... 5.00
I Ain't Got Nobody, Young/Warfield, 1914 .... 7.00

I Ain't Lazy I'm Just Dreamin', Franklin, 1934 .... 2.00
I Ain't Nobody's Darling, Hughes/King, 1921 .... 2.00
I Almost Lost My Mind, 1950 .... 2.00
I Always Do the Heavy, Arnold/Vivian, 1871 .... 12.00
I Always Knew the Girl I'd Love Would Be a Girl Like You 3.00
I Am A Highly Educated Man, 1894 .... 7.00
I Am An American, 1940 .... 2.00
I Am For You, 1910 .... 6.00
I Am the Candy, Graham/Davis, 1904 .... 6.00
I Believe, 1947 .... 2.00
I Bring A Love Song, 1930 .... 3.00
I Called To Say Goodnight, Young/Conrad, 1932 .... 2.00
I Called You My Sweetheart, 1917 .... 3.00
I Came Here To Talk For Joe, 1942 .... 2.00
I Can Dream, Can't I, Fain, 1937 .... 2.00
I Can't Begin To Tell You, Gordon/Monaco, 1945 .... 3.00
I Can't Believe That You're In Love With Me, 1926 .... 10.00
I Can't Believe the Tales of Hoffman, 1927 .... 3.00
I Can't Do Without You, Berlin, 1928 .... 6.00
I Can't Escape From You, 1936 .... 3.00
I Can't Forget Tthe Night We Met, 1933 .... 2.00
I Can't Get Over A Girl Like You, 1926 .... 2.00
I Can't Get Started, Gershwin, 1935 .... 5.00
I Can't Give you Anything But Love, 1928 .... 2.00
I Can't Live Without You, 1914 .... 3.00
I Can't Love you Anymore, 1940 .... 2.00
I Can't Make Her Happy, 1928 .... 2.00
I Can't See the Good In Good Bye, 1919 .... 4.00
I Can't Stop Babying You, 1924 .... 2.00
I Can't Stop Loving You Now, 1914 .... 3.00
I Can't Tell Why I Love You But I Do, 1900 .... 7.00
I Cannot Sleep Without Dreaming of You, 1920 .... 3.00
I Could Have Danced All Night, 1956 .... 2.00
I Couldn't Get To It, Hall, 1924 .... 2.00
I Couldn't Sleep a Wink Last Night, 1943 .... 3.00
I Cover the Waterfront, 1933 .... 3.00
I Cried Like a Baby, 1939 .... 2.00
I Didn't Mean A Word I Said, 1945 .... 2.00
I Didn't Raise My Boy To Be a Slacker, Fries, 1924 .... 2.00
I Didn't Raise My Boy To Be a Soldier, Bryan, 1915 .... 10.00
I Didn't Raise My Ford To Be a Jitney, Frost, 1915 .... 25.00
I Do, 1925 .... 2.00
I Do, I Don't Know Why, 1952 .... 2.00
I Don't Care What Happens To Me Now, Hall 14.00
I Don't Care What You Used To Be, 1924 .... 2.00

48

I Don't Care Who Knows It, 1944 .... 3.00
I Don't Feel No Ways Tired, Burleigh, 1917 .... 6.00
I Don't Mind Being All Alone, 1926 .... 2.00
I Don't Need Atmosphere, 1930 .... 3.00
I Don't See Me In Your Eyes Anymore, 1949 .... 2.00
I Don't Think I'm In Love, Cahn, 1964 .... 2.00
I Don't Think So, Hall, 1925 .... 2.00
I Don't Want To Be Loved, 1944 .... 2.00
I Don't Want To Get Well, 1917 .... 10.00
I Don't Want To See Tomorrow, Wayne/Morris 2.00
I Don't Want To Set the World On Fire, 1941 .... 2.00
I Don't Want to Make History, Robin/Rainger, 1936 .... 5.00
I Don't Want to Play In Your Yard, 1932 .... 2.00
I Don't Want to Walk Without You, 1941 .... 3.00
I Don't Want Your Kisses, 1929 .... 3.00
I Don't Want Your Lips, 1926 .... 2.00
I Dream of Jeannie, 1939 .... 2.00
I Dream of You, 1944 .... 2.00
I Dream Too Much, 1935 .... 3.00
I Dreamed My Boy Was Home Again, Sawyer, 1863 .... 20.00
I Dreamt My Daddy Came Home, Porter/Darcey, 1918 .... 3.00
I Dug A Ditch, 1943 .... 6.00
I Fall In Love Too Easily, Cahn, 1944 .... 5.00
I Faw Down an' Go Boom, Brockman, 1928 .... 6.00
I Feel Like a Feather In the Breeze, Gordon/Revel, 1935 .... 3.00
I Found the Sweetest Rose That Grows in Dixieland, 1919 .... 4.00
I Found You Among the Roses, Pitman, 1915 .... 3.00
I Gave Her That, DeSylva/Jolson, 1919 .... 10.00
I Get the Blues When It Rains, 1929 .... 2.00
I Get The Neck of the Chicken, 1942 .... 4.00
I Go, 1956 .... 2.00
I Got Plenty O'Nuttin, Gershwin, 1935 .... 3.00
I Got Rhythm, Gershwin, 1930 .... 6.00
I Got Spurs That Jingle Jangle Jingle, 1942 .... 2.00
I Gotta Get Myself Somebody to Love, 1926 .... 2.00
I Gotta Go Get My Baby, 1955 .... 2.00
I Gotta Have My Baby Back, 1949 .... 2.00
I Guess I Expected Too Much, Gallop/Saxon 2.00
I Guess I'll Soon Be Back in Dixieland, Rogers, 1915 .... 5.00
I Had a Little Talk With the Lord, Curtis, 1944 .... 5.00
I Had the Craziest Dream, 1942 .... 4.00
I Handed It Over To Riley, McGlennon, 1892, ... 10.00
I Hate to Lose You, Clarke/Gottler, 1918 .... 3.00
I Hate to See Those Summer Days Roll By, Calendar, 1912 .... 6.00
I Have a Big Jazz Band, Bowers, 1918 .... 6.00

I Have But One Heart, 1945 .... 2.00
I Have Eyes, Robin/Rainger, 1938 .... 2.00
I Have to Have You, Robin/Whiting, 1929 .... 3.00
I Haven't Changed a Thing, 1938 .... 2.00
I Hear a Dream, 1939 .... 7.00
I Just Came In To Say Hello, Edwards/Cobb, 1913 .... 2.00
I Just Cannot Say Goodbye, Knight, 1912 .... 20.00
I Just Roll Along, Trent/De Rose, 1927 .... 3.00
I Know De Lord's Laid His Hands On Me, Burleigh, 1925 .... 7.00
I Know I Got More Than My Share (When God Gave Me You) 5.00
I Know Now, Dubin/Warren, 1937 .... 2.00
I Know What It Means to be Lonesome, Kendis, 1919 .... 2.00
I KnowYou, 1917 .... 3.00
I Left Her On the Beach At Honolulu, 1916 .... 3.00
I Left My Door Open, 1919 .... 3.00
I Left My Heart At the Stage Door Canteen, Berlin, 1942 .... 10.00
I Left My Heart In San Francisco, 1954 .... 2.00
I Like It, 1921 .... 3.00
I Like Mountain Music, Weldon, 1933, ... 5.00
I Like My Old Home Town, Lauder, 1923 .... 3.00
I Like the Hat - I Like the Dress, Henry/Bryan, 1911 .... 3.00
I Like You, Carle/Peters 2.00
I Look At Heaven, 1942 .... 2.00
I Lost My Heart in Dixieland, 1919 .... 3.00
I Love a Lassie, 1906 .... 2.00
I Love a Piano, 1915 .... 20.00
I Love America, Garrick, 1941 .... 3.00
I Love But You, Burnette, 1925 .... 2.00
I Love Her Oh-Oh-Oh, Jolson, 1913 .... 20.00
I Love Her, Porter, 1918 .... 2.00
I Love It, Goetz, 1910 .... 5.00
I Love My Billy Sunday, But Oh You Saturday Night, 1914 .... 6.00
I Love My Wife, Lucas/Tilzer, 1909 .... 8.00
I Love Paris, 1953 .... 2.00
I Love the Ladies, 1914 .... 3.00
I Love the Name of Mary, Young, 1910 .... 5.00
I Love the U.S.A., Hardy, 1914 .... 6.00
I Love the Way You Say Goodnight, 1951 .... 3.00
I Love Thee, 1911 .... 5.00
I Love To Quarrel With You, Berlin, 1914 .... 10.00
I Love to Bumpity Bump, Sherman, 1928 .... 6.00
I Love to Whistle, 1938 .... 3.00
I Love You - I Hate You, Meyer, 1929 .... 2.00
I Love You Best of All, Taylor, 1915 .... 5.00
I Love You California, 1913 .... 3.00

**Pictured above is a small selection of
Sheet Music Covers that are listed within this book.**

I Love You So Much, 1930 .... 3.00
I Love You So Much, 1948 .... 2.00
I Love You Truly, Bond, 1906 .... 2.00
I Love You, Believe Me, I Love You, Boutelje, 1929 .... 3.00
I Love You, Porter, 1943 .... 2.00
I Love You, The World Is Thine, Schader, 1907 .... 10.00
I Love You, Thompson/Archer, 1923 .... 2.00
I Love You Today, Allen, 1963 .... 8.00
I Loved Her Ever Since She Was a Baby, Lauder, 1909 .... 2.00
I Loved You Not Your Gold, Curran/Sullivan, 1900 .... 10.00
I Loved You Then, 1928 .... 3.00
I May Be Dancing With Somebody Else, 1926 .... 3.00
I May Be Gone for a Long, Long Time, Brown/Tilzer, 1917 ....20.00
I May Be Wrong, Yellen, 1929 .... 5.00
I Met Him In Paris, Meinardi/Carmichael, 1937 .... 10.00
I Might Be Your Once-In-A-While, 1919 .... 3.00
I Mind Me the Mornin', Waugh/Rosedale, 1910 .... 3.00
I Miss That Mississippi Miss That Misses Me, Wendling,1918 ...... 6.00
I Miss You American, Gilbert/Roberts, 1916 .... 5.00
I Miss You In A Thousand Different Ways, 1906 .... 3.00
I Miss You Most of All, McCarthy/Monaco, 1913 .... 3.00
I Must Be Dreaming, Dubin, 1927 .... 2.00
I Never Knew A Wonderful Wife, 1919 .... 2.00
I Never Knew How Much I Loved You, 1919 .... 3.00
I Never Knew There Was Sunshine, Flanagan, 1918 .... 2.00
I Never Knew What Eyes Could Do, 1912 .... 3.00
I Never Knew What Sweetheart Meant Till I Met You, 1912 .... 3.00
I Never Knew, Williams, Young/Grant, 1913 .... 6.00
I Never See Maggie Alone, Tilsey/Lynton, 1936 .... 3.00
I Poured My Heart Into A Song, Berlin, 1939 .... 6.00
I Promise You, 1931 .... 3.00
I Remember You, 1942 .... 3.00
I Said No, Loesser/Styne, 1941 .... 3.00
I Saw Mommy Kissing Santa Claus, Connor, 1952 .... 3.00
I Sent My Wife to the 1,000 Isles, 1916 .... 15.00
I Should Car, 1944 .... 5.00
I Simply Can't Resist You, Hobart/Hoffman, 1906 .... 5.00
I Still Call You Sweetheart, Yellen/New, 1930 .... 2.00
I Stole A Kiss In the Dark, 1945 .... 5.00
I Stood On De Ribber Ob Jerdon, Burleigh, 1918 .... 10.00
I Take Thee, Dear, Carter/Johnson, 1950 .... 2.00
I Think I Oughtn't Ought to Any More, Bryan, 1907 .... 15.00
I Think I'll Get Wed In the Summer, Lauder, 1919 .... 3.00
I Thought About You, Mercer, 1939 .... 9.00
I Threw A Kiss In the Ocean, Berlin, 1942 .... 5.00

I Trust My Husband Anywhere, But I Like to Stick Around 4.00
I Used To Be Color Blind, Berlin, 1938 .... 10.00
I Used To Love you But It's All Over Now, Brown/Tilzer, 1920 ..... 3.00
I Used to be Afraid to Go Home in the Dark, 1908 .... 10.00
I Used to Sing, I Wish I Had a Girl, But, 1909 .... 5.00
I Walked In, 1944 .... 2.00
I Waltz Alone, 1949 .... 2.00
I Wanna Be Loved By You, 1928 .... 2.00
I Want A Daddy Who Will Rock Me to Sleep, 1919 .... 6.00
I Want A Girl (Just Like the Girl, That Married Dear Old Dad 10.00
I Want a Little Love From You, 1915 .... 3.00
I Want Dem Presents Back, West, 1896 .... 15.00
I Want My Mammy, 1921 .... 12.00
I Want Someone to Love, 1912 .... 3.00
I Want To Be a Lady, 1901 .... 3.00
I Want To Be Happy, 1924 .... 2.00
I Want To Be In Berlin, Berlin/Snyder, 1912 .... 6.00
I Want To Be In Georgia, Levenson, 1915 .... 3.00
I Want To Be Ready, Burleigh, 1917 .... 5.00
I Want To Be Somebody's Baby Girl, Greene/Motzan, 1913 .... 3.00
I Want To Be There, Monaco/Clarke, 1915 .... 2.00
I Want To Be With You, Swan, Garton, 1916 .... 3.00
I Want To Be In Dixie, Berlin, 1912 .... 12.00
I Want To Go Back to Michigan, Berlin, 1914 .... 6.00
I Want To Go To Tokyo, McCarthy/Fischer, 1914 .... 3.00
I Want To Go to the Land Where the Sweet Daddies Grow, 1920 . 3.00
I Want To Linger, Marshall, 1914 .... 3.00
I Want You Morning, Noon, and Night, 1921 .... 2.00
I Want You to Meet My Mother, Dubin/Coolidge, 1914 .... 6.00
I Want You, Arnold & Brown, 1914 .... 6.00
I Was A Dreamer Too, Lewis, 1916 .... 3.00
I Was Coming Thru the Clover, Howard, 1919 .... 3.00
I Was So Young, Gershwin, 1919 .... 6.00
I Will Love You When the Silver Threads Are Shining 2.00
I Will Return Sweetheart Again, Gillespie/Dillea, 1902 .... 5.00
I Wish I Didn't Love You So, Hutton/Lund, 1947 .... 8.00
I Wish I Had a Girl, Kahn/LeBoy, 1907 .... 6.00
I Wish I Had Died In Egypt Land, Klemm, 1926 .... 3.00
I Wish I Was In Dixieland Tonight, 1900 .... 10.00
I Wish I Were Aladdin, 1935 .... 2.00
I Wish My Honeymoon Would Shine, 1912 .... 3.00
I Wish the Band Would Play, Breen/Geary, 1903 .... 10.00
I Wish Today Were Yesterday and Yesterday Today, 1912 .... 3.00
I Wish You All the Luck in the World, Olman, 1917 .... 12.00
I Wish You'd Keep Out of My Dreams, Clark, 1913 .... 3.00

I Won't Dance, 1935 .... 6.00
I Won't Say I Will, Gershwin, 1923 .... 3.00
I Wonder How I Ever Passed You By, 1921 .... 2.00
I Wonder How the Old Folks Are at Home, 1909 .... 3.00
I Wonder If the Old Place Looks the Same, 1898 .... 4.00
I Wonder if You Miss Me, 1904 .... 3.00
I Wonder What He's Doing Tonight, Goodwin/Hanley, 1917 .... 3.00
I Wonder What Will William Tell, 1914 .... 3.00
I Wonder What Would Happen if the Moon Would Tell, 1912 .... 3.00
I Wonder What's Become of Sally, Yellen/Ager, 1924 .... 8.00
I Wonder Where My Baby Is Tonight, 1925 .... 2.00
I Wonder Whether, 1917 .... 3.00
I Wonder Who's Kissing Her Now, 1909 .... 6.00
I Wonder Why She Kept on Saying Si-Si, Jolson, 1918 .... 15.00
I Would Like to Be a Grand Lady, 1905 .... 3.00
I'd Do It All Over Again, 1914 .... 3.00
I'd Feel At Home If They'd Let Me Join the Army, 1917 .... 3.00
I'd Give a Million Tomorrows, 1940 .... 2.00
I'd Give the World to Win the One Who's All the World to Me 3.00
I'd Like To Be In Texas When They Round Up In the Spring 2.00
I'd Like To Be the Fellow That Girl Is Waiting For, 1909 .... 3.00
I'd Like to Go Bathing With Someone, 1914 .... 3.00
I'd Like to See the Kaiser With A Lily In His Hand, 1918 .... 10.00
I'd Like to Wander Back Again to Kidland, 1917 .... 4.00
I'd Love To Meet That Old Sweetheart of Mine, 1926 .... 2.00
I'd Love to Live In Loveland, Williams, 1910 .... 3.00
I'd Rather Be Blue Over You, Rose/Fisher, 1928 .... 5.00
I'd Rather Be Me, 1945 .... 2.00
I'd Rather Float Through a Dreamy Old Waltz with You, You 4.00
I'd Rather Have a Girlie Than An Automobile, Dillon, 1908 .... 20.00
I'd Rather Listen To Your Eyes, 1935 .... 3.00
I'd Rather Love What I Cannot Have, Janis, 1911 .... 7.00
I'd Rather Two Step Than Waltz, Bill, 1907 .... 5.00
I'l Get You, 1913 .... 2.00
I'll Always Be In Love With You, 1929 .... 2.00
I'll Always Love You, Livingston/Evans, 1950 .... 3.00
I'll Always Remember You, Caddigan/Coty, 1917 .... 3.00
I'll Await My Love, Howard, 1883 .... 20.00
I'll Be Back in a Year Little Darling, 1941 .... 3.00
I'll Be Good Because of You, 1930 .... 2.00
I'll Be Loving You, Cahn/Duke, 1952 .... 8.00
I'll Be There Mary Dear, Sterling/Tilzer, 1902 .... 12.00
I'll Be With You Honey in Honeysuckle time, 1910 .... 6.00
I'll Be With You in Apple Blossom Time, 1920 .... 3.00
I'll Be Your Own, Bush, 1900 .... 15.00

I'll Be Yours, 1938 .... 2.00
I'll Build A Bungalow Of Love, 1916 .... 2.00
I'll Build A Fence Around You, Lewis/Mills, 1910 .... 2.00
I'll Change Your Shadows to Sunshine, Griffith, 1912 .... 4.00
I'll Come Back Some Day, Palmer, 1917 .... 2.00
I'll Come Back to You When It's All Over, Brown/Mills, 1917 .... 4.00
I'll Dance My Way Right Back To Dixieland, Clarke, 1919 ....20.00
I'll Do Anything In the World For You, Edwards/Cobb, 1906........ 5.00
I'll Do It All Over Again, Brown/Gumble, 1914 .... 3.00
I'll Dream of You, Rubens, 1902 .... 3.00
I'll Follow My Secret Heart, 1934 .... 2.00
I'll Forget You, Ball/Burns, 1921 .... 3.00
I'll Get By as Long as I Have You, 1943 .... 3.00
I'll Get By, Turk/Ahlert, 1928 .... 2.00
I'll Give You Back your Kisses, 1922 .... 3.00
I'll Go Back to the Ole Bridge Again, Cooper/Skelley, 1884..........20.00
I'll Go Fifty-Fifty With You, Branen/Lange, 1914 .... 5.00
I'll Have Somebody Else, Wills, 1948 .... 2.00
I'll Hop, Skip and Jump, 1923 .... 3.00
I'll Keep On Loving You, 1939 .... 2.00
I'll Love You In My Dreams, 1931 .... 2.00
I'll Make You Happy, Dietz/Schwarts, 1934............................... 10.00
I'll Meet You in the City When the Summer Days are Over 3.00
I'll Never Do It Again, 1923 .... 3.00
I'll Never Let A Day Pass, 1941 .... 3.00
I'll Never Say "I Love You", 1948 .... 3.00
I'll Never Smile Again, Lowe, 1940 .... 5.00
I'll Say She Does, Jolson, 1918 ....20.00
I'll See You Again, 1929 .... 2.00
I'll See You In My Dreams, 1924... 4.00
I'll See You In the Morning, 1932 .... 2.00
I'll See You Later Yankeeland, Harris, 1916 .... 4.00
I'll Soon Be Leaving For My Home Town, 1915 .... 4.00
I'll Stand Beneath Your Window Tonight, 1922 .... 2.00
I'll Still Be Loving You, 1928 .... 3.00
I'll Strew Your Path With Roses, 1912 .... 2.00
I'll String Along With You, 1934 .... 3.00
I'll Take You Back To Italy, Berlin, 1917..................................... 8.00
I'll Take You Home Again, Kathleen, Westendorf, 1922 .... 10.00
I'll Wait For You Till the Cows Come Home, Allen, 1911 .... 3.00
I'll Walk Alone, 1944 .... 3.00
I'll Wed You in the Golden Summertime, Bryan, 1902.................. 5.00
I'm A Long Way From Tipperary, Lewis/Erdman, 1914 .... 5.00
I'm a Dreamer Aren't We All, 1929... 3.00
I'm a Dreamer That's Chasing Bubbles, Magine/Little, 1919 .... 2.00

**Pictured above is a small selection of
Sheet Music Covers that are listed within this book.**

I'm a Lonesome Melody, Young/Meyer, 1915 .... 3.00
I'm A-Longing for You, Tice, 1919.. 2.00
I'm A Lover of Paree, Robin/Rainger, 1933 .... 8.00
I'm Afraid to Come Home in the Dark, Boley................................ 3.00
I'm All Bound 'Round Mason Dixon Line, Schwartz, 1917 .... 14.00
I'm All Dressed Up and No Place To Go, Allen/Daly, 1913 .... 7.00
I'm Always Chasing Rainbows, Carroll/McCarthy, 1918 .... 6.00
I'm Always Chasing Rainbows, Grable/Haver, 1934..................... 8.00
I'm Always Thinking of Georgia, McCarthy, Monaco, 1917 .... 3.00
I'm An Old Cowhand, 1936 .... 3.00
I'm Another, Osborne/Ellis, 1892.. 5.00
I'm As Happy As a Bumble Bee, Kramer/Cooper 3.00
I'm Bringing Up the Family, Franklin/Green, 1909 .... 5.00
I'm Coming Home To You Mother of Mine, Duffy, 1941 .... 2.00
I'm Doin' That Thing, 1930 .... 3.00
I'm Doing What I'm Doing For Love, Yellen/Ager, 1929 .... 5.00
I'm Facing the Music, 1934 .... 2.00
I'm Falling In Love With Someone, Herbert, 1910 .... 7.00
I'm Falling In Love With Your Wonderful Eyes, 1929 .... 3.00
I'm Fit To Be Tied, 1939... 3.00
I'm Following You, 1929 .... 3.00
I'm Forever Blowing Bubbles, 1919 .... 3.00
I'm From Ohio, Brennan/Ball, 1918... 2.00
I'm Gettin' Sentimental Over You, 1932 .... 3.00
I'm Getting Ready For My Mother-in-Law, Norworth, 1906 .... 12.00
I'm Getting Tired So I Can Sleep, Berlin, 1942........................... 8.00
I'm Getting Tired, 1934 .... 2.00
I'm Glad I Can Make You Cry, 1918 .... 3.00
I'm Glad I'm Not Young Anymore, 1957 .... 3.00
I'm Glad My Wife's in Europe, 1914 .... 12.00
I'm Goin Back to Carolina, Erdman, 1914 .... 12.00
I'm Goin' Back to Louisiana, 1913... 2.00
I'm Goin' Home to Mobile, Leap, 1914 .... 3.00
I'm Goin' Shoppin With You, 1935... 2.00
I'm Goin' South, Jolson, 1923 .... 10.00
I'm Going Back To the Farm, Berlin, 1915 .... 15.00
I'm Going Back to California, Brennan/Ball, 1916 .... 3.00
I'm Going Back to Erin, 1915 .... 2.00
I'm Going Back to My Home Town, Goldie/Harlow, 1916............. 3.00
I'm Going Back to Reno, Jerome, 1911 .... 5.00
I'm Going Back to the Girl I Love, Clay, 1915 .... 5.00
I'm Going Back to Tipperary, Dick, 1915.................................... 3.00
I'm Going To Bring A Wedding Ring to You In Spring, 1915 .... 3.00
I'm Going to Climb the Blue Ridge Mountains, 1918................... 4.00
I'm Going to Do What I Please, 1909 .... 3.00

I'm Going to Follow the Boys, Rogers/Monaco, 1917 .... 3.00
I'm Going to Park Myself In Your Arms, Heath, 1926 .... 5.00
I'm Gonna Build a Home In Heaven, 1933 .... 2.00
I'm Gonna Knock Knock Knock, 1922 .... 3.00
I'm Gonna Live Till I Die, 1950 .... 2.00
I'm Gonna Meet My Sweetie Now, Davis, 1927 .... 2.00
I'm Gonna Rise, Gunn, 1941 .... 8.00
I'm Gonna Sit Right Down and Write Myself a Letter, 1935 .... 3.00
I'm Gonna Spend My Honeymoon in Dixie, Rogers, 1919 .... 3.00
I'm Gonna Wander Out Yonder, 1926 .... 2.00
I'm Hearin', Gilbert/Friedland, 1917 .... 5.00
I'm Hitting the Trail to Normandy, Snyder, 1917 .... 4.00
I'm In A Dancing Mood, 1936 .... 3.00
I'm In Love With Vienna, 1938 .... 3.00
I'm In Love With You, 1929 .... 12.00
I'm In the Market For You, McCarthy/Hanley, 1930 .... 5.00
I'm In the Mood For Love, McHugh/Fields, 1935 .... 3.00
I'm in Love With the Mother of My Best Girl, 1913 .... 3.00
I'm Just a Little Blue, 1922 .... 2.00
I'm Just a Little Boy Blue, 1934 .... 2.00
I'm Just Wild About Animal Crackers, 1926 .... 3.00
I'm Just Wild About Harry, Sissle/Blake, 1921 .... 10.00
I'm Learning A Lot From You, Fields/McHugh, 1930 .... 3.00
I'm Like a Ship Without a Sail, Brockman, 1919 .... 10.00
I'm Living In A Great Big Way, 1935 .... 3.00
I'm Longing For Old Virginia and You, 1915 .... 2.00
I'm Looking For a Bluebird, 1921 .... 3.00
I'm Losing My Heart to Someone, 1920 .... 2.00
I'm Lost Without You, Sally, 1932 .... 3.00
I'm Making Hay In the Moonlight, 1933 .... 3.00
I'm Mighty Lonesome Hon' Jes Fo' Yo', Trinkaus, 1925 .... 10.00
I'm Missin' Mammy's Kissin', Pollack, 1921 .... 10.00
I'm Not Jealous, 1919 .... 2.00
I'm Not Weary Yet, Gest, 1925 .... 3.00
I'm On A See Saw, 1934 .... 2.00
I'm On My Way Home, Berlin, 1926 .... 6.00
I'm On My Way to Dublin Bay, Murphy, 1915 .... 3.00
I'm On My Way to Mandalay, Fisher, 1913 .... 5.00
I'm On My Way to Reno, 1910 .... 4.00
I'm On the Road to Happiness, Malcolm/Solman, 1916 .... 5.00
I'm Only A Broken Toy, 1924 .... 3.00
I'm Only a Miner's Daughter, Montroy/Beaver, 1910 .... 5.00
I'm Only Guessing, 1931 .... 2.00
I'm Ridin' For a Fall, 1943 .... 4.00
I'm Sailing on a Sunbeam, 1929 .... 4.00

I'm Satisfied, 1918 .... 3.00
I'm Singing Your Love Songs to Somebody Else, 1930 .... 2.00
I'm Sittin' In a Hill Top, Johnston/Kahn, 1935 .... 3.00
I'm Skipping Rope With a Rainbow, 1953 .... 2.00
I'm So Busy, Greene/Wodehouse/Kern, 1916 .... 15.00
I'm Sorry I Ain't Got It-You Could Have It If I Had It Blues 6.00
I'm Sorry I Made You Cry, Bowers, 1918 .... 5.00
I'm Stepping Out With A Memory Tonight, 1940 .... 2.00
I'm Still In Love With Mollie, Browning/Stanley, 1906 .... 5.00
I'm Strong for Medinah, Stauffer 3.00
I'm That Way About Baby, 1929 .... 3.00
I'm the Echo, 1935 .... 3.00
I'm the Guy, Goldberg/Grant, 1912 .... 12.00
I'm the Last One Left On the Corner, 1930 .... 2.00
I'm Thinking, 1906 .... 3.00
I'm Thirsty For Kisses Hungry For Love, 1928 .... 6.00
I'm Throwing Rice, 1949 .... 2.00
I'm Thru With Love, Kahn/Malneck, 1931 .... 3.00
I'm Too Tired To Make Love, Layton, 1928 .... 3.00
I'm Tying the Leaves So They Won't Come Down, 1907 .... 4.00
I'm Waiting For a Letter, Love, Blake/French, 1878 .... 15.00
I'm Waiting for the Blue Moon to Shine, Williams, 1927 .... 3.00
I'm Walking Around In a Dream, 1929 .... 2.00
I'm Waltzing With A Broken Heart, 1948 .... 2.00
I'm Wastin' My Tears On You, 1944 .... 2.00
I'm Wearing My Heart Away For You, Harris, 1902 .... 5.00
I'm Wild About Horns on Automobiles That Go Ta-Ta-Ta 20.00
I'm Wishing, 1937 .... 15.00
I'm With You, Huston, 1918 .... 5.00
I'm Writing To You Sammy, Brown, 1917 .... 10.00
I'm Yours, 1930 .... 3.00
I've A Cosy Little Cottage In the Country, 1913 .... 3.00
I've A Longing In My Heart For You Louise, Harris, 1900 .... 6.00
I've a Rose For a Sweetheart, Walsh/Shisler, 1910 .... 3.00
I've Been Floating Down the Old Green River, Cooper, 1915 .... 5.00
I've Got A Feeling I'm Falling, 1929 .... 2.00
I've Got A Pocketful of Sunshine, Kahn/Johnston, 1935 .... 3.00
I've Got ADate With a Dream, Gordon/Revel, 1938 .... 3.00
I've Got AFeelin' For You, Madden/Morse, 1904 .... 7.00
I've Got AFeelin' You're Foolin, 1935 .... 3.00
I've Got APocketful of Dreams, 1938 .... 3.00
I've Got My Captain Working for Me, 1919 .... 6.00
I've Got My Eyes On You, Hager, 1902 .... 6.00
I've Got My Love To Keep Me Warm, Berlin, 1937 .... 8.00
I've Got Rings On My Fingers, 1909 .... 3.00

I've Got the Sweetest Girl In Maryland, Donaldson, 1917............. 3.00
I've Got the Time, I've Got the Place, 1910 .... 3.00
I've Got To Sing a Torch Song, Dubin/Warren, 1933 .... 5.00
I've Got You Under My Skin, 1936... 3.00
I've Got Your Number, Bryan/Meyer, 1910 .... 7.00
I've Gotta Get Up and Go To Work, 1933 .... 3.00
I've Grown So Used To You, 1901 .... 3.00
I've Had My Moments, Kahn/Donaldson, 1934.......................... 3.00
I've Lost My Heart But I Don't Care, Hough/Adams, 1908 .... 6.00
I've Lost You, Howard, 1916.. 12.00
I've Loved You Since You Were A Baby, McCarthy, 1914 .... 3.00
I've Painted A Picture in my Mind, 1931 .... 8.00
I've Never Forgotten, 1946.. 3.00
I've Never Seen a Smile Like Yours, 1924................................... 3.00
I've Sent My Wife to the Seashore, Dubin/Cormack, 1914 .... 3.00
I've Waited a Lifetime For You, 1929 .... 3.00
Ice Cream, Johnson, 1927 .... 2.00
Idaho, 1936 .... 2.00
Idle Dreams, Gershwin, 1920.. 3.00
If Absence Makes the Heart Grow Fonder, Why Did You 3.00
If All Girls Were Roses, Cooper/Douglas, 1906 .... 3.00
If All Moons Were Honeymoons, 1909... 3.00
If Dreams Were Only True, Pulford/Dailey, 1912 .... 3.00
If God Sent Me You, 1927 .... 2.00
If He Can Fight Like He Can Love, Good Night, German, 1918 .....20.00
If He Cared, Grey/Stothart, 1929 .... 2.00
If He Comes In, I'm Going Out, Smith/Mack, 1910..................... 8.00
If He Looks Good to Mother Don't Look for Another, 1913........... 4.00
If I Be Your Best Chance, 1965 .... 2.00
If I Can't Have You, 1929 .... 3.00
If I Catch the Guy Who Wrote Poor Butterfly, Green, 1917.......... 5.00
If I Could Call the Years Back, North, 1907 .... 4.00
If I Could Love You, 1914 .... 3.00
If I Had A Dozen Hearts, 1929... 2.00
If I Had A Million Dollars, Mercer/Malneck, 1934 .... 3.00
If I Had A Wishing Ring, 1945 .... 3.00
If I Had a Son For Each Star In Old Glory, 1917 .... 4.00
If I Had My Way, Klein/Kendis, 1913 .... 10.00
If I Knock the "L" Out of Kelly, Grant, 1916 .... 6.00
If I Loved You, 1945 .... 2.00
If I Only Had a Home Sweet Home, McDermott, 1906 .... 5.00
If I Only Had You Back Again, 1926 .... 2.00
If I Should Lose You, Robin/Rainger, 1935 .... 3.00
If I Was A Millionaire, Cobb/Edwards, 1912 .... 15.00
If I Were a Bell, Loesser, 1950 .... 2.00

Pictured above is a small selection of
Sheet Music Covers that are listed within this book.

If I Were Just Your Rose, Dodge, 1916 .... 2.00
If I Were King, 1902 .... 4.00
If I Were Rich, Reden, 1868 .... 7.00
If I Were the Ocean and You Were the Shore, 1914 .... 3.00
If I'm Dreaming, Bolton/Grey, 1929 .... 3.00
If I'm Lucky, 1946 .... 2.00
If I'm Not at the Roll Call, 1918 .... 3.00
If It Takes a Thousand Years, Brennan/Ball, 1915 .... 2.00
If Only She'd Look My Way, Novello, 1950 .... 2.00
If That's Your Idea of a Wonderful Time Take Me Home, 1914 ...... 12.00
If the Man In the Moon Were A Coon, Fischer, 1905 .... 25.00
If the Moon Turns Green, 1935 .... 2.00
If You Are But A Dream, 1941 .... 2.00
If You Are There, Bishop, 1904 .... 3.00
If You Can't Get A Girl In the Summertime, 1915 .... 2.00
If You Can't Sing, Dance, Bowers/Smith, 1909 .... 3.00
If You Could Care, 1920 .... 2.00
If You Could See Mother Today, 1913 .... 2.00
If You Don't Want Me, Berlin, 1913 .... 12.00
If You Ever Get Lonely, Kahn/Marshall, 1916 .... 3.00
If You Look in Her Eyes, Harbach, 1917 .... 3.00
If You Love Me, 1949 .... 2.00
If You Loved Me Truly, Porter, 1953 .... 2.00
If You Only Had My Disposition, McCarron/VonTilzer, 1915 .... 10.00
If You Please, 1943 .... 1.00
If You Talk In Your Sleep Don't Mention My Name, 1911 .... 2.00
If You Want the Rainbow, 1928 .... 3.00
If You Won't Be Good to Me, Corin, 1908 .... 8.00
If You're Crazy About the Women You're Not Crazy At All 4.00
Illinois, 1948 .... 2.00
Imagination, Mullen/Bryan, 1904 .... 5.00
In A Blue And Pensive Mood, 1934 .... 2.00
In A Kitchenette, Dubin/Burke, 1929 .... 3.00
In A Little Hula Heaven, Robin/Rainger, 1937 .... 3.00
In a Blue Sunbonnet and a Gingham Gown, 1911 .... 4.00
In a Hupmobile for Two, Brady/Alexander, 1910 .... 25.00
In a Little Spanish Town, 1926 .... 3.00
In A One Room Flat, Robin/Rainger, 1933 .... 8.00
In Acapulco, 1945 .... 3.00
In an Auto Car, Sutton, 1908 .... 20.00
In Dear Old Tennessee, Fields/Newman, 1909 .... 3.00
In Dixie Land With Dixie Lou, 1912 .... 6.00
In Flanders' Fields, Tours, 1918 .... 10.00
In Florida Among the Palms, Berlin, 1916 .... 15.00
In Great Falls Virginia, Tait/Bernard, 1922 .... 3.00

In Her Cute Little Automobile, Travaline, 1916 .... 30.00
In Loves Garden, Just You and I, Gillespie/Osborne, 1913 .... 3.00
In Maytime, Snyder, 1921 .... 2.00
In Mexico, 1933 .... 2.00
In My Arms, 1943 .... 3.00
In My Canoe, Jones/Story, 1913 .... 3.00
In My Dreams of You, 1900 .... 4.00
In My Garden of Golden Dreams, 1910 .... 3.00
In My Garden, Firestone, 1929 .... 2.00
In My Harem, Berlin, 1913 .... 6.00
In My Home Town, Kalmar/Ruby, 1922 .... 2.00
In My Honolulu Garden, Rudd, 1916 .... 10.00
In My Little Red Book, Stillma/Bloch/Simon, 1938 .... 3.00
In My Merry Oldsmobile, Edwards/Bryan, 1905 .... 25.00
In My Old Home Town, Walsh, 1910 .... 14.00
In Old California With You, 1922 .... 2.00
In Old Kentucky, Stewart, 1919 .... 3.00
In Old Madrid, 1905 .... 3.00
In Old New Hampshire Far Away, 1930 .... 2.00
In Our Bungalow, 1919 .... 2.00
In Our Kingdom of Our Own, 1919 .... 2.00
In Philadelphia, Edwards, 1909 .... 6.00
In Room 202, 1919 .... 2.00
In Rotterdam, Caryll/Monckton, 1906 .... 3.00
In San Domingo, Snyder, 1917 .... 2.00
In Soudan, 1919 .... 2.00
In Sunny Africa, Trahern/Barron, 1902 .... 5.00
In Sweetheart Time, Drummond, 1911 .... 5.00
In the Baggage Coach Ahead, Davis, 1896 .... 20.00
In the Bright Moonlight, Jerome/Mack, 1893 .... 15.00
In the Candle Light, 1913 .... 2.00
In the Chapel in the Moonlight, Hill, 1936 .... 3.00
In the City of Broken Hearts, Allen, 1916 .... 3.00
In the City of Sighs and Tears, Sterling/Mills, 1902 .... 5.00
In the Cool, Cool of the Evening, 1951 .... 2.00
In the Dark, 1916 .... 2.00
In the Days of Old Black Joe, Brockman, 1917 .... 20.00
In the Days of Old, 1903 .... 3.00
In the Evening By the Moonlight, Bland, 1937 .... 2.00
In the Evening, Donaldson, 1924 .... 6.00
In the Garden of My Heart, Roma/Ball, 1908 .... 6.00
In the Garden of the Gods, Brennan/Ball, 1914 .... 6.00
In the Glory of the Moonlight, Wenrich, 1915 .... 6.00
In the Gold Fields of Nevada, Leslie/Gottler, 1915 .... 3.00
In the Golden Harvest Time, 1912 .... 3.00

In the Good Old Fashioned Way, Harris, 1901 .... 5.00
In the Good Old Summer Time, Evans, 1903.............................. 5.00
In the Harbor of Home Sweet Home, Denison, 1910 .... 6.00
In the Heart of a Rose, 1912 .... 2.00
In the Heart of an Irish Rose, Keithley, 1916 .... 5.00
In the Heart of the City, Allen/Daly, 1913 .... 5.00
In the Hills of Old Kentucky, Johnson, 1914 ....20.00
In the House of Too Much Trouble, Paine, 1901 .... 6.00
In the Hush of the Night, 1929.. 2.00
In the Land of Beginning Again, 1918 .... 3.00
In the Land of Harmony, 1911 .... 3.00
In the Land of Honeymoon, Spurr, 1912.................................... 3.00
In the Land of Let's Pretend, 1929.. 3.00
In the Land of Sweet Sixteen, 1923 .... 3.00
In the Land of the Beginning, 1918 .... 3.00
In the Land Where the Shamrock Grows, Beardsley, 1919.......... 3.00
In the Maytime, Hamilton/Bunning, 1906................................. 2.00
In The Mood, Garland, 1941 ....15.00
In the Palace of Dreams, Friedman, 1914 .... 3.00
In the Quiet Eve, Stevenson/Carew, 1920 .... 2.00
In the Shade of the Coconut Tree, Merritt, 1914 .... 3.00
In the Still of the Night, 1937 .... 3.00
In the Sunsets Golden Glow, Concannon/Hoyt, 1909 .... 5.00
In the Sweet Long Ago, Heath/Lange, 1916 .... 3.00
In the Town Where I Was Born, Howard, 1914 .... 6.00
In the Vale of the Old Berkshire Hills, Stoddard, 1905 .... 5.00
In the Valley of Sunshine and Love, 1917 .... 2.00
In the Valley of the Moon, 1913.. 3.00
In the Valley Where the Bluebirds Sing, Solman, 1906 .... 5.00
In the Village By the Sea, Langdon, 1903 .... 6.00
Indian Cradle Song, Kahn, 1927 .... 3.00
Indian Love Call, 1924 .... 3.00
Indian Summer, Herbert, 1934 .... 3.00
Indiana, MacDonald, 1917... 5.00
Indianola, Henry, 1918 .... 5.00
Infantry, Loesser, 1943 .... 3.00
International Rag, 1913 ....15.00
Invitation, 1906 .... 4.00
Ireland I'm For You, Byers/Wilson/Newhoff, 1916 ....10.00
Ireland Is Calling, 1917 .... 6.00
Ireland Is Heaven to Me, Griffin, 1923...................................... 2.00
Ireland Is Ireland to Me, Brennan/O'Hara/Ball, 1915 .... 5.00
Ireland Must Be Heaven for My Mother Came From There 5.00
Ireland Will Go On Forever, Ellis, 1918.................................... 2.00
Irene, Tierney/McCarthy, 1919.. 2.00

Irish Eyes of Love, Ball, 1914 .... 8.00
Irrestible You, 1944 .... 3.00
Is It Warm Enough for You?, Kendis, 1906 .... 6.00
Is My Darling True to Me, Cooper/Pratt, 1875 .... 10.00
Is There Still Room For Me Neath the Old Apple Tree, 1915 .... 2.00
Is You Is, Or Is You Ain't Ma' Baby, 1944 .... 4.00
Isle D'Amour, Carroll/Edwards, 1913 .... 3.00
Isn't It Kinda Fun, 1945 .... 3.00
Isn't It Romantic, 1933 .... 3.00
Isn't This A Lovely Day, Berlin, 1935 .... 6.00
Isn't This A Night For Love, Burton/Jason, 1933 .... 3.00
It Ain't Gonna Rain No Mo, Hall, 1923 .... 2.00
It All Depends On You, Jolson, 1926 .... 6.00
It Can't Be Wrong, 1942 .... 7.00
It Had to Be You, Jones, 1924 .... 3.00
It Happened in Monterey, Wayne, 1930 .... 2.00
It Looks Like a Big Night Tonight, 1908 .... 3.00
It Made You Happy, Donaldson, 1926 .... 2.00
It Makes Me Think of Home Sweet Home, Bryan, 1904 .... 5.00
It Makes No Difference Now, 1939 .... 2.00
It May Be Far to Tipperary, It's a Longer Way to Tennessee 4.00
It Might As Well Be You, 1918 .... 3.00
It Might Have Been Me, Coslow, 1924 .... 2.00
It Only Happens When I Dance With You, Berlin, 1947 .... 10.00
It Seemed to Me As If the Stars Were Singing, Perrins, 1916 .... 2.00
It Was Cotton Time in Dixie, 1904 .... 3.00
It Was Written In the Stars, Robin/Arlen, 1948 .... 3.00
It Won't Be Long Before We're Home, 1918 .... 4.00
It's A Bird, Kaufman, 1917 .... 3.00
It's A Girl Like You That Keeps a Fellow Guessing, 1910 .... 2.00
It's A Great Life, Spaulding/Daly, 1917 .... 2.00
It's A Hap-Hap-Happy Day, 1929 .... 3.00
It's A Long Way Back to Mother's Knee, Lange, 1917 .... 5.00
It's A Long Way to Berlin, Fields/Flatow, 1917 .... 3.00
It's A Long, Long Time, Vail, 1916 .... 2.00
It's A Most Unusual Day, 1948 .... 3.00
It's A Very Easy Thing to Put A Ring Upon A Finger, 1914 .... 2.00
It's All Over Now, Tilzer/Brown, 1920 .... 3.00
It's A Long, Long Way to Tipperary, Judge/Williams, 1912 .... 15.00
It's Been So Long, Adamson/Donaldson, 1935 .... 5.00
It's Beginning to Look Like Christmas, Wilson, 1951 .... 2.00
It's Dark On Observatory Hill, Burke/Spina, 1934 .... 2.00
It's Easy to Remember, 1935 .... 5.00
It's Good To Be Alive, Rome, 1965 .... 2.00
It's Great To Be A Soldier Man, 1907 .... 8.00

**Pictured above is a small selection of
Sheet Music Covers that are listed within this book.**

It's Just Because I Love You So, Davis, 1900 .... 5.00
It's Love, Bernstein, 1953 .... 2.00
It's Love, My Darling, It's Love, Tore, 1950 .... 8.00
It's Magic, 1948 .... 4.00
It's Not Your Nationality, McCarthy, 1916 .... 3.00
It's Only A Paper Moon, 1933 .... 3.00
It's Swell Of You, Gordon/Revel, 1937 .... 5.00
It's the Picture of a Mother, Layne, 1897 .... 5.00
It's the Pretty Things You Say, 1908 .... 4.00
It's the Same Old Dream, 1947 .... 3.00
It's the Talk of the Town, Levinson, 1933 .... 2.00
It's the Three Leaves of Shamrock, Allen/Daly, 1915 .... 2.00
It's Time for Every Boy To Be a Soldier, Bryan, 1917 .... 3.00
It's Tulip Time In Holland, Whiting/Radford, 1915 .... 2.00
It's You I Love, 1929 .... 3.00
It's You or No One, 1948 .... 3.00
It's You, Jolson, 1921 .... 6.00
Italy, Edwards/Meyer, 1912 .... 3.00
Ivy, Fontaine, 1947 .... 6.00
Ja-Da-Carelton -USNRF, 1918 .... 3.00
Jack O'Lantern Song, Mack/Rohans, 1899 .... 15.00
Jack Rabbit Rag, Garcia, 1909 .... 20.00
Jagtime Johnson's Ragtime March, Ryder, 1905 .... 20.00
Janette, O'Reilley, 1867 .... 25.00
Jasper Jenkins De Cake Walk Coon, Vogel, 1898 .... 25.00
Java, Friday, 1958 .... 5.00
Jazz Baby, Merrill, 1919 .... 8.00
Jazz Band Blues, Graham/Hirsch/White, 1919 .... 7.00
Jazzin' the Blues Away, Branen, 1918 .... 8.00
Jealous Heart, Carson/Perryman, 1944 .... 2.00
Jeanette And Jeannot, Jefferys/Glover 5.00
Jerry,You Warra a Warrior, Baskette, 1919 .... 7.00
Jes' Come Aroun' Wid an Automobile, Baker, 1902 .... 23.00
Jim, 1941 .... 2.00
Jingo, Gale, 1902 .... 12.00
Joan of Arc, They are Calling You, Wells, 1917 .... 15.00
John Henry, March, 1903 .... 7.00
Johnnie Took the One I Wanted, Dillon, 1896 .... 10.00
Johnny Doughboy Found A Rose In Ireland, 1936 .... 2.00
Johnny Get A Girl, Murphy/Puck, 1916 .... 5.00
Johnny One Note, Hart/Rodgers, 1937 .... 3.00
Johnny Zero, David/Lawnhurst, 1943 .... 8.00
Johnson Rag, 1917 .... 10.00
Jolly Fellows, Vollsterdt, 1905 .... 10.00
Josephine My Jo, McPherson/Brymn, 1901 .... 7.00

Jubilation T. Cornpone, Mercer/DePaul, 1956 .... 13.00
Judy, Carmichael/Lerner 2.00
Jumping Jupiter, Carle, 1910 .... 5.00
June In January, Robin/Rainger, 1934 .... 2.00
June Is Bustin' Out All Over, 1945 .... 2.00
June Time, Hoomes, 1910 .... 3.00
Just A Baby's Prayer at Twilight, Jerome, 1918 .... 7.00
Just A Chain of Daisies, Owen, 1911 .... 3.00
Just A Dream of You Dear, McNamara/Klickman, 1910 .... 3.00
Just A Girl of Yesterday, Meyer, 1916 .... 3.00
Just A Girl That Men Forget, Dubin, ... 2.00
Just A Kiss, Barth/Reeg, 1916 .... 3.00
Just A Little After Taps, 1918 .... 4.00
Just A Little Closer, 1930 .... 4.00
Just A Little Cottage, 1917 .... 4.00
Just A Little Longer, 1926 .... 3.00
Just A Little Love By the Way, 1917 .... 3.00
Just A Little Love Song, 1921 .... 2.00
Just A Little Picture In A Little Frame of Gold, 1913 .... 3.00
Just A Little Piece of Sage, Stayner, 1912 .... 2.00
Just A Little Smile, 1911 .... 4.00
Just A Little Song At Twilight, Howard, 1916 .... 3.00
Just A Little Sunshine, Buckley, 1914 .... 3.00
Just A Little Town Sweetheart, Clay, 1915 .... 3.00
Just A Lonely Hobo, Calaway/Lowry, 1932 .... 3.00
Just A Night In Dreamland, 1915 .... 3.00
Just A Picture of You, 1904 .... 4.00
Just A Prayer Away, Kapp, 1944 .... 2.00
Just A Small Town Sweetheart, Clay, 1916 .... 3.00
Just A Sweetheart, Pasternack, 1928 .... 2.00
Just A Thought of Yesterday, 1917 .... 3.00
Just Across the Bridge of Gold, Sterling/Tilzer, 1905 .... 10.00
Just Across the Bridge of Years, 1912 .... 3.00
Just and I, Weston, 1913 .... 3.00
Just Any Little Girl, Vincent/Bimberg, 1909 .... 5.00
Just As Happy In her Plain Old Home, 1904 .... 3.00
Just As Long As the Swanee Flows, Bryan 5.00
Just As the Boat Went Down, Lee, 1912 .... 20.00
Just As the Ship Went Down, Lessing, 1912 .... 20.00
Just As the Sun Went Down, Udall, 1898 .... 15.00
Just As You Say, Swains, 1881 .... 15.00
Just A Wearying For You, Bond, 1901 .... 7.00
Just Because It Reminds Me of You, Perkins/Norton, 1906 .... 3.00
Just Because It's You, 1913 .... 3.00
Just Because She Made Dem Goo-Goo Eyes, Queen/Cannon 2.00

Just Close Your Eyes Big Moon, Whitson, 1913 .... 3.00
Just Dreaming of You, Eastman/Heltman, 1915 .... 3.00
Just For A Dear Little Girl, Allen/Daly, 1910 .... 3.00
Just For the Sake of Your Mother, Schaeffer, 1917 .... 3.00
Just For Tonight, Cobb, 1914 .... 3.00
Just For You Dear, Sullivan/Pittman, 1917 .... 3.00
Just In the Same Old Way, 1895 .... 7.00
Just Let Me Call You Sweetheart, Schwartz, 1925 .... 2.00
Just Like In a Story Book, 1930 .... 4.00
Just Like the Rose You Gave, 1913 .... 2.00
Just Like Washington Crossed the Delaware, General 40.00
Just Like You, Loan, 1921 .... 2.00
Just Like You, Steinberg, 1906 .... 3.00
Just My Style, 1904 .... 3.00
Just One Day, 1916 .... 3.00
Just Someone, Anderson, 1907 .... 5.00
Just To Hear My Mother Sing Again, Barnes/White, 1914 .... 3.00
Just Walking in The Rain, 1953 .... 5.00
Just You, 1917 .... 3.00
Just You, Greene/Motzan, 1914 .... 3.00
K-K-K-Katy, Ohara, 1918 .... 5.00
Ka-Lu-A, Caldwell/Kern, 1921 .... 2.00
Kangaroo Hop, Morris, 1915 .... 3.00
Kansas City Kitty, Donaldson, 1929 .... 3.00
Karavan, 1919 .... 2.00
Karma, Hanson, 1921 .... 2.00
Kate, Potter, 1906 .... 3.00
Kathleen Mine, Heyman/Youmans, 1931 .... 5.00
Katinkitschka, Gershwin, 1931 .... 5.00
Keep A Little Song Handy, Lerner/Timberg, 1932 .... 8.00
Keep Away From the Fellow Who Owns an Automobile, 1912 ...... 23.00
Keep Moving March, Pond, 1911 .... 12.00
Keep On the Sunny Side, Drislane/Morse, 1906 .... 5.00
Keep On Walking, 1913 .... 12.00
Keep Smiling the Cobwebs Off the Moon, Lewis/Young, 1927 ...... 2.00
Keep the Home Fires Burning, 1915 .... 5.00
Keep the Lovelight Burning In the Window Till the Boys - - - 6.00
Keep the Trench Fires Going, Moran/Tilzer, 1918 .... 5.00
Keep Your Eye On the Girlie You Love, 1916 .... 3.00
Keep Your Foot On the Sot Pedal, Dillon/Tilzer, 1909 .... 5.00
Keep Your Love For Me, 1914 .... 3.00
Kentucky Babe, Geibel, 1898 .... 10.00
Kentucky Blues, Gaskill, 1921 .... 2.00
Kentucky Days, Wenrich/Mahoney, 1912 .... 3.00
Kentucky Dream, Henry, 1918 .... 5.00

Kentucky Echoes, Gilbert/Reilly, 1922 .... 2.00
Kentucky Smiles, Otto/Kenton, 1920 .... 2.00
Kentucky Waltz, Monroe/Smith, 1947 .... 3.00
Kentucky, 1943 .... 2.00
Kerry Mills Barn Dance, Mills, 1908 .... 6.00
Kerry Mills Palmetto Slide, Mills, 1910 .... 6.00
Kewpie, Rose, 1929 .... 3.00
Khaki Sammy, Carpenter, 1917 .... 10.00
Kid Days, Glick/Wilson, 1919 .... 2.00
Killarney, Balfe 3.00
King Cupid, Blake, 1903 .... 7.00
King Mammon, Meyer, 1882 .... 10.00
King Of Good Fellows March, Yeager, 1906 .... 3.00
King Of the Air, Johnson, 1910 .... 30.00
Kingdom Coming, Work, 1862 .... 20.00
Kiss Burglar, 1918 .... 3.00
Kiss Mama, Kiss Papa, Fairman, 1922 .... 2.00
Kiss Me Dearie, Darry/Sigman, 1908 .... 3.00
Kiss Me Goodnight Dear Love, 1904 .... 3.00
Kiss Me Goodnight, Not Goodbye, Furthman/Hanley 3.00
Kiss Me Honey Do, Smith/Stromberg, 1898 .... 15.00
Kiss Me Honey, Kiss Me, 1910 .... 15.00
Kiss Me Pretty, 1917 .... 3.00
Kiss Me, My Love, 1910 .... 3.00
Kiss Of Spring, Staals/Rolfe, 1910 .... 3.00
Kiss Pappa Goodnight, Irving, 1866 .... 20.00
Kiss That Made You Mine, 1915 .... 2.00
Kiss Waltz, Dubin/Burke, 1930 .... 5.00
Kiss Your Sailor Boy Good-Bye, Berlin, 1913 .... 20.00
Kisses, Harlow/Kaper, 1964 .... 10.00
Kitchen Stove Rag, 1918 .... 6.00
Kitty And Ben, Ardor/Webster, 1872 .... 20.00
Kitty McGee, 1914 .... 3.00
Knock At the Door, Olson, 1924 .... 6.00
Kokomo, Indiana, Gordon/Myrow, 1947 .... 5.00
Koonville Koonlets, Weidt 20.00
La Ballerina, Sternberg, 1897 .... 6.00
La Detroit, Fraser, 1905 .... 3.00
La Marseillaise, Lisle, 1917 .... 3.00
La Veeda, 1920 .... 2.00
Laddie Boy, Cobb/Edwards, 1917 .... 3.00
Laddie In Kahaki, Novello, 1915 .... 3.00
Laddie, Lawton/Moore, 1914 .... 2.00
Lady Angeline, Reed/Christie, 1912 .... 3.00
Lady April Waltz, Fancher, 1898 .... 5.00

**Pictured above is a small selection of
Sheet Music Covers that are listed within this book.**

Lady Bird Cha Cha Cha, Starr, 1968 .... 23.00
Lady Divine, 1929 .... 2.00
Lady Laughter, 1908 .... 3.00
Lady Love, McKenna/Gumble, 1909 .... 5.00
Lady Of Dreams, Daniels, 1909 .... 3.00
Lady of the Evening, 1922 .... 4.00
Lafayette, Earl, 1918 .... 12.00
Lambeth Walk, 1937 .... 2.00
Lasses White All Star Minstrels, White, 1922 .... 2.00
Last Night On the Back Porch, Brown, 1923 .... 3.00
Last Night Was the End Of the World, Sterling/Tilzer, 1912 .... 3.00
Last Night, Heinzman, 1912 .... 2.00
Laugh Clown Laugh, 1928 .... 7.00
Laughing Eyes, Powell, 1913 .... 3.00
Laughing Love Train, 1909 .... 3.00
Laughing Marionette, Collins, 1929 .... 2.00
Laura, Raskin, 1945 .... 2.00
Lay Me Down To Sleep In Carolina, Yellen/Ager, 1926 .... 2.00
Lazy Day, Kahn, 1931 .... 2.00
Lazy Louisiana Moon, Donaldson, 1930 .... 5.00
Lazy River, 1931 .... 2.00
Lazy Silv'ry Moon, McConnell, 1931 .... 2.00
Lazy, 1924 .... 3.00
Lazybones, 1933 .... 2.00
Lead Me To That Beautiful Band, Goetz, Berlin, 1912 .... 15.00
Leaf By Leaf the Roses Fall, Vane, 1867 .... 20.00
Leanin' On the Ole Top Rail, Kenny, 1939 .... 2.00
Learn To Sing A Love Song, 1927 .... 3.00
Learn To Smile, Harbach, 1921 .... 2.00
Learning, Heagney/Gregory, 1925 .... 3.00
Leave Me With A Smile, Burtnett, 1921 .... 2.00
Led Astray, Frazer/Williams, 189 .... 10.00
Left All Alone Again Blues, Caldwell, 1920 .... 7.00
Lehigh Polka, Dresher, 1875 .... 35.00
Lemon Tree, Madden, 1907 .... 3.00
Less Than Tomorrow, Menzies/Mullen, 1953 .... 2.00
Let A Smile Be Your Umbrella, 1927 .... 2.00
Let Me Be the One, 1953 .... 2.00
Let Me Be Your Rain-Beau, Hansen, 1922 .... 2.00
Let Me Call You Sweetheart, Whitson, 1910 .... 3.00
Let Me Go Back, Stoddard, 1904 .... 5.00
Let Me Have My Dreams, Clarke/Akst, 1929 .... 3.00
Let Me Hear the Song My Mother Used To Sing, 1906 .... 3.00
Let Me Hear Thy Voice Again, Millard, 1876 .... 15.00
Let Me Kiss You Little Dear, White, 1910 .... 3.00

Let Me Know, Willet, 1953 .... 2.00
Let Me See Your Rainbow Smile, Havez/Barron, 1913 .... 3.00
Let Me Sing In Echo Valley, Nelson/Rose, 1936 .... 3.00
Let Me Waltz To That Melody, Garton, 1912 .... 3.00
Let the Dead And the Beautiful Rest, 1868 .... 20.00
Let Us Cheer the Weary Traveller, Burleigh, 1919 .... 10.00
Let Yourself Go, 1936 .... 3.00
Let'er Go, Wood, 1912 .... 3.00
Let's All Be Americans Now, Berlin, 1917 .... 20.00
Let's All Sing Like the Birdies Sing, Hargreaves 3.00
Let's All Sing Together, 1940 .... 2.00
Let's Be Friendly, 1956 .... 3.00
Let's Be Prepared, Heath/James, 1916 .... 3.00
Let's Bring New Glory To Old Glory, Gordon/Warren, 1942 .... 3.00
Let's Call the Whole Thing Off, Gershwin, 1937 .... 7.00
Let's Dance, Cohen, 1922 .... 3.00
Let's Fill the Old Oaken Bucket With Love, Bryan, ... 3.00
Let's Finish the Job, Watson, 1919 .... 10.00
Let's Get Lost, 1943 .... 3.00
Let's Get Together, Merchant, 1950 .... 2.00
Let's Go Down To Cradle Town, Bergman/Handman, 1921 .... 3.00
Let's Go Home, Burt, 1908 .... 3.00
Let's Go To Church, 1950 .... 2.00
Let's Grow Old Together, Brockman, 1926 .... 3.00
Let's Harmonize, 1949 .... 2.00
Let's Kiss and Make Up, Gershwin, 1927 .... 3.00
Let's Live A Little, 1951 .... 2.00
Let's Make Our Own Sunshine, Gerard/Armstrong, 1914 .... 3.00
Let's Make Up, Little, 1933 .... 3.00
Let's Take A Ride On the Jitney Bus, McConnell, 1915 .... 20.00
Let's Take An Old Fashioned Walk, 1948 .... 4.00
Let's Take the Long Way Home, Mercer/Arlen, 1944 .... 2.00
Let's Try Again, Newman/Jones, 1932 .... 3.00
Let's Wait For the Last Train Home, Cunningham, 1914 .... 15.00
Let's You And I Just Say Goodbye, Cohan, 1923 .... 3.00
Letter Song, Straus/Strange, 1908 .... 6.00
Letters From Those You Love, 1907 .... 3.00
Levee Lou, Edwards, 1907 .... 5.00
Leven Thirty, 1930 .... 2.00
Li'l Liza Jane, 1916 .... 3.00
Liberty Bell, Goodwin/Mohr, 1917 .... 10.00
Liberty Loan March, Sousa, 1918 .... 6.00
Lies, Barris/Springer, 1931 .... 2.00
Life Is A See-Saw, Smith/Hubbel, 1906 .... 3.00
Life Is But A Fading Flower, Hockey, 1911 .... 3.00

Life Isn't All Roses, Rosie, 1911 .... 3.00
Life Of a Rose, 1923 .... 3.00
Life's A Dance, Harburg/Arlen, 1937 .... 8.00
Life's What You Make It, 1919 .... 12.00
Life, Let Me Live My Life For You, 1919 .... 6.00
Light's Out, Hill, 1935 .... 2.00
Lightning Express, Fitzpatrick, 1905 .... 12.00
Lightning Rag, Hylands, 1912 .... 14.00
Lights Of My home Town, Harris, 1915 .... 3.00
Like A Beautiful Wild Red Rose, Perrins, 1917 .... 3.00
Like A Breath of Springtime, 1929 .... 8.00
Like A Ship That Drifted Away, 1916 .... 3.00
Like the Breeze Blows, 1965 .... 2.00
Lili Marlene, Park/David, 1943 .... 2.00
Lillette, Gold, 1948 .... 2.00
Lilly Of the Prairie, Mills, 1909 .... 6.00
Lily Of the Valley, Gilbert/Friedland, 1917 .... 3.00
Limited Express March, Duss, 1894 .... 17.00
Lincoln Centennial Grand March, Paull 24.00
Lindbergh (The Eagle of the USA), Johnson/Sherman, 1927 .... 30.00
Linger A Little Longer In the Twilight, Woods, 1932 .... 3.00
Lips Of Wine, Wolfe/Soloway, 1957 .... 2.00
Lips, Ott, 1917 .... 3.00
Listen To That Dixie Band, Yellen/Cobb, 1914 .... 3.00
Listen To the Mocking Bird, Drumheller, 1908 .... 9.00
Listen To the Mocking Bird, Hawthorne/Scats, 1936 .... 2.00
Listening, Berlin, 1924 .... 10.00
Little Alabama Coon, Starr, 1898 .... 25.00
Little Annie Rooney, Nolan, 1925 .... 6.00
Little Bit Independent, Leslie/Burke, 1935 .... 3.00
Little Blue Eyes, 1893 .... 6.00
Little Blue Moon, Talbot, 1905 .... 5.00
Little Bo Peep Has Lost Her Jeep, Browne, 1942 .... 20.00
Little Boy And A Little Girl, 1940 .... 2.00
Little Brown Jug, Eastburn, 1941 .... 2.00
Little Cotton Dolly, Buck/Geibel, 1897 .... 5.00
Little Cotton Pickers, 1944 .... 20.00
Little David, Play On Your Harp, Burleigh, 1921 .... 5.00
Little Did I Know, Kenny, 1943 .... 2.00
Little Dutch Mill, Freed/Barris, 1934 .... 2.00
Little Ford Rambled Right Along, Gay, 1914 .... 25.00
Little Game Of Love, Lolomon/Osias, 1911 .... 3.00
Little Girl, A Little Boy, A Little Moon, 1927 .... 4.00
Little Girl, Clayton, 1918 .... 2.00
Little Girls We Met Upon The Train, Stauffer, 1896 .... 25.00

Little Grey Home In the West, Wilmot/Lohr, 1911 .... 3.00
Little Grey Mother, Grossman/DeCosta, 1915 .... 5.00
Little House Upon the Hill, MacDonald, 1914 .... 3.00
Little Love, Little Kiss, Ross/Silesu, 1912 .... 3.00
Little Man-You've Had A Busy Day, Sigler, 1934 .... 2.00
Little Mother Of the Hills, 1932 .... 2.00
Little Old Church Near Leicester Square, Carr/Goell, 1949 .... 2.00
Little Old Clock On the Mantel, Fiorito, 1924 .... 2.00
Little Old Lady, 1936 .... 2.00
Little Old Red Schoolhouse, Wheeler/Durham, 1890 .... 20.00
Little Old Sod Shanty On the Claim, 1935 .... 3.00
Little Pal, Dowling/Hanley, 1929 .... 5.00
Little Rover, Kahn/Donaldson, 1923 .... 2.00
Little Street Where Old Friends Meet, Kahn/Woods, 1932 .... 2.00
Little Sweetheart Of the Mountains, 1931 .... 2.00
Little Sweetheart Of the Prairie, Brown, 1931 .... 2.00
Little Things In Life, 1930 .... 3.00
Little Things Mean A Lot, 1954 .... 2.00
Little White Rose, Cadman, 1925 .... 13.00
Little Wheel A Turnin' In My Heart, Fisher, 1919 .... 3.00
Little Yaller Dog, Gallatly, 1919 .... 3.00
Living A Life Of Dreams, 1930 .... 2.00
Liza Jane, Creamer/Layton, 1918 .... 3.00
Loading Up the Mandy Lee, Murphy, 1915 .... 9.00
Lonely And Blue, 1924 .... 3.00
Lonely Corral, 1947 .... 2.00
Lonely Little Bluebird, Woods, 1928 .... 3.00
Lonely Troubadour, Klenner, 1929 .... 3.00
Lonely, Carlisle, 1945 .... 2.00
Lonesome And Blue, Tillman, 1922 .... 2.00
Lonesome Baby, Goodwin, 1913 .... 5.00
Lonesome Heart, Strickland, 1925 .... 3.00
Lonesome In the Moonlight, 1928 .... 2.00
Lonesome Land, Costello, 1909 .... 3.00
Lonesome Little Doll, 1929 .... 4.00
Lonesome Road, Shilkret, 1928 .... 2.00
Lonesome, Nyers, 1909 .... 5.00
Lonesome, Rosey/Tilzer, 1904 .... 5.00
Long Ago, 1944 .... 10.00
Long Beach By the Sea, Kitchen/Hill, 1918 .... 3.00
Long Boy, Herschell/Walker, 1917 .... 5.00
Long Live the Twenty Sixth, Ryan, 1919 .... 6.00
Longing For Home, Jungman, 1907 .... 5.00
Look Around, 1955 .... 2.00
Look For the Silver Lining, Bolton, 1920 .... 3.00

**Pictured above is a small selection of
Sheet Music Covers that are listed within this book.**

Look Out Mary, Lambert, 1914 .... 3.00
Look Out! Here Comes An American, Tilzer, 1908 .... 15.00
Look What My Boy Got In France, Dillon/Conrad, 1918 .... 6.00
Look What You've Done, Creamer, 1928 .... 5.00
Looking At the World Thru Rose Colored Glasses, Malie 2.00
Looking For a Boy, 1925 .... 4.00
Lookout Mountain, Goodwin/Mohr, 1917 .... 3.00
Lorelei, Herendeen/Horan, 1935 .... 10.00
Lorena, Webster, 1857 .... 20.00
Lorraine, Bryan/Fisher, 1917 .... 2.00
Lost Chord, Sullivan 2.00
Lost, Davis, 1922 .... 6.00
Lotus Land, Wilson, 1915 .... 2.00
Louise, Robin/Whiting, 1929 .... 3.00
Louise, Van Alstyne, 1906 .... 5.00
Louisiana Lou, Stuart, 1894 .... 10.00
Louisiana, Freed/Wallace, 1920 .... 2.00
Louisville Lou, Yellen/Ager, 1922 .... 3.00
Lovable And Sweet, Clare/Levant, 1929 .... 2.00
Love Ain't Nothin' But the Blues, Alter, 1929 .... 5.00
Love Among the Daisies, Tours, 1906 .... 3.00
Love And Devotion, Drumheller, 1907 .... 3.00
Love And Passion, Messina, 1902 .... 3.00
Love and Honor Dear Old Dad, Bonner, 1915 .... 3.00
Love and Marriage, 1955 .... 3.00
Love Bird, Earl, 1921 .... 5.00
Love Came Smiling Through, Tobias/Moret, 1947 .... 2.00
Love Days, Mohr, 1916 .... 3.00
Love Dreams, 1910 .... 2.00
Love Here Is My Heart, Ross/Silesu, 1915 .... 3.00
Love I Adore You, Cooper, 1896 .... 14.00
Love In An Automobile, Dixon, 1899 .... 30.00
Love In Bloom, 1934 .... 4.00
Love In the Gleaming, 1908 .... 3.00
Love Is All In All, Ellis/Wilson, 1900 .... 5.00
Love Is Everywhere, 1906 .... 4.00
Love Is Just Around the Corner, Robin/Gensler, 1934 .... 2.00
Love Is the Best Of All, Blossom/Herbert, 1890 .... 5.00
Love Is Where You Find It, Brent/Brown, 1948 .... 2.00
Love Letters, 1945 .... 2.00
Love Light, Bloom, 1907 .... 3.00
Love Makes the World a Merry-Go-Round, Lauder, 1923 .... 3.00
Love Me Again, Costa, 1931 .... 2.00
Love Me Again, Stults, 1910 .... 3.00
Love Me And the World Is Mine, Ball, 1906 .... 5.00

Love Me Just Like Romeo Loved Miss Juliet, 1909 .... 5.00
Love Me Like You Used To Love A Sugar Lump, 1912 .... 3.00
Love Me Little, Love Me Long, Gaunt, 1898 .... 5.00
Love Me Or Leave Me, Kahn/Donaldson, 1928 .... 5.00
Love Me To-Day, Onivas, 1917 .... 3.00
Love Me Tonight, 1931 .... 4.00
Love Me When the Lilacs Bloom Again, 1913 .... 3.00
Love Me, Let the World Go By, 1911 .... 4.00
Love Me, Madden/Gumble, 1911 .... 3.00
Love Never Dies, 1912 .... 2.00
Love Of Mine, Duncan, 1919 .... 3.00
Love On A Greyhound Bus, 1945 .... 4.00
Love Passes By, 1935 .... 3.00
Love Secrets, Zamecnik, 1911 .... 3.00
Love Somebody, 1948 .... 5.00
Love Songs Of the Nile, Freed/Brown, 1933 .... 5.00
Love Story, Sigman/Lai, 1970 .... 3.00
Love Thy Neighbor, Gordon/Revel, 1934 .... 2.00
Love Walked In, 1938 .... 3.00
Love's Dreamland, 1907 .... 3.00
Love's Golden Star, 1907 .... 3.00
Love's Madrigal, Teschemacher/Rae, 1903 .... 3.00
Love's Melody, Shannon, 1917 .... 3.00
Love's Own Sweet Song, Wilhelm, 1912 .... 3.00
Love's Pleading, Ford, 1905 .... 4.00
Love, 1903 .... 2.00
Love, Goulding/Janis, 1929 .... 2.00
Love, Here Is My Heart, Ross/Silseu, 1915 .... 3.00
Love, Huerter, 1917 .... 3.00
Love, You Didn't Do Me Right, Berlin, 1953 .... 7.00
Love, You're A Wonderful Game, Rubens, 1902 .... 5.00
Loveable Eyes, 1922 .... 2.00
Loveland, Robinson/Fleming, 1910 .... 3.00
Lovelight Be Always Shining, Weasner, 1918 .... 3.00
Lovelight In the Starlight, Freed/Hollander, 1938 .... 3.00
Lovelight, Harrett/Bennett, 1909 .... 5.00
Lovely Hula Hands, Anderson, 1940 .... 2.00
Lovely Katie, Shelley, 1914 .... 3.00
Lovely To Look At, Harbach/Kern, 1935 .... 6.00
Lovely Woman, Duncan, 1885 .... 5.00
Lover, Come Back To Me, 1928 .... 3.00
Lovers' Lane, Heartz, 1902 .... 5.00
Loves Enchantment, Vardley, 1919 .... 3.00
Loves Wooing, Fink, 1904 .... 3.00
Lovey Came Back, Handman, 1923 .... 2.00

Loving Time, Brown, 1908 .... 5.00
Loving, Klein, 1910 .... 3.00
Low Down Rhythm, 1929 .... 4.00
Luana, Hiller, 1916 .... 3.00
Lucia, 1906 .... 2.00
Lucky Lady, Ebb/Kander, 1975 .... 8.00
Lucky Lindy, Baer, 1927 .... 20.00
Lucky Me-Lovable You, Yellen/Ager, 1929 .... 5.00
Lucky Moon, Stevens, 1909 .... 3.00
Lucy Linda Lady, Reed, 1904 .... 15.00
Luella Lee, Esrom, 1912 .... 5.00
Lullaby Of Broadway, Dubin/Warren, 1935 .... 3.00
Lulu Belle & Skyland Scotty, 1937 .... 6.00
Lulu Lou, Hall, 1926 .... 3.00
Lulu's Back In Town, Warren/Dubin, 1935 .... 3.00
Luna, Friedman, 1914 .... 3.00
Lustspiel, 1905 .... 3.00
M'Hoss, M'Dog An' Me, Ingraham, 1934 .... 3.00
M-O-T-H-E-R A Word That Means the World To Me, 1915 .... 6.00
Ma Black Tulip, Harris, 1900 .... 20.00
Ma Blushin' Rosie, 1940 .... 3.00
Ma Curly Headed Baby, Clutsam 7.00
Ma Ebony Belle, Levi, 1901 .... 25.00
Ma L'il Batteau, Strickland, 1921 .... 5.00
Ma Lady Lu, Brill, 1899 .... 25.00
Ma Mississippi Babe, Harris, 1920 .... 3.00
Ma Pickaninny Babe, Johnson, 1913 .... 20.00
Ma Says I Can't Go For A Ride, Howe, 1914 .... 20.00
Mack the Knife, 1928 .... 3.00
Mack's Swell Car Was A Maxwell, Patrick, 1915 .... 25.00
Mack's Swing Song, Mack, 1895 .... 6.00
Macnamara's Band, Stamford, 1917 .... 2.00
Madelon, Bryan, 1919 .... 6.00
Magic Is the Moonlight, 1930 .... 3.00
Mah Lindy Lou, Strickland, 1920 .... 7.00
Maid From Nicobar, 1904 .... 6.00
Maidens Prayer, 1914 .... 3.00
Make A Noise Like A Hoop And Roll Away, Helf, 1908 .... 8.00
Make A Wish, 1937 .... 3.00
Make Believe, 1927 .... 4.00
Makin' Whoopee, Donaldson/Kahn, 1928 .... 3.00
Malindy, Golden, 1915 .... 7.00
Mam'selle, Power, 1947 .... 8.00
Mama I Wanna Make Rhythm, 1937 .... 3.00
Mama's Waltz and Papa' Waltz, Rosewig, 1898 .... 3.00

Mamie, Cobb/Edwards, 1901 .... 7.00
Mammy O'Mine, Pinkard, 1919 .... 7.00
Mammy's Chocolate Soldier, Mitchell/Gottler, 1918 .... 7.00
Mammy's Jinny's Jubilee, Gilbert/Muhr, 1913 .... 15.00
Mammy's Little Coal Black Rose, Rowland, 1916 .... 20.00
Mammy's Little Pumpkin Colored Coons, Hillman, 1897 .... 25.00
Mammy's Lullaby, 1919 .... 12.00
Mammy's Shufflin' Dance, Gilbert, 1911 .... 8.00
Man On the Flying Trapeze, Manoloff, 1935 .... 3.00
Manague Nicaragua, Fields/Gamse, 1946 .... 3.00
Mandy And the Spiders, Tombo, 1927 .... 5.00
Mandy Lane, McKenna, 1908 .... 8.00
Mandy Lou, Allen, 1911 .... 15.00
Mandy's Ragtime Waltz, Zamecnik, 1912 .... 20.00
Mandy, 1919 .... 4.00
Manhattan Serenade, Alter/Adamson, 1928 .... 3.00
Many Happy Returns Of the Day, Dubin/Burke, 1959 .... 2.00
Maple Leaf Rag, Joplin, 1899 .... 25.00
March Of the Iron Horse, Rapee, 1924 .... 25.00
March Of the Junior Commandos, Pearson, 1942 .... 7.00
March Of the Mannikins, Onivas, 1923 .... 12.00
March Of the Nations, Pond, 1910 .... 6.00
March To the White House, Harris, 1924 .... 19.00
Margie, Davis/Conrad, 1920 .... 3.00
Maria Elena, Darcelata, 1933 .... 3.00
Maria, Porter, 1938 .... 2.00
Marianne, Turk/Ahlert, 1929 .... 5.00
Marie, 1929 .... 6.00
Marine's Hymn, 1942 .... 6.00
Martyres Of the Maine, Gebest, 1898 .... 30.00
Mary Malone, Carter, 1908 .... 5.00
Mary Regan, Stewart, 1919 .... 3.00
Mary Was My Mother's Name, 1912 .... 3.00
Mary You're A Big Girl Now, 1909 .... 5.00
Mary's A Grand Old Name, Cohan, 1932 .... 10.00
Mary, Frey, 1918 .... 3.00
Mary, You're A Little Old Fashioned, 1914 .... 4.00
May I Have the Next Dream With You?, 1968 .... 2.00
May I Sleep In Your Barn Tonight Mister, Manoloff, 1935 .... 2.00
May the Good Lord Bless and Keep You, 1950 .... 2.00
Maybe It's Love, 1930 .... 10.00
Maybe That Is Why I'm Lonely, Meyer/Goodwin, 1911 .... 3.00
Maybe This Is Love, 1928 .... 2.00
Maybe You're Not the Only One Who Loves Me, 1910 .... 3.00
Maybe, Turk, 1924 .... 5.00

**Pictured above is a small selection of
Sheet Music Covers that are listed within this book.**

Maytime In the Air, 1936 .... 2.00
Mazurka de Concert, 1887 .... 15.00
McKinley's Funeral March, Ikeler, 1901 .... 15.00
Me An' Mah Pardner, Strickland, 1922 .... 7.00
Me And Marie, Porter, 1935 .... 2.00
Me And My Shadow, Jolson, 1927... 10.00
Me And the Boy Friend, Clare, 1924.. 9.00
Me-Ow, Kerr/Kaufman, 1919... 5.00
Meadowbrook Fox Trot, Kraus, 1914.. 3.00
Meadowland, Knipper, 1945... 3.00
Medic Rag, Woolsey, 1910 .... 14.00
Meet Me At Twilight, Harris, 1914 .... 5.00
Meet Me In Bubble Land, 1919 .... 3.00
Meet Me In Rose Time Rosie, Schwartz/Jerome, 1908 .... 3.00
Meet Me In St, Louis, Louis, Sterling/Mills, 1931 .... 6.00
Meet Me In St. Louis, 1904 .... 5.00
Meet Me Tonight In Dreamland, Whitson, 1909.......................... 6.00
Meet Me Tonight, Taylor, 1913 .... 2.00
Meet Me When the Roses Bloom, 1910 .... 3.00
Meet Me Where the Lanterns Glow, Klein, 1909 .... 3.00
Meet Me Where the Shadows Fall, Johnson, 1912 .... 3.00
Melancholy, Norton/Barnett, 1911 .... 3.00
Melinda's Wedding Day Rag, Piantadosi, 1913............................ 14.00
Melody In Spring, 1934.. 3.00
Melody Of Love, 1904 .... 3.00
Memories Of France, Dubin/Robinson, 1928 .... 3.00
Memories Of the South, Thaler, 1908 .... 20.00
Memories Of Virginia, 1918... 3.00
Memories, 1915... 3.00
Memphis Blues, 1913 .... 4.00
Men Of America, Deyo, 1942 .... 3.00
Merrily We'll Float Along, Kennedy, 1910................................... 14.00
Merry Madcap, Bell, 1908 .... 8.00
Message Of Peace, Engelmann, 1905 .... 5.00
Message Of the Violet, 1902 .... 3.00
Message On the Train, Grimm, 1897... 25.00
Mexico, Cole/Johnson, 1904 .... 3.00
Miami Shore, Jacobi, 1919 .... 5.00
Mickey, Williams/Moret, 1918 .... 5.00
Mid the Blue Grass of Kentucky, Harris, 1909 .... 15.00
Mid the Green Fields Of Virginia, 1898....................................... 6.00
Mid the Light Ripples, Schubert, 1857 .... 35.00
Mid the Purple Tinted Hills Of Tennessee, 1913 .... 5.00
Midnight Flyer, Paull, 1903 .... 34.00
Midnight Special, Lincoln, 1910 .... 24.00

Military Parade, Chapman, 1905 .... 5.00
Milkman, Keep Those Bottles Quiet, 1944 .... 6.00
Mine, Chapine/Hinshaw, 1912 .... 3.00
Mine, Gershwin, 1933 .... 5.00
Minnie Shimmie For Me, Frisch, 1918 .... 15.00
Mira, Merrill, 1961 .... 8.00
Mirandy, Hoffman/Lewis, 1901 .... 3.00
Miss You, Tobias, 1929 .... 2.00
Mississippi Mamie, Sterling/Silver, 1904 .... 7.00
Mississippi Mud, 1927 .... 3.00
Mississippi Shore, Alstyne, 1919 .... 3.00
Missouri Waltz, Shannon, 1915 .... 7.00
Missouri, Logan, 1914 .... 3.00
Mister Five By Five, Raye/DePaul, 1942 .... 3.00
Mister Tap Toe, 1952 .... 5.00
Mister Whitney's Little Jitney Bus, Gaskill, 1915 .... 30.00
Mixing In Dixie, Edwards, 1917 .... 5.00
Moanin' Low, 1929 .... 3.00
Mocking Bird Rag, Walsh, 1912 .... 15.00
Molly Dear, It's You I'm After, Pether, 1915 .... 5.00
Molly Malone, Cohan, 1927 .... 5.00
Mona Lisa, 1949 .... 3.00
Money Burns A Hole In My Pocket, 1953 .... 3.00
Monkey Doodle Dandy, Drislane, 1909 .... 15.00
Monkey Lane, Drislane,1907 .... 3.00
Montmart, Porter, 1935 .... 2.00
Moon And Sea, 1909 .... 3.00
Moon Baby, Miller, 1904 .... 5.00
Moon Burn, Heyman/Carmichael, 1935 .... 6.00
Moon Dear, Klein, 1905 .... 5.00
Moon River, Mercer, 1961 .... 2.00
Moon Song, 1932 .... 3.00
Moon Winks, Stevens, 1904 .... 6.00
Moonbeams And Dreams Of You, 1907 .... 4.00
Moonlight & Shadows, 1936 .... 6.00
Moonlight Bay, Madden/Wenrich, 1912 .... 5.00
Moonlight Becomes You, Burke/Van Heusen, 1942 .... 3.00
Moonlight Kisses, 1923 .... 2.00
Moonlight Lane, 1923 .... 2.00
Moonlight Love Song, 1901 .... 3.00
Moonlight On the Danube, 1927 .... 3.00
Moonlight On the Lake, White, 1873 .... 25.00
Moonlight on the Prairie, Nolan/Spencer, 1934 .... 8.00
Moonlight On the Waves, Verner, 1891 .... 15.00
Moonlight Serenade, 1939 .... 3.00

Moonlight Waltz, Logan, 1916 .... 3.00
Moonstruck, Coslow/Johnston, 1938 .... 3.00
Moontime, Spink, 1909 .... 3.00
More And More, Kern, 1944 .... 5.00
More Candy, 1917 .... 3.00
More, 1923 .... 2.00
Morning Will Come, Jolson, 1923 .... 8.00
Morning, Teschemacher/Ronald, 1901 .... 3.00
Mother Kissed Me In My Dream, Cooper/Thomas, 1854 .... 15.00
Mother Machree, Ball, 1910 .... 3.00
Mother O'Mine, Hughes/Richardson, 1914 .... 3.00
Mother's Good Night Song, 1916 .... 3.00
Mother's Rosary Of Love, Wood, 1919 .... 3.00
Mother, 1915 .... 3.00
Mother, Dixie and You, Johnson, 1927 .... 3.00
Mother, Is the Battle Over, 1862 .... 40.00
Mother, Smith, 1919 .... 3.00
Motor Girl, Edwards, 1909 .... 20.00
Motor King, Frantzen, 1910 .... 25.00
Motor March, Rosey, 1906 .... 30.00
Mountain Belle, Kinkel, 1902 .... 5.00
Moxie One Step, 1921 .... 9.00
Mr. & Mrs. Is the Name, 1934 .... 5.00
Mr. Black Man, Pryor, 1904 .... 20.00
Mr. Ford, You've Got the Right Idea, 1916 .... 30.00
Mr. Jazz Himself, Berlin, 1917 .... 20.00
Mr. Johnson, Don't Get Gay, Reed, 1898 .... 8.00
Mr. Moon Man, Turn Off Your Light, 1910 .... 3.00
Mr. Pee Wee, Smith/Penn, 1904 .... 5.00
Mrs. Brady's Daughter, Kennedy, 1882 .... 15.00
Mrs. Casey Jones (The Brave Engineers Widow), Newton, ... 50.00
Mule Train, Lange, 1949 .... 3.00
Music Caressing Of Violins, Smith/Fall, 1911 .... 3.00
Music Makes Me, Youmans/Kahn, 1933 .... 5.00
Musical Michael Magan, 1916 .... 4.00
Must Be In Love, 1964 .... 2.00
Must We Then Meet As Strangers, 1875 .... 10.00
Mutiny In the Nursery, Mercer 5.00
My Angel Of the Flaming Cross, Gay, 1918 .... 3.00
My Auto Lady, Atkins, 1901 .... 20.00
My Automobile Girl From New Orleans, Davis, 1900 .... 20.00
My Automobile Girl, Morris, 1900 .... 20.00
My Baby Just Cares For Me, Donaldson/Kahn, 1930 .... 5.00
My Baby Said Yes, 1945 .... 3.00
My Baby's Arms, Tierney, 1919 .... 3.00

My Balckbirds Are Bluebirds Now, 1928 .... 4.00
My Barney Lies Over the Ocean, 1919 .... 3.00
My Beautiful Passion Flower, 1915 .... 3.00
My Belgian Rose, Benoit/Levenson/Garton, 1918 .... 6.00
My Beloved Is Rugged, Ellis, 1942 .... 3.00
My Best Girl, Robey, 1895 .... 5.00
My Bird Of Paradise, Berlin, 1915 .... 10.00
My Black Bess, Sterling/Tilzer, 1899 .... 20.00
My Blue Heaven, Whiting, 1927 .... 6.00
My Boy, Breuer/Lee, 1913 .... 3.00
My Buddy, Jolson, 1922 .... 10.00
My Concerto, 1951 .... 2.00
My Country Has First Call, Gordon, 1910 .... 10.00
My Croony Melody, Goodwin/Goetz, 1914 .... 3.00
My Cutey's Due At Two To Two, Robin/Tilzer, 1926 .... 3.00
My Dad's the Engineer, Graham, 1895 .... 25.00
My Daddy's Dreamtime Lullaby, Herscher/Keefer, 1924 .... 3.00
My Daddy, 1921 .... 2.00
My Darling Clara Bell, 1943 .... 2.00
My Darling, 1932 .... 2.00
My Darling, My Darling, 1948 .... 2.00
My Defenses Are Down, 1949 .... 10.00
My Down East Rose, Orum/Everett, 1927 .... 3.00
My Dream Girl, 1924 .... 3.00
My Dream Melody, 1929 .... 3.00
My Dream Memory, Clare/Levant, 1929 .... 2.00
My Dream Of Life, Rourke/Wynne, 1942 .... 2.00
My Dream Of Love, Schleiffarth, 1899 .... 10.00
My Dream Of the Big Parade, Dubin/McHugh, 1926 .... 3.00
My Dream Of the USA, Click, 1908 .... 15.00
My Dream World, 1945 .... 2.00
My Dreamy Rose, Johnson, 1912 .... 3.00
My Fate Is In Your Hands, Waller, 1929 .... 3.00
My Foolish Heart, Andrews/Hayward, 1949 .... 8.00
My Gal Don't Love Me Anymore, 1924 .... 2.00
My Geisha, Waxman, 1962 .... 8.00
My Georgiana Lou, Allen, 1912 .... 5.00
My Girl From Tennessee, Sterling/Smith, ... 8.00
My Girl In Lovey Loveland, Glaser, 1916 .... 3.00
My Guy's Come Back, 1945 .... 3.00
My Hannah Lady, Reed, 1899 .... 20.00
My Hawaiian Melody, 1921 .... 3.00
My Heart Beats Faster, Loesser, 1948 .... 3.00
My Heart Belongs To Daddy, 1938 .... 2.00
My Heart Goes Crazy, Burke/Van Heusen, 1946 .... 3.00

**Pictured above is a small selection of
Sheet Music Covers that are listed within this book.**

My Heart Has Eyes To Watch Over You, 1946 .... 2.00
My Heart Has Learned To Love You, Ball/Reed, 1910 .... 3.00
My Heart Is A Hobo, 1947 .... 3.00
My Heart Is An Open Book, 1935 .... 3.00
My Heart Is In the Violet, Gardner, 1905 .... 3.00
My Heart Sings, 1941 .... 2.00
My Heart Stood Still, 1927 .... 2.00
My Heart Tells Me, Gordon/Warren, 1943 .... 5.00
My Hero, Stange/Straus, 1908 .... 3.00
My Home Town Is Good Enough For Me, Brennan, 1911 .... 5.00
My Honey's Lovin Arms, Ruby/Meyer, 1922 .... 3.00
My Honeymoon Man, Sanford/Williams, 1913 .... 5.00
My Hula-Hula Love, Madden/Wenrich, 1911 .... 5.00
My Ideal, Robin, 1930 .... 5.00
My Irish Molly O, 1905 .... 6.00
My Irish Song Of Songs, Sullivan, 1917 .... 3.00
My Isle Of Golden Dreams, 1919 .... 3.00
My Keepsake Is A Heartache, Lamb/Jones, 1915 .... 3.00
My Kinda Love, Trent/Alter, 1929 .... 2.00
My Kingdom For A Kiss, 1936 .... 3.00
My Laddie, Thayer, 1906 .... 3.00
My Lady Of the Nile, Barron/Ralph, 1917 .... 5.00
My Last Affair, Johnson/Martin, 1936 .... 2.00
My Life, My Heart, My Soul, 1914 .... 3.00
My Little Belle Of Japan, Robb/Bratton, 1901 .... 10.00
My Little Blue-Eyed Girl, Ketchum, 1912 .... 8.00
My Little Buckaroo, 1937 .... 3.00
My Little Climbing Rose, 1913 .... 3.00
My Little Coney Isle, Sterling, 1903 .... 10.00
My Little Dream Girl, Gilbert/Friedland, 1905 .... 6.00
My Little Girl, Lewis/Tilzer, 1915 .... 3.00
My Little Grass Shack, 1933 .... 2.00
My Little Nest Of Heavenly Blue, 1922 .... 2.00
My Little Rambling Rose, Freeman, 1917 .... 3.00
My Little Red Book, David/Bacharach, 1965 .... 8.00
My Little Swanee Sue, 1932 .... 3.00
My Little Zambezi, Golden, 1905 .... 6.00
My Lord What A Mornin', Burleigh, 1918 .... 10.00
My Love For You Grows Fonder As Your Golden Hair Turns 3.00
My Love Is A Muleteer, 1916 .... 2.00
My Love Is Young, 1936 .... 2.00
My Love Parade, 1929 .... 3.00
My Lovin' Melody Man, Ward, 1913 .... 3.00
My Madagascar Maid, Carle, 1902 .... 15.00
My Magnolia Maid, 1901 .... 15.00

My Mama Lives Up In the Sky, Harris, 1915................................. 5.00
My Mammy Knows, DeCasta, 1921 .... 10.00
My Mammy, Jolson, 1921 .... 10.00
My Man, Pollock, 1921 .... 3.00
My Margarita, Hirsch/Grever, 1938 .... 2.00
My Melancholy Baby, 1911 .... 3.00
My Mind's On You, Roy, 1953 .... 2.00
My Mobile Gal, MacConnell, 1900 .... 20.00
My Mom, Donaldson/Kay, 1932... 3.00
My Mother's Kiss Was Sweetest Of Them All, 1890 .... 10.00
My Mother's Lullaby, 1923... 2.00
My Mother's Photograph, 1929 .... 2.00
My Mother's Rosary, Lewis/Meyer, 1915 .... 3.00
My Mother's Song, 1904 .... 3.00
My Mother's Waltz, 1945.. 2.00
My Mother, My Dad, And My Girl, Dubin/McConnell, 1916 .... 3.00
My Northern Light, 1930... 3.00
My Old Fashioned Sweetheart, 1917 .... 3.00
My Old Girl's My New Girl Now, Caesar, 1928 .... 2.00
My Old Kentucky Home, Foster, 1905 .... 10.00
My Old Town, Klein, 1911 .... 3.00
My One Ambition Is You, 1930 .... 3.00
My Own Home Town In Ireland, Costello/Solman, 1915 .... 3.00
My Own Iona, 1916 .... 6.00
My Own Sweetheart, Scofield/Smith, 1910 .... 5.00
My Own United States, Edwards, 1902 .... 10.00
My Own, McHugh/Adamson, 1938 .... 3.00
My Own, My Gypsy Bride, Hall, 1903 .... 8.00
My Pretty Poppy, Levenson/Mendelsohn, 1918 .... 3.00
My Rainbow Girl, Wolf/Hirsch, 1917 .... 3.00
My Regular Gal, 1927 .... 2.00
My River Home, Petkere, 1932 .... 2.00
My Rocky Mountain Sweetheart, 1932 .... 2.00
My Romance, 1935 .... 2.00
My Shining Hour, Mercer/Arlen, 1943 .... 6.00
My Skylark Love, Bowles, 1913 .... 16.00
My Soldier Boy, Hollenbeck, 1918.. 3.00
My Soul to God, My Heart to Thee!, Frey, 1870 .... 15.00
My Soul, Bond, 1910 .... 3.00
My South Sea Island, 1906 .... 3.00
My Southern Rose, Taylor, 1909 .... 10.00
My Special Angel, 1957.. 2.00
My Sugar Coated Chocolate Boy, 1919 .... 20.00
My Sulu Lulu Loo, 1901 .... 3.00
My Summer Girl, Paxson, 1912 .... 3.00

My Sunny Tennessee, 1921 .... 2.00
My Suppressed Desire, Miller/Cohn, 1928 .... 3.00
My Swanee Home, Hamilton, 1919 .... 5.00
My Sweet Adair, Gilbert/Friedland, 1915 .... 3.00
My Sweeter Than Sweet, 1929 .... 3.00
My Sweetheart Is Somewhere In France, Earl, 1917 .... 10.00
My Sweetie Knows, 1920 .... 2.00
My Sweetie, 1917 .... 10.00
My Ten Ton Baby And Me, Wilson, 1942 .... 7.00
My Tonia, 1928 .... 3.00
My Trust In You, Dean/Houghton, 1919 .... 3.00
My Two Front Teeth, 1948 .... 2.00
My Uncle Sam, 1919 .... 3.00
My Walking Stick, Berlin, 1938 .... 10.00
My Waltz Queen, 1916 .... 3.00
My Way's Cloudy, Burleigh, 1917 .... 3.00
My What A Funny Little World This Is, 1910 .... 3.00
My Wife's Gone To the Country, Whiting/Berlin, 1909 .... 10.00
My Wife's Up In An Airship, Edwards, 1911 .... 20.00
My Wild Irish Rose, Olcott, 1898 .... 6.00
My Wonderful Dream Girl, 1913 .... 3.00
My Yellow Jacket Girl, Atteridge, 1913 .... 7.00
My, My, 1940 .... 4.00
N' Everything, Jolson, 1918 .... 12.00
Nagasaki, Dixon/Warren, 1928 .... 6.00
Nancy with the Laughing Face, 1944 .... 7.00
Napolean's Last Charge, Ellis, Paull, 1910 .... 30.00
Nasty Man, Henderson/Yellen, 1934 .... 5.00
National Emblem March, 1919 .... 10.00
Native Dancer, 1953 .... 2.00
Naughty-Naughty-Naughty, 1916 .... 4.00
Navy Blue, Zimmerman, 1902 .... 15.00
Navy Blues, Turk/Ahlert, 1929 .... 5.00
NC-4 March, Bigelow, 1919 .... 35.00
Near You, Goell/Craig, 1947 .... 2.00
Nearer and Deaer, Heyman, Friml, 1947 .... 10.00
Neath the Carolina Moon, 1923 .... 2.00
Neath the Old Cherry Tree, Sweet Marie, 1907 .... 5.00
Neath the South Sea Moon, 1922 .... 3.00
Neath the Stars And Stripes, Morrison, 1943 .... 3.00
Needin' You Like I Do, 1929 .... 2.00
Nellie Kelly I Love You, Cohan, 1922 .... 7.00
Nelly Was A Lady, Foster, 1849 .... 25.00
Neptune, Zimmerman, 1904 .... 15.00
Nesting Time, Hirsch/Hanley, 1921 .... 2.00

Nestle By My Side, Pixley/Lauders, 1906 .... 3.00
Never Before, David/Livingston, 1951 .... 3.00
Never Give Anything Away, Porter, 1953 .... 3.00
Never In A Million Years, Gordon/Revel, 1937 .... 5.00
Never Lay A Mother's Gift Aside, Elm, 1904 .... 3.00
Never Mind, Breau/Sanders, 1922 .... 3.00
Never So Beautiful, 1953 .... 3.00
Never, 1951 .... 2.00
Nevertheless, 1931 .... 3.00
New Express Galop, Evans, 1869 .... 65.00
New York and Coney Island Cycle March, E.T. Paull, 1896 .... 40.00
New York, New York, Bernstein, 1945 .... 2.00
Newport Belles, Ascher, 1901 .... 12.00
Next To Your Mother Who Do You Love, Berlin,1909 .... 15.00
Nice Work If You Can Get It, Gershwin, 1937 .... 5.00
Nigger Blues, Bush, 1908 .... 25.00
Nigger War Bride Blues, Goggan, 1917 .... 25.00
Night And Day, Porter, 1932 .... 3.00
Night In Paradise, Brooks/Skinner, 1945 .... 8.00
Night Of Gladness, Ancliffe, 1912 .... 5.00
Night Over Shanghai, Mercer/Warren, 1937 .... 5.00
Night Owl, 1923 .... 3.00
Night Shall Be Filled With Music, 1932 .... 2.00
Night Winds, Clare/Levant, 1929 .... 8.00
Nightingale, Coburn, 1920 .... 5.00
Nights Of Gladness, Ancliffe, 1912 .... 2.00
No Blossoms, Ford, 1905 .... 5.00
No Can Do, Tobias/Simon, 1945 .... 2.00
No Greater Love, 1936 .... 2.00
No Help Wanted, 1952 .... 2.00
No Letter Today, Brown/Wills, 1943 .... 3.00
No Love, No Nothin', 1943 .... 3.00
No Man Is An Island, 1954 .... 2.00
No No Nazi, You Too, Jappy, Jahnke, 1943 .... 10.00
No One But You, 1911 .... 3.00
No One Else Can Take Your Place, Harris, 1913 .... 7.00
No One Loves You Any Better Than Your M-A-Double M-Y 10.00
No One, Ager/Yellen, 1952 .... 2.00
No Wedding Bells For Me, Moran, 1906 .... 5.00
No Wonder (That I Love You), Burke, 1924 .... 2.00
Nobles Of the Mystic Shrine March, Sousa, 1923 .... 3.00
Nobody But You, Gershwin, 1919 .... 10.00
Nobody Cares If I'm Blue, Clarke/Akst, 1929 .... 5.00
Nobody Knows De Trouble I've Seen, Burleigh, 1917 .... 7.00
Nobody Knows Where Rosie Goes, Walker, 1917 .... 20.00

**Pictured above is a small selection of
Sheet Music Covers that are listed within this book.**

Nobody's Chasing Me, Porter, 1950 .... 2.00
Nobody, Rodgers, 1905 .... 15.00
Nokomis, 1903 .... 15.00
Nona, Shannon/Vandersloot, 1918 .... 5.00
Nora, My Irish Queen, Mittenthal, 1911 .... 3.00
Noreen, 1924 .... 2.00
Normandy Chimes, Powell, 1913 .... 5.00
North To Alaska, Phillips, 1960 .... 18.00
North Western Railway Polka, Ward, 1859 .... 75.00
Northern Route March, Smith, 1876 .... 50.00
Norway, McCarthy/Fisher, 1915 .... 3.00
Not For all the Rice In China, Berlin,1933 .... 15.00
Nothin' But Love, Alsop/Bond, 1912 .... 5.00
Nothing Lives Longer Than Love, Lewis, 1935 .... 2.00
Nothing Really Matters After All, Fleeson/Daly, 1925 .... 2.00
Nothing Seems the Same, Davis/Greer, 1926 .... 2.00
Now And Then, 1920 .... 2.00
Now I Know, Arlen/Koehler, 1943 .... 3.00
Now I Know, Henry, 1919 .... 3.00
Now I Lay Me Down To Dream, 1940 .... 2.00
Now I Lay Me Down To Sleep, 1920 .... 2.00
Now Is the Hour, Kaihan, 1913 .... 3.00
Now It Can Be Told, Berlin, 1938 .... 3.00
Now That I Need You, Loesser, 1949 .... 3.00
Now That I Need You, You're Gone, 1923 .... 5.00
Now's The Time To Fall In Love, 1931 .... 8.00
Number Ten Lullaby Lane, 1940 .... 2.00
Nutin', Carpenter, 1915 .... 3.00
Nuttin' For Christmas, 1955 .... 2.00
O Canada, Weir 2.00
O Dry Those Tears, 1901 .... 4.00
O Katharina, Gilbert/Fall, 1924 .... 2.00
O Lafayette We're Here, Geiger, 1918 .... 5.00
O Restless Sea, White, 1871 .... 15.00
O Won't You Be My Teddy Bear, 1907 .... 4.00
O'Brien Is Learning Hawaiian, Cormack, 1916 .... 15.00
O'Briens Tryin' To Talk Hawaiian, Dubin/Cormack, 1916 .... 15.00
O'Sole Mio, 1916 .... 2.00
Ocean Must Be Free, Kohn/Flint, 1917 .... 6.00
Oceana Roll, Lewis/Denni, 1911 .... 11.00
Of Thee I Sing, Gershwin, 1931 .... 3.00
Oh Baby, Ager/Murphy, 1928 .... 3.00
Oh Boy! Couldn't You Care For That, Kahal, 1927 .... 2.00
Oh Brother, 1945 .... 2.00
Oh Bury Me Out On the Prairie, Hale/Fitzer, 1927 .... 3.00

Oh By Jingo!, Tilzer, 1919 .... 10.00
Oh Death, Where Is Thy Sting, Stout, 1918 .... 15.00
Oh Didn't It Rain, Burleigh, 1919 .... 7.00
Oh Frenchy, Conrad, 1918 .... 10.00
Oh Friends, McGlennon, 1893 .... 6.00
Oh How I Wish I Could Sleep Till Daddy's Home, 1918 .... 10.00
Oh Johnny, Oh Johnny , Rose/Olman, 1939 .... 5.00
Oh Lady Be Good, Gershwin, 1924 .... 5.00
Oh Moon of the Summer Night, Flynn, 1918 .... 3.00
Oh Papa, Oh Papa, Vancent/Hanley, 1917 .... 5.00
Oh Peter Go Ring Dem Bells, Burleigh, 1918 .... 7.00
Oh Promise Me, Scott, 1889 .... 7.00
Oh Say! Can I See You Tonight, Creamer, 1925 .... 6.00
Oh What A Beautiful Ocean, Gray, 1897 .... 20.00
Oh You Circus Day, Lessing, 1912 .... 5.00
Oh You Little Sun-Uv-Er Gun, Howard/Solman, 1923 .... 3.00
Oh! Boy, What A Girl, Green, 1925 .... 8.00
Oh! Gay, 1919 .... 6.00
Oh! Gee, Oh! Gosh, Oh! Golly I'm In Love, 1923 .... 3.00
Oh! How I Hate To Get Up In the Morning, Berlin, 1918 .... 10.00
Oh! How She Can Dance, 1919 .... 2.00
Oh! Mama, Buy Me That, Himan, 1890 .... 6.00
Oh! Were I Rich And Mighty, Lohr, 1893 .... 7.00
Oh! What A Time For the Girlies, Lewis/Young/Ruby, 1918 .... 3.00
Oh! You Georgia Rose, Cole, 1912 .... 6.00
Oh! You Irrestible Child, Lerner, 1914 .... 5.00
Oh! You Rah! Rah! Boy, Morse/Mahoney, 1910 .... 6.00
Oh, How I Love You, 1930 .... 6.00
Oh, How I Want You, Lamb/Jones, 1916 .... 5.00
Oh, How She Could Yacki Hacki Wicki Wacki Woo, 1916 .... 5.00
Oh, Lady Be Good, Gershwin, 1924 .... 5.00
Oh, Moon Of the Summer Night, Flynn, 1918 .... 6.00
Oh, The Good Ship Lollipop, 1934 .... 15.00
Oh, What A Beautiful Mornin', 1943 .... 2.00
Oh, What I'd Do For A Girl Like You, Whiting, 1909 .... 6.00
Oh, You Beautiful Doll, Brown, 1911 .... 6.00
Oh-Susanna, Foster, 1935 .... 3.00
Ohio, Bernstein, 1953 .... 2.00
Ohio, Lauder, 1921 .... 5.00
Ol' Man River, 1927 .... 3.00
Old Black Joe, Drumheller, 1906 .... 12.00
Old Calico Of Blue, Loveday, 1922 .... 2.00
Old Cathedral Door, Lamb/Solman, 1912 .... 3.00
Old Chapel Bell, Holst, 1896 .... 10.00
Old Fall River Line, Tilzer, 1913 .... 17.00

Old Fashioned Garden, 1919 .... 5.00
Old Fashioned Girl, Jolson, 1922 .... 15.00
Old Grey Mare, 1915 .... 3.00
Old Home Down On the Farm, Dubois, 1888, ... 12.00
Old Homestead Fox Trot, Penn, 1914 .... 3.00
Old Homestead, 1915 .... 3.00
Old King Tut, Jerome/Tilzer, 1923 .... 5.00
Old MacDonald Had A Farm, 1935... 2.00
Old Maid's Ball, Berlin, 1913 .... 13.00
Old Man Jazz, Quaw, 1920 .... 2.00
Old Man Shay, Burt, 1905 .... 15.00
Old Oaken Bucket, Durkee, 1882 .... 10.00
Old Piano Roll Blues, Coben, 1949.. 2.00
Old Rag Carpet, 1897 .... 10.00
Old Spinning Wheel, Hill, 1933 .... 3.00
Old Time Rag, Madden/Morse, 1908... 20.00
Old Times Sake, Harris, 1900 .... 3.00
Old Town Is Looking Mighty Good Tonight, Mills, 1911 .... 10.00
Old Treasured Memories, Gifford, 1917..................................... 3.00
Ole Buttermilk Sky, 1946 .... 5.00
Ole South, Lodge, 1909... 12.00
On A Joy Ride, Kenna, 1909 .... 12.00
On A Little Farm In Normandie, 1919 .... 5.00
On A Monkey Honeymoon, Mahoney, 1909 .... 3.00
On A Moonlight Night, Gilbert, 1922 .... 3.00
On A Steamer Coming Over, Goodwin, 1933.............................. 13.00
On A Saturday Night, Bratton, 1922 .... 6.00
On A Starlight Night, 1903... 3.00
On A Starry Night, 1912 .... 3.00
On A Summer Night, Cobb, 1914 .... 3.00
On An Automobile Honeymoon, Schwartz, 1905.......................... 25.00
On Broadway, 1895 .... 3.00
On Dreamy Bay, Jerome, 1912 .... 3.00
On Her Veranda, Ponce, 1913 .... 3.00
On Lake Champlain, Bryan, 1916 .... 8.00
On Mobile Bay, Jones/Daniels, 1910 .... 3.00
On Old Broadway, Forrester, 1906 .... 5.00
On Our Honeymoon, Harris, 1907 .... 6.00
On the 'Gin 'Ginny Shore, Leslie, 1922...................................... 3.00
On the 5:15, Marshall, 1914 .... 20.00
On the 7:28, Marshall, 1915 .... 20.00
On the Alamo, Kahn/Jones, 1922 .... 2.00
On the Arm Of the Old Armchair, Lange/Heath, 1916 .... 3.00
On the Atchison, Topeka And the Santa Fe, 1945....................... 7.00
On the Banks Of Killarney, Bohannon, 1913.............................. 3.00

On the Banks Of Lovelight Bay, Williams, 1913 .... 3.00
On the Banks Of the Wabash, Far Away, Dressler, 1897 .... 15.00
On the Bay Of Old Bombay, Madden/Morris, 1915 .... 3.00
On the Beach At Bali-Bali, Sherman/Meskill, 1936 .... 2.00
On the Beach At Waikiki, Stover, 1916 .... 5.00
On the Boardwalk, Gordon, 1946 .... 3.00
On the Bombiloo Islands, Tobias, 1915 .... 5.00
On the Corner of Sunshine and Main, Gannon/Styne, 1943 .... 10.00
On the First Dark Night Next Week, Leslie, 1911 .... 5.00
On the Hoko Moko Isle, Klein/Tilzer, 1916 .... 6.00
On the Island Of Pines, Bryan/Carroll, 1914 .... 3.00
On the Mississippi, MacDonald/Carroll, 1912 .... 3.00
On the New York, New Haven and Hartford, Conroy, 1911 .... 25.00
On the Old Back Seat Of the Henry Ford, Dillon, 1916 .... 30.00
On the Old Front Porch, Heath/Lange, 1913 .... 3.00
On the Old See-Saw, Gardenier, 1907 .... 6.00
On the Old Virginia Shore, Browning, 1905 .... 5.00
On the Old West Side, Dillon, 1920 .... 3.00
On the Road That Leads Back Home, Rice, 1918 .... 5.00
On the Road To Home Sweet Home, 1917 .... 3.00
On the Rockin' Rosa Lee, Overstreet, 1917 .... 15.00
On the Same Old Road, Flynn/Piantadosi, 1916 .... 3.00
On the Sentimental Side, 1938 .... 3.00
On the Shore At Le Lei Wi, 1916 .... 3.00
On the Shores Of Italy, Glogau/Piantadosi, 1916 .... 3.00
On the Sidewalks Of Berlin, Keithley, 1918 .... 5.00
On the Silvery Sea, Campbell/Hamilton, 1913 .... 5.00
On the South Sea Isle, Tilzer, 1916 .... 3.00
On the Street Where You Live, Loewe/Lerner, 1956 .... 2.00
On the Sunny Side Of the Street, 1930 .... 3.00
On the Trail Of the Honeymoon, Cormack/Dubin, 1914 .... 3.00
On the Way To Home Sweet Home, Lewis/Meyer, 1915 .... 3.00
On To Plattsburg, Lowe, 1916 .... 5.00
On Wisconsin, Purdy/Beck, 1909 .... 3.00
On Your Toes, 1936 .... 2.00
Once A Pal, Always A Pal, Brockman, 1910 .... 3.00
Once In A Lifetime, Klages/Greer, 1928 .... 3.00
Once In A Million, Mitchell/Pollack, 1936 .... 5.00
Once In A While, Green/Edwards, 1937 .... 5.00
Once More Upon the Sea, Buckley 25.00
Once Upon A Time, Coburn, 1921 .... 2.00
One Alone, Harbach, 1926 .... 2.00
One Called Mother And the Other Home Sweet Home, 1905 .... 5.00
One Day In June, Goodwin/Hanley, 1917 .... 3.00
One Day When We Were Young, 1938 .... 3.00

**Pictured above is a small selection of
Sheet Music Covers that are listed within this book.**

One Fleeting Hour, Fuhram/Lee, 1915 .... 3.00
One Hamburger For Madame, 1936 .... 2.00
One Hand, One Heart, Bernstein, 1957 .... 3.00
One Happy Day, De Costa, 1917 .... 3.00
One Hour With You, 1932 .... 3.00
One Last Love Song, 1945 .... 2.00
One Little Girlie Can Do, Yellen/Schuster, 1917 .... 3.00
One Little Raindrop, Richman, 1930 .... 2.00
One Little Smile, 1916 .... 2.00
One Moment Alone, Kern/Harbach, 1931 .... 2.00
One Never Knows, Does One?, Gordon/Revel, 1936 .... 15.00
One Night In June, Harris, 1899 .... 6.00
One Night Of Love, Kahn, 1934 .... 3.00
One O'Clock Baby, Jolson, 1927 .... 6.00
One Second of Sex, Heyman/Green, 1931 .... 10.00
One Sunday Afternoon, Blane, 1948 .... 2.00
One Sweetly Solemn Thought, Ambrose, 1914 .... 3.00
One Wonderful Night, Jones, 1914 .... 3.00
One, Two, Button Your Shoe, 1936 .... 3.00
Only A Message From Home Sweet Home, Fleming/Florant 3.00
Only A Rose Of Yesterday, Spurr, 1918 .... 3.00
Only A Rose, Post/Hooker, 1925 .... 3.00
Only A Tangle Of Golden Curls, Harris, 1892 .... 6.00
Only A Year Ago, Bowles/Albers, 1915 .... 3.00
Only Another Boy and Girl, Porter, 1944 .... 10.00
Only Lonely Little Me, Ellwood/Snyder, 1909 .... 3.00
Only Me, Brown/Bibo, 1919 .... 2.00
Only Me, Ford/Bratton, 1894 .... 10.00
Only One Daisy Left, 1908 .... 5.00
OO-LA-LA-WEE-WEE, Ruby, 1919 .... 6.00
Ooh La La I'm Having A Wonderful Time, Green, 1918 .... 3.00
Ooh That Kiss, Dixon/Young, 1931 .... 2.00
Oops!, Warren/Mercer, 1951 .... 8.00
Open Up the Golden Gates To Dixieland, Yellen, 1919 .... 3.00
Open Up Your Heart, Gilbert, 1915 .... 3.00
Orange Blossom Time In Loveland, 1915 .... 5.00
Orange Blossom, Ludovic, 1902 .... 5.00
Oregon Trail, DeRose, 1935 .... 3.00
Organ Grinders Swing, Hudson, 1936 .... 2.00
Oriental Love Dreams, Kerr, 1924 .... 2.00
Oriental Melody, Saunders, 1920 .... 2.00
Otto, You Ought To Take Me In Your Auto, Speck, 1905 .... 20.00
Our Boys And Girls Of California, Ascher, 1916 .... 6.00
Our Boys And Girls, Kaiser, 1903 .... 12.00
Our Childhood Days, Wade, 1897 .... 8.00

Our Country's Heroes, Barrett, 1910 .... 6.00
Our Country's Voice Is Calling, Ebel, 1917 .... 3.00
Our Director, Bigelow, 1901 .... 5.00
Our Flag, Clark, 1859 .... 35.00
Our Flag, Torhorst, 1941 .... 2.00
Our Flag-Our Country For Country Dear, 1898 .... 10.00
Our Glorious Land, 1917 .... 3.00
Our Little Home On the Highway, Coslow, 1937 .... 5.00
Our Love Affair, Freed/Edens, 1940 .... 10.00
Our Melody the Phonograph Song, 1956 .... 2.00
Our Penthouse On Third Avenue, 1937 .... 5.00
Our Song, 1937 .... 3.00
Our "V" For Victory, Wheeler, 1942 .... 3.00
Our Very Own, 1950 .... 2.00
Out In An Automobile, Evans, 1905 .... 20.00
Out in the New Mown Hay, Tracey/Ehrlich/Dougherty, 1926 ...... 2.00
Out Of My Life Forever, Verona, 1903 .... 3.00
Out of The Blue, Nemo/Jason, 1947 .... 8.00
Out Of the Cradle, Into My Heart, Gilbert, 1916 .... 3.00
Out Of the Dawn, Donaldson, 1928 .... 7.00
Out Of This World, Mercer/Arlen, 1945 .... 3.00
Out On the Deep, Lohr, 1900 .... 6.00
Out Side Of That You're All Right, Tracey/McGavisk, 1910 .... 3.00
Out Where the Billows Roll High, Brannen, 1901 .... 15.00
Outside Of You, Warren/Dubin, 1935 .... 5.00
Outside, 1915 .... 3.00
Over On the Jersey Side, 1908 .... 3.00
Over the Deep Sea Of Love, Favor, 1912 .... 3.00
Over the Hills And Far Away, Jerome/Schwartz, 1908 .... 3.00
Over the Hills To Mary, Bryan/Wells, 1915 .... 5.00
Over the Phone, Olman, 1917 .... 5.00
Over the Rainbow, Arlen, 1939 .... 12.00
Over the Sea To Skye, Stevenson 3.00
Over the Seas For Liberty, Stanley, 1917 .... 5.00
Over the Top, Bryan/Wells, 1917 .... 6.00
Over There, Cohan, 1917 .... 25.00
Pack Up Your Blues and Smile, Trent, 1927 .... 13.00
Pack Up Your Sins And Go To the Devil, Berlin, 1922 .... 7.00
Packard And the Ford, Carroll, 1915 .... 25.00
Paddlin' Madelin' Home, Woods, 1925 .... 3.00
Paddy Day, 1905 .... 3.00
Pagan Love Song, Freed/Brown, 1929 .... 3.00
Paint A Rainbow, 1962 .... 2.00
Painting That Mother Of Mine, Sturgis, 1915 .... 3.00
Pal That I Loved Stole the Gal That I Loved, 1924 .... 2.00

Pale Hands, Hope/Finden, 1903 .... 5.00
Palesteena, Conrad, 1920 .... 2.00
Palestine, Kendis/Brockman/Bryan, 1918 .... 5.00
Palm Limited, Lincoln, 1905 .... 20.00
Pals, Just Pals, 1928 .... 5.00
Pansies Mean Thoughts And Thoughts Mean You, 1908 .... 3.00
Papa Come Back To Mama, 1894 .... 15.00
Parade March Of Union Grays, 1862 .... 40.00
Paradise, Kerr, 1928 .... 5.00
Pardon Came Too Late, Dresser, 1896 .... 10.00
Pardon My Southern Accent, Mercer, 1934 .... 2.00
Paris In the Spring, Gordon/Revel, 1935 .... 5.00
Parisian Maxine, Nazareth, 1914 .... 5.00
Parisiola, Gerber/Silver, 1920 .... 2.00
Parkin' In the Park With You, Denniker, 1932 .... 7.00
Pass Me By, Leigh/Coleman, 1964 .... 2.00
Pass That Peace Pipe, 1947 .... 5.00
Pass the Pickles, 1913 .... 10.00
Passion Flower, Berlin, 1921 .... 6.00
Paul Revere's Ride, Paull, 1905 .... 20.00
Pawn Broker East Side, Wegern, 1894 .... 6.00
Peace In the Valley, Dorsey, 1939 .... 3.00
Peacock Walk, 1920 .... 2.00
Peek-A-Boo Rag, Johnson, 1914 .... 15.00
Peg Away, Bevan, 1904 .... 5.00
Peg O' My Heart, Bryan/Fisher, 1913 .... 5.00
Peggy, Williams, 1919 .... 7.00
Pennies From Heaven, Johnston, 1936 .... 6.00
People Will Say We're In Love, 1943 .... 2.00
People, 1963 .... 2.00
Pepper Pot, Ivers, 1913 .... 12.00
Perhaps, 1901 .... 3.00
Perhaps, Perhaps, Perhaps, Davis, 1947 .... 3.00
Perry's Victory March, Martin, 1913 .... 20.00
Pershing's Crusaders, Paull, 1918 .... 35.00
Personality, 1945 .... 5.00
Pet Of the Ranch, Kaiser, 1906 .... 6.00
Peter Cottontail, 1950 .... 2.00
Peter Pan, I Love You, 1924 .... 5.00
Pettin' In the Park, Dubin/Warren, 1933 .... 5.00
Philosophy, 1904 .... 3.00
Pianist Rag, Schwartz, 1917 .... 10.00
Pick A Chicken, Kaufman, 1914 .... 5.00
Pick Me Up And Lay Me Down In Dear Old Dixieland, 1922 .... 6.00
Pick, Pick, Pick On the Mandolin, Berlin, 1912 .... 14.00

Pickaninny Blues, Frost, 1919 .... 5.00
Pickaninny Sam, Havez, 1920 .... 3.00
Pickaninny's Lullaby, Conrad, 1920 .... 7.00
Pickaninny's Paradise, Ehrlich, 1918 .... 12.00
Pickin' Cotton, 1928 .... 5.00
Pickin' Petals Off O' Daisies, 1929 .... 5.00
Pickles & Peppers, Sheperd, 1907 .... 7.00
Pierrot, Pierette, Edwards, 1916 .... 5.00
Pig Foot Pete, Raye/DePaul, 1941 .... 13.00
Piney Ridge, Mohr, 1915 .... 3.00
Pinkie, 1902 .... 2.00
Pioneer Limited, Lincoln, 1910 .... 25.00
Pistol Packin' Mama, Dexter, 1943 .... 3.00
Pitter Patter Rag, Daly, 1910 .... 12.00
Pitter Patter, Hough, 1920 .... 3.00
Pity the Homeless One Tonight, Pratt, 1878 .... 8.00
Planning, 1920 .... 2.00
Plantation Boogie, Horton/Dee, 1954 .... 2.00
Play A Simple Melody, Berlin, 1942 .... 8.00
Play Me Something I Can Dance To, Smith/Herbert, 1920 .... 8.00
Play That Barber Shop Chord, Tracey/Muhr, 1910 .... 7.00
Please Don't Jazz My Mammy's Lullaby, Broderick, 1920 .... 20.00
Please Don't Lean On the Bell, Harris/Vincent, 1917 .... 6.00
Please Don't Love Anybody Else But Me, Smith, 1913 .... 6.00
Please Don't Say No, Freed/Fain, 1944 .... 2.00
Please Don't Talk About Me When I'm Gone, 1930 .... 5.00
Please Give Me A Penny Sir, Seibert, 1868 .... 15.00
Please Let Me Sleep, Brymn, 1902 .... 8.00
Please Pass the Word Around, 1934 .... 2.00
Please, Robin/Rainger, 1932 .... 5.00
Plenty To Be Thankful For, Berlin, 1942 .... 6.00
Poet & Peasant, 1914 .... 6.00
Poinsettia, Storer, 1911 .... 5.00
Polar Bear Polka, 1865 .... 50.00
Polly, Zamecnik, 1929 .... 2.00
Pompanola, 1928 .... 2.00
Poor Butterfly, 1916 .... 3.00
Poor Little Butterfly Is A Fly Girl Now, Lewis, 1919 .... 15.00
Poor Little Midnight, Rich/Clifford, 1926 .... 8.00
Poor Little Rhode Island, 1944 .... 3.00
Poor Little Rich Girl, Caddigan/Brennan, 1914 .... 5.00
Poor Lizzie, Silver, 1928 .... 15.00
Poor Mother Willie's Gone, Seward 3.00
Poor Papa, Rose/Woods, 1926 .... 5.00
Poor Pauline, McCarron/Walker, 1914 .... 3.00

**Pictured above is a small selection of
Sheet Music Covers that are listed within this book.**

Poor Whip Poor Will, 1951 .... 2.00
Poppies Carry On, Green, 1932 .... 3.00
Porcelain Maid, Berlin, 1922 .... 5.00
Porgy And Bess, Gershwin, 1923 .... 12.00
Portrait Of Jennie, 1948 .... 3.00
Portrait Of My Love, 1960 .... 2.00
Powder Rag, Birch, 1908 .... 10.00
Prairie Lullaby, Hill, 1934 .... 2.00
Praise the Lord And Pass the Ammunition, Loesser, 1941 .... 5.00
Precious Little One, 1935 .... 2.00
Pretty Baby, 1916 .... 3.00
Pretty Girl Is Like A Melody, Berlin, 1919 .... 7.00
Pretty Kitty Kelly, Nelson, 1920 .... 3.00
Pretty Little Rainbow, Levenson, 1919 .... 3.00
Prince Of Tonight (I Wonder Who's Kissing Her Now), 1909 .... 6.00
Prohibition Blues, Sweet 20.00
Pucker Up And Whistle, Franklyn, 1921 .... 2.00
Pull the Cork Out Of Erin, 1917 .... 7.00
Pullman Porter Man, Murphy, 1911 .... 10.00
Pullman Porter's Parade, Abrahams, 1913 .... 20.00
Pumping the Pump Pump Pump, 1899 .... 8.00
Punchinello, Wright/Forrest, 1940 .... 8.00
Put 'Em In A Box, 1948 .... 2.00
Put Me To Sleep With An Old Fashioned Melody, 1915 .... 3.00
Put On Your Old Gray Bonnet, Murphy, 1909 .... 12.00
Put On Your Slippers And Fill Your Pipe, 1916 .... 3.00
Put Your Arms Around Me, Honey, McCree/Tilzer, 1910 .... 7.00
Put Your Arms Where They Belong, 1926 .... 2.00
Put Your Little Foot Right Out, 1939 .... 3.00
Put Your Shoes On Lucy, Fort, 1947 .... 2.00
Puttin' On the Ritz, Berlin, 1929 .... 6.00
Q Galop, Leggett, 1884 .... 30.00
Quality, Scott, 1911 .... 7.00
Queen Of the Bungalow, Hoffman, 1903 .... 3.00
Queen Of the Carnival March, Warner, 1923 .... 2.00
Quit Cryin', Charlotte/Irving, 1931 .... 12.00
R-e-m-o-r-s-e, 1902 .... 5.00
Racing Down the Rapids, Lawrence, 1888 .... 30.00
Rackety Coo, 1915 .... 3.00
Rag Baby Rag, 1909 .... 15.00
Rag Doll, Brown, 1928 .... 3.00
Rag Of Rags, Bee, 1951 .... 6.00
Raggedy Man, Riley/Krull, 1908 .... 3.00
Ragging the Scale, Claypoole, 1915 .... 8.00
Ragmuffin Rag, Drake, 1957 .... 6.00

Ragmuffin, Janssen, 1920 .... 3.00
Rags and Silk, Morelle/McCarthy, 1925 .... 8.00
Ragtime Automobile, Greensfelder, 1914 .... 25.00
Ragtime In the Air, Klein, 1913 .... 14.00
Ragtime Organ Morgan, Gaskill, 1912 .... 14.00
Ragtime Soldier Man, Berlin, 1912 .... 25.00
Ragtime Violin, 1911 .... 20.00
Ragtime Wedding Bells, Meyer, 1913 .... 14.00
Rail-Road, Meineke, 1828 .... 125.00
Railroad Galop, Treloar, 1893 .... 35.00
Railroad Rag, Bimberg, 1911 .... 25.00
Rain On the Roof, Ronell/Whiteman, 1932 .... 2.00
Rain Or Shine, Yellen/Ager, 1928 .... 3.00
Rain With the Sunshine, 1913 .... 3.00
Rain, DeRose, 1934 .... 3.00
Rainbow Of Waikiki, Marley, 1926 .... 2.00
Rainbow On the River, 1936 .... 5.00
Rainbow Sal, 1920 .... 2.00
Rainbow-Pretty Little Rainbow, 1918 .... 3.00
Raindrops Keep Fallin' On My Head, 1969 .... 2.00
Raise The Dust, Eliscu/Meyer, 1929 .... 10.00
Rambling Rose, McCarthy/Burke, 1948 .... 2.00
Ramona, Gilbert/Wayne, 1927 .... 2.00
Rastus Rag, Fischler 15.00
Reaching For the Moon, 1930 .... 3.00
Ready, Willing and Able, Rinker/Huddleston, 1954 .... 5.00
Rebecca of Sunnybrook Farm, Gumble, 1914 .... 5.00
Rebecca, 1921 .... 2.00
Recollections, 1926 .... 2.00
Red Ball Express, 1946 .... 3.00
Red Feather, 1903 .... 5.00
Red Hair, Bryan, 1928 .... 6.00
Red Hot Mamma, Wells, 1924 .... 3.00
Red Peppers, Giles, 1907 .... 12.00
Red River Valley, Potter, 1933 .... 3.00
Red, Red As A Rose, 1919 .... 2.00
Redhead, Franklin/Green, 1908 .... 3.00
Redskin, Kerr, 1929 .... 3.00
Remember Me, Dubin/Warren, 1937 .... 5.00
Remember Me, Woman, 1907 .... 3.00
Remember Mo?, 1937 .... 2.00
Remember My Forgotten Man, Dubin/Warren, 1933 .... 5.00
Remember the Rose, 1921 .... 2.00
Remember You've A Sister Of Your Own, 1894 .... 10.00
Remember, Berlin,1925 .... 6.00

Remus Takes the Cake, Becker, 1897 .... 15.00
Renee Waltzes, 1897 .... 6.00
Repasz Band, Sweeney, 1901 .... 6.00
Restless Heart, 1954 .... 2.00
Retreat, 1952 .... 2.00
Return To Paradise, 1953 .... 3.00
Reuben And Rachel, Gooch, 1910 .... 2.00
Revenge, 1928 .... 3.00
Rhapsody In Blue, Gershwin, 1939 .... 5.00
Rhythm Of the Rain, 1935 .... 3.00
Rhythm On The Ice, Carlton/Condor, 1938 .... 10.00
Ricochet, Coleman/Gimbel/Darion, 1953 .... 3.00
Ride Me In A Big Balloon, Kerr, 1910 .... 20.00
Ride On Vaquero, 1929 .... 3.00
Ride Tenderfoot Ride, Mercer/Whiting, 1938 .... 3.00
Riders In the Sky, Jones, 1949 .... 2.00
Riding Up the River Road, Woods, 1935 .... 5.00
Right From My Heart, Allen, 1912 .... 3.00
Right Or Wrong, 1928 .... 2.00
Rigoletto, Murfree, 1911 .... 3.00
Ring Down the Curtain, I Can't Sing Tonight, 1902 .... 5.00
Ring Me Up In Heaven, Please Central, 1908 .... 3.00
Ring Ting A Ling, 1912 .... 3.00
Rio Rita, Tierney/McCarthy, 1926 .... 2.00
Riptide, 1934 .... 6.00
River Shannon Moon, 1923 .... 2.00
River, Stay Way From My Door, 1931 .... 6.00
Riverside I Stray, 1861 .... 15.00
Ro Ro Rollin' Along, 1930 .... 3.00
Roamin' In the Gloamin', Lauder, 1911 .... 8.00
Roaring Volcano, Paull, 1912 .... 35.00
Robin Hood, Prima/Miketta 2.00
Robinson Crusoe's Isle, Jones/Willis, 1913 .... 6.00
Rock & Rye Polka, 1940 .... 2.00
Rock A Bye To Sleep In Dixie, 1930 .... 2.00
Rock Me In A Cradle Of Kalua, Bryan/Wendling, 1931 .... 2.00
Rock Me In the Cradle Of the Rockies, 1939 .... 5.00
Rock the Cradle, Mother, Hand, 1898 .... 3.00
Rock-A-Bye Your Baby With A Dixie Melody, 1918 .... 10.00
Rockaway, Roberts/Johnson, 1917 .... 10.00
Rocked In the Cradle Of the Deep, Knight 7.00
Rodger Young, 1945 .... 2.00
Roll Em Girls, 1925 .... 2.00
Rollin' Home, De Rose, 1934 .... 5.00
Romance Of A Rose, O'Connor, 1908 .... 5.00

Romance Runs In the Family, 1939 .... 2.00
Romance, Harbach/Hammerstein, 1926 .... 3.00
Romance, Leslie/Donaldson, 1929 .... 3.00
Romany Love, Zamecnik, 1922 .... 2.00
Romeo And Juliet, 1968.. 2.00
Rondino, Kreisler, 1915 .... 5.00
Roo Te Too Toot, 1912 .... 5.00
Rosalie, 1937, Cole Porter 6.00
Rosalinda, 1948 .... 2.00
Rosary-My Rosary, My Mother's Rosary, 1901 .... 5.00
Rose Ann Of Charing Cross, 1942 .... 2.00
Rose Dreams, Statsny, 1916 .... 10.00
Rose O'Mine, Allan, 1917 .... 3.00
Rose Of My Heart, 1919 .... 2.00
Rose Of No Man's Land, Brennan, 1918 .... 10.00
Rose Of the Morning, 1923 .... 2.00
Rose Of the Mountain Trail, Caddigan/Brennan, 1914 .... 5.00
Rose Of Washington Square, 1920 .... 2.00
Rose Petals, Pierson, 1910 .... 3.00
Rose Room Fox Trot, Hickman, 1917 .... 3.00
Rose-Mary-Fay, 1915... 3.00
Rosemary, 1928... 3.00
Roses And Lilacs, Harris, 1904 .... 3.00
Roses And Violets, Daly, 1911 .... 3.00
Roses At Twilight, Black/Marple, 1918 .... 3.00
Roses Bloom For Lovers, 1908 .... 2.00
Roses Bring Dreams Of You, Ingraham, 1908 .... 5.00
Roses In December, 1937... 3.00
Roses In the Rain, 1947 .... 2.00
Roses Mean Memories, Cobb/Yellen, 1915 .... 3.00
Roses Of Beautiful Memories, Pitman, 1916 .... 2.00
Roses Of Picardy, Wood, 1916... 5.00
Roses Of Yesterday, 1928... 3.00
Roses, Ingraham, 1908 .... 3.00
Rosiana, 1909 .... 2.00
Rosie O'Ryan, 1926 .... 2.00
Round Hill Quick Step, 1840 .... 40.00
Row Gentle Here, My Gondolier, Heinrich, 1913 .... 6.00
Row-Row-Row, Monaco, 1912 .... 5.00
Rub-A-Dub Dub, 1953.. 2.00
Ruby, Parish, 1953 .... 3.00
Rudolph the Red-Nosed Reindeer, Marks, 1949 .... 2.00
Rum And Coca-Cola, 1944.. 5.00
Rum Tum Tiddle, Jolson, 1912 .... 15.00
Rumble Seat, Morgan, 1929... 12.00

**Pictured above is a small selection of
Sheet Music Covers that are listed within this book.**

Run Home And Tell Your Mother, 1911 .... 14.00
Runaway June, 1915 .... 2.00
Runnin' Wild, 1922 .... 10.00
Running Between the Rain Drops, 1931 .... 2.00
Russian Lullaby, Berlin, 1927 .... 6.00
Russian March, Mack, 1861 .... 30.00
Russian Pony Rag, Ramsay, 1910 .... 11.00
Russian Rag, Cobb, 1918 .... 10.00
Rustic Dance, 1905 .... 5.00
'S Wonderful, Gershwin, 1927 .... 3.00
'Scuse Me To-Day, Harris, 1909 .... 12.00
Saddle Your Blues To A Wild Mustang, Whiting, 1936 .... 3.00
Sadie Salome Go Home, Berlin, 1909 .... 25.00
Sadie Won't You Be My Little Lady, Edwards, 1905 .... 7.00
Sahara, 1919 .... 3.00
Sail Along Silvery Moon, Tobias/Wenrich, 1937 .... 3.00
Sail On Silvery Moon, Downs/Erdman, 1912 .... 5.00
Sail On the Ceylon, 1916 .... 5.00
Sailing Down the Chesapeake Bay, Havez, 1913 .... 5.00
Sailing Down the River In the Moonlight, Mandy and I, 1914 ...... 8.00
Sailing In My Balloon, Scott, 1907 .... 12.00
Saint Louis Blues, 1942 .... 4.00
Sally In Our Alley, Carey, 1935 .... 2.00
Sally, 1921 .... 2.00
Salt Water Cowboy, Evans/Haines, 1944 .... 2.00
Salvation Lassie Of Mine, Story, 1919 .... 10.00
Sam's Laugh, O'Connor, 1906 .... 12.00
Sam's Song, 1950 .... 2.00
Sambo & Dinah, 1904 .... 10.00
Same Sort Of Girl, 1914 .... 3.00
San Antonio Rose, Wills, 1940 .... 2.00
San Antonio, Williams, 1907 .... 5.00
San Fernando Valley, Jenkins, 1943 .... 2.00
San Francisco Bound, Berlin, 1913 .... 15.00
Sand Dunes, Gay/Brandt, 1919 .... 3.00
Santa Claus Is Comin' To Town, 1934 .... 3.00
Satan's A Liar An' A Conjur Too, Guion, 1918 .... 8.00
Save the Last Dance For Me, 1931 .... 2.00
Saw Mill River Road, 1921 .... 2.00
Say A Little Prayer For Me, 1930 .... 2.00
Say A Prayer For the Boys Out There, Marr, 1917 .... 15.00
Say Boys, I've Found A Girl, Kahn, 1909 .... 5.00
Say It Again, 1923 .... 2.00
Say It With Music, Berlin, 1921 .... 6.00
Say It With Your Heart, 1952 .... 2.00

Say Sis! Give Us A Kiss, Clark, 1907 .... 5.00
Say So, 1928 .... 2.00
Say Suz! How 'Bout You?, Thatcher, 1899 .... 15.00
Say When, 1940 .... 2.00
Say You Haven't Sacrificed At All, Dulmage, 1918 .... 10.00
Say You'll Be A Friend Of Mine, 1903 .... 5.00
Say You'll Be My Lady, Dinad, 1906 .... 3.00
Scandal Of Little Lizzie Ford, Tilzer, 1921 .... 20.00
Scandinavia, 1921 .... 3.00
Scented Roses, Daly, 1909 .... 3.00
School Day Sweethearts, Edwards, 1923 .... 2.00
Sea Shell, Baer/Shisler, 1910 .... 5.00
Seal It With A Kiss, 1936 .... 3.00
Secret Love, 1953 .... 3.00
See Saw, Crowe, 1884 .... 8.00
Seeing Denver, Brohm, 1906 .... 15.00
Seek, Strike and Destroy, Waring, 1944 .... 15.00
Seems Like Old Times, Loeb/Lombardo, 1946 .... 3.00
Semper Paratus, Boskerck, 1928 .... 3.00
Sen'imental Sal, Ellis, 1900 .... 12.00
Send A Little Love My Way, David/Mancini, ... 2.00
Send For Me, Leslie/Meyer, 1911 .... 3.00
Send Me A Letter From Over the Sea, Jackson, 1880 .... 20.00
Send Me An Answer From Over the Sea, Pratt, 1870 .... 20.00
Send Me Away With A Smile, Weslyn/Piantadosi, 1917 .... 5.00
Senora, 1907 .... 3.00
Sentimental Baby, Palmer/Grogan, 1928 .... 2.00
Sentimental Tears, 1951 .... 2.00
September In the Rain, 1937 .... 3.00
September, 1894 .... 6.00
Serenade In Blue, Gordon/Warren, 1942 .... 5.00
Serenade In the Night, 1934 .... 3.00
Serenade, Schubert, 1905 .... 5.00
Shade Of the Palm, Stuart, 1900 .... 6.00
Shades Of Night, 1916 .... 3.00
Shadow Time, Johnson, 1913 .... 3.00
Shadows Of Flame, 1916 .... 3.00
Shake Your Little Shoulder, MacBoyle/Rosemont, 1920 .... 3.00
Shamrock Waltzes, 1918 .... 3.00
Shanghai Lil, Dubin/Warren, 1933 .... 5.00
She Ain't What She Used To Be, 1925 .... 3.00
She Didn't Even Say Goodbye, 1955 .... 2.00
She Didn't Say Yes, 1931 .... 2.00
She Don't Wanna, Yellen/Ager, 1927 .... 3.00
She Is the Sunshine Of Virginia, MacDonald, 1916 .... 7.00

She Knows Her Onions, Yellen/Ager, 1926 .... 5.00
She Knows It, Jolson, 1921 .... 9.00
She Loves Me, She Loves Me Not, 1921 .... 2.00
She Never Flirts, Williams, 1869 .... 12.00
She Reminds Me Of You, Gordon/Revel, 1934 .... 5.00
She Rested By the Broken Brook, 1906 .... 3.00
She Sang Aloha To Me, Carey, 1915 .... 3.00
She Shall Have Music, Sigler/Goodhart, 1935 .... 3.00
She Was A Good Old Soul, 1904 .... 3.00
She Was Bred In Old Kentucky, Carter, 1898 .... 20.00
She Was Happy Till She Met You, 1899 .... 8.00
She Was Not So Bad For A Country Girl, De Sylva, 1918 .... 5.00
She Wears Red Feathers, 1952 .... 2.00
She Wore A Yellow Ribbon, 1949 .... 3.00
She Wouldn't Do, 1923 .... 2.00
She'll Be Comin' Round the Mountain, 1935 .... 2.00
She's A Gorgeous, Thing, 1930 .... 2.00
She's A Great, Great Girl, Woods, 1928 .... 2.00
She's Dancing Her Heart Away, Gilbert/Mills, 1914 .... 5.00
She's Funny That Way, 1928 .... 2.00
She's Got the Gimmes, 1918 .... 3.00
She's Just A Little Different From the Others I Know, 1904 .... 6.00
She's Just Sweet Sixteen Years Old, Talbert, 1885 .... 15.00
She's Like A Great Big Bouquet, 1919 .... 3.00
She's My Girl, 1923 .... 2.00
She's My Love, Merrill, 1961 .... 8.00
She's One Sweet Show Girl, 1928 .... 10.00
She's Still My Baby, 1926 .... 2.00
She's the Apple Of My Eye, 1907 .... 3.00
She's the Daughter Of Mother Machree, Ball, 1915 .... 5.00
She's the Sweetheart Of Six Other Guys, 1928 .... 2.00
She's Too Far Above Me, Heneker, 1963 .... 2.00
Shepherd Of the Alps, 1906 .... 5.00
Shine On Arizona Moon, Donovan/Freeman, 1915 .... 3.00
Shine On Harvest Moon, Bayes, 1908 .... 10.00
Shine, 1924 .... 2.00
Ship Of My Dreams, Solman/Lamb, 1912 .... 5.00
Shipmates Forever, Don't Give Up the Ship, 1935 .... 10.00
Ships That Pass In the Night, 1918 .... 3.00
Shoe Shine Boy, 1936 .... 3.00
Shoo Shoo Baby, 1943 .... 3.00
Should I?, 1929 .... 3.00
Show Me the Way To Go Home, King, 1925 .... 4.00
Show Me the Way, 1924 .... 2.00
Show Us How To Do the Fox Trot, Berlin, 1913 .... 14.00

Shrewsbury Waltz, 1890 .... 3.00
Shuffle Off To Buffalo, Dubin/Warren, 1932 .... 5.00
Siam, 1915 .... 3.00
Sierra Madre, 1947 .... 2.00
Sierra Sue, Carey, 1916 .... 2.00
Silent Lips, 1957 .... 2.00
Silent Night, Shields, 1910 .... 5.00
Silk & Rags 12.00
Silk Stockings, 1954 .... 2.00
Silver And Gold, 1951 .... 2.00
Silver Bay, Wenrich, 1916 .... 3.00
Silver Bell, Wenrich, 1910 .... 3.00
Silver Moon, 1927 .... 2.00
Silver On the Sage, Robin/Rainger, 1938 .... 5.00
Silver Sleighbells, Paull, 1906 .... 35.00
Silver Threads Among the Gold, 1873 .... 10.00
Silver Wings In the Moonlight, 1943 .... 2.00
Sin, Manney, 1926 .... 3.00
Since Casey Runs the Flat, Janssen, 1890 .... 15.00
Since Sally Left Our Alley, 1923 .... 2.00
Since You Called Me Dearie, 1906 .... 3.00
Since You Called Me Sweetheart, Weil/Klickmann, 1925 .... 2.00
Since You Came Along, 1931 .... 2.00
Since You Went Away, 1913 .... 3.00
Sing A Little Love Song, 1929 .... 5.00
Sing A Song Of Sunbeams, 1939 .... 3.00
Sing Again That Sweet Refrain, Davis 2.00
Sing Baby Sing, Yellen, 1936 .... 5.00
Sing Me A Song Of the Islands, Gordon/Owens, 1942 .... 3.00
Sing Me Loves Lullaby, Terriss/Morse, 1917 .... 3.00
Sing Me the Rosary, Lewis/Klickman, 1913 .... 3.00
Sing Me To Sleep, Bingham/Greene, 1902 .... 5.00
Sing Me To Sleep, Harris, 1919 .... 3.00
Sing Rock-A-Bye Baby To Me, Kirkpatrick/Long, 1913 .... 3.00
Sing Something Simple, 1930 .... 2.00
Sing With Gracie Fields, 1943 .... 3.00
Sing You Sinners, 1930 .... 3.00
Singin' In the Rain, 1929 .... 6.00
Singin' the Blues, 1920 .... 2.00
Singing A Happy Song, 1935 .... 3.00
Singing A Song Of Love, 1932 .... 2.00
Singing A Song To the Stars, 1930 .... 3.00
Singing A Vagabond Song, 1930 .... 3.00
Singing Sands, 1923 .... 2.00
Singing the Blues, 1954 .... 2.00

**Pictured above is a small selection of
Sheet Music Covers that are listed within this book.**

Singing the Dear Little Baby To Sleep, Armstrong, 1896 .... 8.00
Sinner Please Don't Let This Harvest Pass, Burleigh, 1917 .... 7.00
Sioux City Sue, 1945 .... 2.00
Sippin' Cider Thru A Straw, 1919 .... 20.00
Siren Of A Southern Sea, 1921 .... 3.00
Sissy, 1938 .... 2.00
Sister Louisa, Hardy, 1913 .... 3.00
Sister Susie Sewing Shirts For Soldiers, Jolson, 1914 .... 20.00
Sit Down! You're Rocking the Boat, Jerome, 1914 .... 14.00
Sittin' On A Backyard Fence, Kahal/Fain, 1933 .... 8.00
Sitting By the Window, 1929 .... 3.00
Sixteen Tons, Travis, 1947 .... 3.00
Skokiaan, 1952 .... 2.00
Sky Anchors, Waring, 1942 .... 15.00
Skylark, Mercer, 1942 .... 3.00
Slap'er Down Again, Paw, 1947 .... 2.00
Sleep And Forget, Bingham/White, 1906 .... 5.00
Sleep Baby Sleep, 1928 .... 2.00
Sleep Little Baby Of Mine, 1891 .... 5.00
Sleep Soldier Boy, 1926 .... 3.00
Sleep, Come On And Take Me, 1932 .... 2.00
Sleep, Ma Little Pickaninny, Crockett, 1928 .... 12.00
Sleepy Head, Kahn/Donaldson, 1934 .... 5.00
Sleepy Lagoon, Coates/Lawrence, 1930 .... 2.00
Sleepy Sidney, Scheu, 1907 .... 10.00
Sleepy Time Down South, 1931 .... 3.00
Sleepy Time Gal, 1925 .... 3.00
Sleepy Valley, 1929 .... 5.00
Sleighride in July, Scott/Shore/Lee, 1944 .... 8.00
Slippery Hank, Losey, 1917 .... 5.00
Slipping Around, 1949 .... 2.00
Slow Poke, Price, 1951 .... 3.00
Slowly, Raskin/Goell, 1945 .... 3.00
Slue Foot, 1927 .... 2.00
Slumberland, Ott, 1917 .... 3.00
Small World, 1959 .... 2.00
Smarty, Horworth/Tilzer, 1908 .... 8.00
Smile All the While, 1925 .... 2.00
Smile And Show Your Dimple, Berlin, 1917 .... 15.00
Smile Darn Ya Smile, 1931 .... 2.00
Smile, Smile, Smile, 1915 .... 3.00
Smiles, 1917 .... 5.00
Smilin Star, Drislane/Morse, 1909 .... 5.00
Smiling Irish Eyes, Perkins, 1929 .... 3.00
Smith's March, 1848 .... 25.00

Smoke From A Chimney, Hill, 1928 .... 3.00
Smoke Gets In Your Eyes, Harbach/Kern, 1933 .... 10.00
Smoke Rings, 1920 .... 2.00
Smoke! Smoke! Smoke!, 1947 .... 2.00
Snap Shot Sal, Williams/Walker, 1899 .... 20.00
Snookey Ookums, Berlin, 1913 .... 15.00
Snow Deer, Mahoney/Wenrich, 1913 .... 5.00
Snow Flakes, Gershwin, 1920 .... 5.00
Snow River, 1927 .... 2.00
Snowbird, Lynden, 1916 .... 3.00
Snowflakes Also Christmas Chimes, 1917 .... 3.00
Snuggled On Your Shoulder, 1932 .... 2.00
So Am I, Gershwin, 1924 .... 5.00
So Beats My Heart For You, 1930 .... 2.00
So Dear To My Heart, Taylor/Freeman, 1948 .... 6.00
So Do I, Burke, 1936 .... 2.00
So I Took the $5,000.00, 1923 .... 3.00
So Is Your Old Lady, Burke, 1926 .... 3.00
So Long Letty, Carroll, 1916 .... 5.00
So Long Mother, Jolson, 1917 .... 12.00
So Long Sal, Sterlin/Lange, 1918 .... 7.00
So Long, Mary, Cohan, 1932 .... 12.00
So This Is Love, 1923 .... 2.00
So Will I, Brown, 1926 .... 2.00
Society Cake Walk, Street, 1900 .... 12.00
Soldiers In the Park, 1893 .... 6.00
Soliloquy, 1945 .... 2.00
Some Boy, Buck/Stamper, 1912 .... 8.00
Some Day Dear, With You, 1935 .... 2.00
Some Day Dearie, Winzel, 1909 .... 5.00
Some Day My Prince Will Come, 1937 .... 7.00
Some Day the Shadows Will All Fade Away, 1915 .... 5.00
Some Day You'll Want Me, 1916 .... 3.00
Some Day, Herbert, 1917 .... 7.00
Some Day, Post/Hooker, 1925 .... 3.00
Some Day-Somehow, 1918 .... 3.00
Some Enchanted Evening, 1949 .... 2.00
Some Girls Do And Some Girls Don't, 1916 .... 8.00
Some Heart Is Sighing, Rose, 1908 .... 3.00
Some Of These Days, Brooks, 1910 .... 3.00
Some One Like You, 1919 .... 3.00
Some Other Day, 1905 .... 3.00
Some Other Day, Some Other Girl, 1924 .... 2.00
Some Sleigh Ride, Hardy, 1913 .... 3.00
Some Sunday Morning, Kahn/Whiting, 1917 .... 8.00

Some Sunny Day, Berlin, 1922 .... 6.00
Some Sweet Day, 1929 .... 3.00
Somebody Else Is Crazy Bout Me, 1913 .... 3.00
Somebody Else Is Getting It, Sterling/Tilzer, 1912 .... 6.00
Somebody Else It's Always Somebody Else, 1910 .... 3.00
Somebody Else, 1927 .... 2.00
Somebody Loves Me, 1924 .... 2.00
Somebody Loves You, Dear, Hawley, 1907 .... 3.00
Somebody Said, Clare/Woods, 1927 .... 2.00
Somebody Stole My Heart, Smith, 1917 .... 5.00
Somebody That I Know And You Know Too, Helf, 1908 .... 5.00
Somebody's Coming To My House, Berlin, 1913 .... 15.00
Somebody's Coming To Town, 1912 .... 3.00
Somebody's Knocking At Your Door, Dett, 1919 .... 3.00
Somebody's Lonesome, Allen, 1909 .... 5.00
Somebody's Love, 1900 .... 3.00
Somebody's Waiting For Me, Sterling/Tilzer, 1902 .... 5.00
Somebody's Waiting For You, Bryan, 1906 .... 3.00
Somebody, Havez, 1911 .... 3.00
Someday They're Coming Home Again, Hilbert, 1917 .... 3.00
Someday You'll Cry Over Someone, 1922 .... 3.00
Someday, 1940 .... 2.00
Someday, I'll Meet You Again, 1944 .... 3.00
Somehow I Can't Forget You, Mayson, 1920 .... 3.00
Someone Else May Be There While I'm Gone, Berlin, 1917 .... 15.00
Someone Is Longing For Home Sweet Home, 1918 .... 3.00
Someone Like You, Blane/Warren, 1949 .... 8.00
Someone Loves You After All, 1923 .... 3.00
Someone Thinks Of Someone, 1905 .... 3.00
Someone To Watch Over Me, Gershwin, 1926 .... 3.00
Someone's Falling In Love, Little, 1928 .... 2.00
Someone, Gershwin, 1922 .... 5.00
Someone, Steiger/Dailey, 1914 .... 3.00
Something Seems Tingle-Ingleing, 1913 .... 3.00
Something To Remember You By, 1930 .... 2.00
Sometime Between Midnight And Dawn, 1918 .... 3.00
Sometime In Springtime, Bryan/Meyer, 1909 .... 5.00
Sometime Somewhere, Mack/Williams, 1908 .... 5.00
Sometime, Bryan/Tilzer, 1908 .... 5.00
Sometime, Jerome/Tierney, 1916 .... 3.00
Sometimes I Feel Like A Motherless Child, Burleigh, 1918 .... 8.00
Sometimes I'm Happy, 1927 .... 3.00
Somewhere A Heart Is Breaking And Calling Me Back - -........... 5.00
Somewhere A Voice Is Calling, 1911 .... 3.00
Somewhere In Dixie, 1912 .... 3.00

Somewhere In France Is Daddy, Howard, 1917 .... 15.00
Somewhere In France Is the Lily, Howard, 1917 .... 15.00
Somewhere In Georgia, 1917 .... 3.00
Somewhere In Ireland, Brennan, 1917 .... 3.00
Somewhere On Broadway, Murphy/Carroll, 1917 .... 3.00
Somewhere, Harris, 1906 .... 3.00
Song Birds Are Singing For You, Lamb/Sullivan, 1904 .... 5.00
Song For the Union, Scott, 1850 .... 35.00
Song Is Ended, Berlin, 1927 .... 6.00
Song Of Love, 1921 .... 3.00
Song Of Omar, Edwards, 1919 .... 2.00
Song Of the Flame, Gershwin, 1925 .... 5.00
Song of the Rodeo, Ritter/Sanucci, 1937 .... 10.00
Song Of the Vagabonds, Hooker/Post, 1925 .... 3.00
Song Of the Wanderer, Moret, 1926 .... 2.00
Songs Of Safety, 1937 .... 20.00
Songs Of Yesterday, Harris, 1916 .... 5.00
Sonny Boy, Jolson, 1928 .... 12.00
Sooner Or Later, 1946 .... 3.00
Sooner Or Later, Rose/Olman, 1915 .... 5.00
Sophisticated Lady, 1933 .... 2.00
Sorority, Roat, 1908 .... 5.00
Sorry And Blue, Elbel, 1925 .... 2.00
Sounds From the Alps, Deinzer, 1892 .... 20.00
Sounds From the Rockies, Ronaud, 1919 .... 20.00
South America, Take It Away, 1946 .... 2.00
South American Way, Dubin/McHugh, 1939 .... 2.00
South, 1941 .... 2.00
Southern Beauty, 1904 .... 3.00
Southern Blossoms, Pryor 12.00
Southern California, 1914 .... 3.00
Southern Gals, Gumble, 1917 .... 5.00
Southern Nights, Roberts, 1917 .... 3.00
Sowing the Wind, 1895 .... 6.00
Spaghetti Rag, Lyons/Yosco, 1910 .... 15.00
Spanish Two-Step, Duncan/Wills, 1942 .... 2.00
Spare the Love And Spoil the Dream, 1946 .... 2.00
Speckled Spider Rag, French, 1910 .... 15.00
Spellbound, Rozsa/David, 1945 .... 6.00
Spirit Of '76, Cox, 1917 .... 12.00
Spirit Of France, Paull, 1919 .... 30.00
Spooks, Eckstein, 1932 .... 2.00
Spoony Moon, 1914 .... 3.00
Spread Out Your White Sails, White, 1887 .... 25.00
Spreading New England's Fame, 1940 .... 3.00

**Pictured above is a small selection of
Sheet Music Covers that are listed within this book.**

Spring & Fall, Berlin, 1912 .... 20.00
Spring Is In My Heart Again, Mercer, 1932 .... 2.00
Springtime Reverie, 1915 .... 5.00
Sprinkle Me With Kisses, Carroll/Ball, 1915 .... 3.00
Squad-Fischer-March, 1916 .... 3.00
Square Dance, Dietz/Schwartz, 1934 .... 10.00
St. Lawrence Tubular Bridge Mazurka-Polka, Montreal 30.00
St. Louis Blues, Handy, 1914 .... 15.00
Stairway To the Stars, 1935 .... 2.00
Standard American Airs, Rosey, 1906 .... 6.00
Standin' In De Need O'Prayer, Reddick, 1918 .... 3.00
Standing On the Corner, Loesser, 1956 .... 3.00
Star Eyes, 1943 .... 4.00
Star Of Gold, 1918 .... 3.00
Star Of Hope, Kennedy, 1902 .... 3.00
Star Of My Dreams, Shine On, 1910 .... 3.00
Star Of the East, Cooper/Kennedy, 1890 .... 15.00
Star Of the Sea, Kennedy, 1848 .... 35.00
Stardust, Carmichael, 1929 .... 5.00
Starlight, Madden/Morse, 1905 .... 3.00
Stars Fell On Alabama, Perkins, 1934 .... 2.00
Stay In Your Own Backyard, Kennett/Udall, 1899 .... 15.00
Stay Out Of the South, Dixon, 1927 .... 2.00
Steal Away, Burleigh, 1921 .... 3.00
Steamboat Bill, Leighton, 1910 .... 20.00
Stein Song, Fenstad, 1930 .... 5.00
Stella, Roberts/Newman, 1950 .... 6.00
Step Along Henry, Olman, 1916 .... 14.00
Step This Way, Grant, 1916 .... 3.00
Steppin' Out With My Baby, Berlin, 1947 .... 6.00
Sterling Waltz, Fry/Yarborough, 1914 .... 3.00
Stick To the Dear Old Flag, Taylor, 1914 .... 5.00
Stick To Your Mother Mary, Allen/Daly, 1913 .... 3.00
Stingy Kid, Bryan, 1909 .... 5.00
Stop Stop Stop, Berlin, 1910 .... 13.00
Stop the Sun, Stop the Moon, 1932 .... 2.00
Stop Your Quittin', Get Away Closer, Carlyle, 1911 .... 5.00
Stop! You're Breaking My Heart, Lane, 1937 .... 2.00
Stories Mother Told, Gurney, 1895 .... 4.00
Storm Of Life, Vanalstyne, 1903 .... 3.00
Storm On the Ocean-Sailboat In Storm, Martin, 1911 .... 10.00
Stormy Weather, Koehler/Arlen, 1933 .... 6.00
Story Book Ball, Montgomery/Perry, 1917 .... 10.00
Story Of Three Loves, Tucker/Keyser, 1953 .... 2.00
Strange Music, 1945 .... 2.00

Stranger In Paradise, 1953 .... 2.00
Streets Of NY, 1906 .... 3.00
Strike Up a Bagpipe Tune, Madden/Edwards, 1910 .... 5.00
Strike Up the Band, Gershwin, 1927 .... 3.00
Strut, Miss Lizzie, Creamer/Layton, 1921 .... 6.00
Struttin' With Some Barbecue, Dixieland Ragtime Blues 15.00
Style Song Of Spring, Cherry/Webb 3.00
Suddenly, 1953 .... 2.00
Sugar Baby, 1919 .... 3.00
Sugar Foot Stomp, 1926 .... 3.00
Sugar Moon, Murphy/Wenrich, 1910 .... 3.00
Sugar Moon, Wills/Walker, 1947 .... 2.00
Summer Days, 1911 .... 3.00
Summer, Rutter, 1910 .... 10.00
Summertime, Mahoney/Tilzer, 1908 .... 5.00
Summertime, Heywood/Gershwin, 1935 .... 18.00
Sunbeams (Isle Of Beauty), 1912 .... 3.00
Sunbonnet Days, Bayha 3.00
Sunbonnet Sue, Cobb, 1908 .... 8.00
Sunday Night At Nellie's Home, Moore, 1894 .... 3.00
Sunday, Miller, 1926 .... 5.00
Sunflower Tickle, Richmond, 1908 .... 10.00
Sunny California, 1930 .... 2.00
Sunny Disposish, Gershwin, 1926 .... 3.00
Sunny Side Up, 1929 .... 3.00
Sunrise, Santly, 1927 .... 2.00
Sunset Land (Aloha), Kawelo/Shannon, 1916 .... 3.00
Sunset Limited March, Bartell, 1910 .... 20.00
Sunshine & Roses, Alstyne, 1913 .... 3.00
Sunshine For Us Now Nellie, Homer, 1906 .... 5.00
Sunshine Valley, Shannon, 1917 .... 3.00
Sunshine, Berlin, 1928 .... 3.00
Suppose I Met You Face To Face, Harris, 1913 .... 3.00
Susie, Jolson, 1925 .... 10.00
Susquehanna Sue, Buzzell/Marshall, 1916 .... 3.00
Swanee River Trail, Jolson, 1927 .... 15.00
Swanee Rose, Jolson, 1921 .... 12.00
Swanee Shore, Hess, 1927 .... 8.00
Swanee Smiles, 1922 .... 3.00
Swanee, Jolson, 1919 .... 12.00
Sweepin' the Clouds Away, Coslow, 1903 .... 5.00
Sweet And Lovely, Johnson/Allyson, 1931 .... 7.00
Sweet And Low Down, Gershwin, 1925 .... 5.00
Sweet And Low, 1919 .... 3.00
Sweet As A Song, 1937 .... 3.00

Sweet Bunch Of Daisies, Owen, 1894 .... 5.00
Sweet By And By, Webster, 1898 .... 5.00
Sweet Caroline, Webber, 1904 .... 3.00
Sweet Cider Time When You Were Mine, 1916 .... 3.00
Sweet Clover, Trahern, 1902 .... 7.00
Sweet Dreams, My Love, Sweet Dreams, Edwards, 1909 .... 6.00
Sweet Dreams, Sweetheart, 1944 .... 5.00
Sweet Emalina, My Gal, Creamer/Layton, 1917 .... 5.00
Sweet Genevieve, Cooper/Tucker, 1916 .... 3.00
Sweet Georgia Brown, Pinkard/Bernie/Casey, 1925 .... 3.00
Sweet Girl Of My Dreams, 1908 .... 3.00
Sweet Henry the Pride Of Tennessee, Davis/Akst, 1923 .... 15.00
Sweet Italian Love, Berlin, 1910 .... 15.00
Sweet Julienne, Havez, 1906 .... 6.00
Sweet Kentucky Lady, Hirsch, 1914 .... 15.00
Sweet Lady, 1921 .... 3.00
Sweet Leilani, Owens, 1937 .... 3.00
Sweet Little Buttercup, Paley, 1917 .... 3.00
Sweet Little Jesus Boy, 1934 .... 3.00
Sweet Little Katie, West, 1895 .... 5.00
Sweet Memories Of Thee, Welby, 1849 .... 20.00
Sweet Miss Mary, 1914 .... 2.00
Sweet Music, Warren/Dubin, 1934 .... 3.00
Sweet Siamese, Earl, 1919 .... 5.00
Sweet Sixteen, Mills, 1908 .... 3.00
Sweeter Than Sugar, Berlin, 1919 .... 12.00
Sweetest Girl In Dixie, O'Dea/Adams, 1904 .... 6.00
Sweetest Girl In Monterey, 1915 .... 3.00
Sweetest Melody Of All, 1916 .... 5.00
Sweetest Story Ever Told, 1892 .... 6.00
Sweetheart Days, Dailey, 1907 .... 3.00
Sweetheart I'm Calling You, 1917 .... 3.00
Sweetheart Of All My Dreams, Fitch, 1928 .... 2.00
Sweetheart Of My Dreams, 1924 .... 2.00
Sweetheart, Gould/Heller, 1916 .... 3.00
Sweetheart, Johnson, 1921 .... 3.00
Sweetheart, We Need Each Other, Tierney/McCarthy, 1929 .... 3.00
Sweethearts Forever, Friend/Caesar, 1932 .... 3.00
Sweethearts On Parade, 1928 .... 2.00
Sweethearts True, Ryder, 1901 .... 3.00
Sweethearts, Wives And Good Fellows, 1908 .... 3.00
Sweetness, Leonard/Stern, 1917 .... 7.00
Swing Low, Sweet Chariot, Fisher, 1925 .... 3.00
Sympathy, Kendis/Paley, 1905 .... 3.00
Syncopate, Harbach/Darling, 1922 .... 3.00

32 Feet, Eight Little Tails, Weldon, 1951 .... 3.00
Tabby the Cat, Dickinson/Gibeling, 1944 .... 2.00
Take A Car, Rose, 1905 .... 20.00
Take A Little One Step, 1933 .... 2.00
Take A Little Ride With Me, Morse, 1906 .... 20.00
Take A Little Tip From Father, Berlin, 1912 .... 15.00
Take Care Of Mother, 1913 .... 3.00
Take Me 'Round In A Taxicab, Gibeon, 1908 .... 20.00
Take Me Back To Home, Sweet Home, Hoomes, 1910 .... 3.00
Take Me Back To My Boots And Saddle, 1935 .... 3.00
Take Me Back To the Garden Of Love, Goetz/Osborne, 1911 .... 5.00
Take Me Back To Your Garden Of Roses, Freeman, 1917 .... 3.00
Take Me On a Buick Honeymoon, Black, 1922 .... 30.00
Take Me Out For A Joy Ride, Mills, 1909 .... 15.00
Take Me Out In A Velie Car, O'Connor, 1911 .... 15.00
Take Me To That Land Of Jazz, Wendling, 1919 .... 7.00
Take Me To That Swanee Shore, 1912 .... 3.00
Take Me To the Midnight Cake Walk Ball, Cox, 1915 .... 3.00
Take Me Up With You Dearie, McCree, 1909 .... 12.00
Take Off Your Worry and Put On a Smile, 1929 .... 2.00
Take These Flowers Old Lady, 1904 .... 3.00
Take Your Girlie to the Movies, 1919 .... 2.00
Taking a Chance On Love, 1940 .... 6.00
Tale of the Sea Shell, 1902 .... 3.00
Talk To the Animals, 1967 .... 6.00
Tangerine, Mercer, 1942 .... 3.00
Tapping on the Pines, Canning, 1887 .... 15.00
Taxi, Kaufman, 1919 .... 15.00
Taxi, Kerr, 1909 .... 15.00
Taxicab, Sawyer, 1910 .... 16.00
Tea For Two, 1924 .... 4.00
Tears Of Love, Henry, 1918 .... 3.00
Teasing, Mack/Tilzer, 1904 .... 5.00
Tee Oodle Um Bum Bo, Gershwin, 1919 .... 10.00
Tell Me Again You Love Me, 1911 .... 2.00
Tell Me the Old, Old Story, Weaver, 1908 .... 5.00
Tell Me Why You Smile, Mona Lisa, 1931 .... 3.00
Tell My Little Gipsy, Berlin, 1920 .... 6.00
Tell Tale Eyes, 1903 .... 2.00
Tell That To the Marines, Atteridge, 1918 .... 10.00
Tell the Last Rose Of Summer Good-Bye, 1917 .... 2.00
Tell Them I'm All Right, West, 1894 .... 6.00
Temple Bells, Klein, 1912 .... 3.00
Temptation Rag, Lodge, 1909 .... 8.00
Temptation, Freed/Brown, 1933 .... 3.00

**Pictured above is a small selection of
Sheet Music Covers that are listed within this book.**

Ten Baby Fingers, Sanders, 1920 .... 3.00
Ten Cents A Dance, 1930 .... 2.00
Ten-Ten-Tenn, Meyer, 1923 .... 3.00
Tennessee I Hear You Calling Me, Jolson, 1914 .... 15.00
Tennessee Moon, 1912 .... 3.00
Tessie, Perkins, 1924 .... 2.00
Texas Ranger Song, Coslow/Behn, 1936 .... 10.00
Thanks For the Memory, 1937 .... 6.00
Thanks, Johnston/Coslow, 1933 .... 3.00
That Aeroplane Glide, Israel, 1912 .... 20.00
That Auto Rag, Smith, 1914 .... 20.00
That Baboon Baby Dance, 1911 .... 7.00
That Beautiful Rag, Berlin, 1910 .... 15.00
That Briny Dip, Vose/Dennison, 1912 .... 15.00
That Certain Feeling, Gershwin, 1925 .... 6.00
That Certain Party, Kahn/Donaldson, 1925 .... 3.00
That Chinatown Rag, Drislane, 1910 .... 15.00
That Christmas Feeling, Weiss/Benjamin, 1946 .... 3.00
That Darn Cat, Sherman, 1964 .... 6.00
That Girl Next Door, Corey, 1890 .... 5.00
That Grant Amen, Harding, 1901 .... 5.00
That Haunting Melody, Cohan, 1911 .... 12.00
That Indian Rag, Bestor, 1910 .... 8.00
That International Rag, Berlin, 1913 .... 8.00
That Italian Serenade, McCarthy/Piantadosi, 1911 .... 7.00
That Little Lamb Was Me, Crawford, 1914 .... 3.00
That Lovin' Traumerei, Stauffer, 1910 .... 12.00
That Lucky Old Sun, 1949 .... 3.00
That Mellow Melody, 1912 .... 5.00
That Mesmerizing Mendelshon Tune, Berlin, 1909 .... 12.00
That Mysterious Rag, Berlin, 1911 .... 12.00
That Naughty Melody, 1913 .... 3.00
That Naughty Waltz, 1919 .... 3.00
That Old Familiar Tune, Cunningham/Seymour, 1911 .... 3.00
That Old Gang Of Mine, Rose/Dixon, 1923 .... 2.00
That Old Girl Of Mine, 1912 .... 3.00
That Old Irish Mother Of Mine, Tilzer, 1920 .... 3.00
That Old Sweetheart Of Mine, 1928 .... 2.00
That Railroad Rag, Bimberg, 1911 .... 15.00
That Redhead Gal, 1923 .... 2.00
That Saxophone Waltz, 1925 .... 2.00
That Silver Haired Daddy Of Mine, 1932 .... 10.00
That Sly Old Gentleman, 1939 .... 3.00
That Society Bear, Berlin, 1912 .... 15.00
That St. Louis Jitney Bus, Mellinger, 1915 .... 20.00

That Tango Tokio, Bryan/Wells, 1913 .... 5.00
That Two-Step Strain, Strain, 1913 .... 2.00
That Wonderful Dengosa Strain, 1914 .... 5.00
That Wonderful Mother Of Mine, Hager, 1918 .... 2.00
That Wonderful Mother You'd Be, 1915 .... 3.00
That's A Mother's Liberty Loan, Gaskill, 1917 .... 3.00
That's A Very Different Thing, Rubens, 1902 .... 3.00
That's All Love Means To You, 1929 .... 8.00
That's Amoro', 1953 .... 5.00
That's An Irish Lullaby, Shannon, 1944 .... 3.00
That's How I Need You, Goodwin/McCarthy, 1912 .... 3.00
That's How Much I Love You, 1946 .... 2.00
That's For Me, Burke/Monaco, 1940 .... 10.00
That's My Gal, 1926 .... 2.00
That's Neither Here Nor There, Abraham, 1885 .... 15.00
That's Some Honeymoon, Hardy, 1911 .... 7.00
That's the Song Of Songs For Me, 1915 .... 5.00
That's What God Made Mothers For, Wood, 1918 .... 6.00
That's What I Call Sweet Music, 1929 .... 2.00
That's What I'd Do For You, 1914 .... 2.00
That's What the Mill Wheel Said, Denison/Holmes, 1913 .... 5.00
That's What the Red, White And Blue Means, 1918 .... 5.00
That's What the Rose Said To Me, 1906 .... 3.00
That's When I Learned To Love You, 1929 .... 2.00
That's Why My Heart Is Lonely, Garton, 1913 .... 3.00
That's Why the Rose Never Dies, 1913 .... 2.00
That's Why You Make Me Cry, 1923 .... 2.00
That's Why, Dixon/Henderson, 1926 .... 2.00
The 3rd Man Theme, 1949 .... 5.00
The Alcoholic Blues, Laska, 1919 .... 15.00
The American Guard March, Bergh, 1924 .... 3.00
The American Legion, Vandersloot, 1920 .... 3.00
The Amethyst March, Lucas, 1957 .... 8.00
The Army Air Corp, Crawford, 1939 .... 3.00
The Band Played "Nearer My God To Thee" As the Ship - - 5.00
The Barber's Bear, Clarke, 1912 .... 15.00
The Battle Of Gettysburg, Paull, 1917 .... 30.00
The Battle Ship Rag, Allen, 1915 .... 15.00
The Battle Song of Liberty, Yellen, 1917 .... 3.00
The Bells Of Normandy, 1944 .... 2.00
The Best Things In Life Are Free, 1927 .... 5.00
The Bible Tells Me So, Dal Evans, 1945 .... 3.00
The Big Brown Bear, 1919 .... 3.00
The Birth Of the Blues, DeSylva, 1926 .... 15.00
The Bolo Rag, Gumble, 1907 .... 8.00

The Boys From Yankee Land, Franks, 1916 .... 3.00
The Boys In the Trenches Are Calling You, Allen, 1918 .... 3.00
The Boys Of London Town, 1900 .... 5.00
The Boys Who Won't Come Home, Hamilton/Thomas, 1919 .... 5.00
The Breeze And I, 1928 .... 3.00
The Bright Little Lantern I Swing, Cake, 1893 .... 30.00
The Brookside Inn, Jerome/Schwartz, 1911 .... 5.00
The Brotherhood Of Man, 1901 .... 5.00
The Brunette Polka, Wallerstein, 1850 .... 35.00
The Bubble, Triml, 1913 .... 3.00
The Bullfrog And the Coon, Feist, 1906 .... 20.00
The Burning Iroquois, 1904 .... 6.00
The Burning Of Rome, Paull, 1903 .... 15.00
The Buzz Saw And the Bee, Mullen, 1906 .... 5.00
The Caissons Go Rolling Along, 1921 .... 2.00
The Call Of the Cozy Little Home, 1918 .... 3.00
The Cat's Whiskers, 1923 .... 2.00
The Charis, 1932 .... 2.00
The Chauffeur, Cobb, 1906 .... 15.00
The Chicago Express, Wenrich, 1905 .... 20.00
The Chimes, Armstrong, 1912 .... 3.00
The Co-Ed, 1925 .... 3.00
The Continental, Conrad, 1934 .... 7.00
The Convict and the Rose, Chapin, 1925 .... 3.00
The Cop On the Beat, The Man In the Moon And Me, 1932 .... 3.00
The Cowboy At Church, 1935 .... 2.00
The Cradle And the Music Box, 1934 .... 2.00
The Crazy Otto Rag, 1955 .... 2.00
The Cricket on the Hearth, Herbert/Smith, 1938 .... 13.00
The Cry Of the Wild Goose, 1949 .... 2.00
The Cubanola Glide, Bryan, 1909 .... 3.00
The Cutest Kids In Town, Weaver, 1928 .... 2.00
The Dark Song, Leavitt/Goldsmith, 1968 .... 12.00
The Darktown Strutter's Ball, Brooks, 1917 .... 15.00
The Darling Girls (I like 'em all), Barr, 1924 .... 7.00
The Day After Forever, 1944 .... 3.00
The Day You Came Along, 1933 .... 3.00
The Deacon Told Me I was Good, Smythe/Gillham, 1924 .... 7.00
The Desert Song, 1926 .... 3.00
The Dixie Volunteers, 1917 .... 5.00
The Dixieland Polka, 1943 .... 2.00
The Dog of Flanders, Stillman/DeLugg, 1969 .... 8.00
The Donkey Serenade,1937 .... 3.00
The Doodle Song, Miller/Whitman/Goodwin, 1946 .... 6.00
The Dream Of A Soldier Boy, 1918 .... 3.00

The Dreamer, Loesser, 1943 .... 5.00
The Drugstore Song, Rome, 1946 .... 10.00
The Easter Sunday Parade, Cohan, 1927 .... 7.00
The End Of A Perfect Day, Bond, 1910 .... 3.00
The Entertainers Rag, Roberts, 1912 .... 10.00
The Eternal Flame, Brenna/Ball, 1922 .... 7.00
The Exodus Song, 1960 .... 3.00
The Eyes Of Heaven, 1916 .... 3.00
The Fatal Ring, McCarron, 1917 .... 3.00
The Fatal Wedding, 1898 .... 10.00
The Fawn, Schiller, 1912 .... 3.00
The Fightining 26th, 1920 .... 5.00
The First Night of the Full Moon, David/Perry, 1964 .... 6.00
The First Time I Saw You, 1937 .... 3.00
The First Time I Saw You, Wrubel/Shilkret, 1937 .... 6.00
The Five Pennies, 1959 .... 10.00
The Five Step, DeSylva/Gensler, 1927 .... 8.00
The Flag That Had Never Retreated, Hogan, 1918 .... 3.00
The Flapper Wife, Rupp/Burton, 1925 .... 5.00
The Fleet's In, Mercer 5.00
The Four Horseman Of the Apocalypse, Paull, 1924 .... 35.00
The Freedom Train, Berlin, 1947 .... 8.00
The Funny Old Hills, Robin/Rainger, 1938 .... 5.00
The Futuristic Rag, Bloom, 1923 .... 20.00
The Gal With The Yaller Shoes, 1955 .... 3.00
The Gallant Seventh, Sousa, 1922 .... 20.00
The Gangsters Warning, Autry, 1932 .... 7.00
The Gay Chauffeur, Valentine, 1906 .... 30.00
The Girl I Loved Out In the Golden West, 1903 .... 5.00
The Girl Of the Golden West, 1923 .... 3.00
The Girl On the Magazine, Berlin, 1915 .... 15.00
The Girl On the Police Gazette, Berlin, 1937 .... 10.00
The Girl That He Loves Best, 1902 .... 3.00
The Girl Who Threw Me Down, 1907 .... 3.00
The Gold Digger (Dig A Little Deeper), 1923 .... 6.00
The Gondolier, Posell, 1904 .... 6.00
The Goo Goo Man, 1903 .... 3.00
The Great Graphic Balloon Galop, Fitch, 1873 .... 35.00
The Greatest Nation On Earth, Marcus, 1916 .... 3.00
The Green Grass Grew All Around, 1912 .... 3.00
The Gunner's Mate, Brown, 1901 .... 12.00
The Hangman, 1959 .... 3.00
The Heel, 1954 .... 2.00
The Hen And the Cow, 1920 .... 3.00
The High And the Mighty, 1954 .... 7.00

**Pictured above is a small selection of
Sheet Music Covers that are listed within this book.**

The Homecoming, Paull, 1908 .... 30.00
The Honey Song, Gibson, 1942 .... 2.00
The Honeysuckle And the Bee, 1901 .... 3.00
The Hoodlum, 1919 .... 7.00
The Hot Canary, Gilbert, 1949 .... 2.00
The Hot Dogs' Fancy Ball, 1916 .... 12.00
The Hour Of Triumph, Flynn/Jerome, 1901 .... 12.00
The Hour That Gave Me You, 1911 .... 3.00
The Hours I Spent With Thee, 1914 .... 3.00
The House I Live In, 1942 .... 4.00
The House Of Singing Bamboo, 1950 .... 3.00
The Huckle-Buck, 1949 .... 5.00
The Hula Blues, 1920 .... 3.00
The Hush Song, Cooper, 1903 .... 5.00
The Illfated Gen'l Slogum, 1904 .... 4.00
The Jack O Lantern Girl, Herbert, 1905 .... 10.00
The Jacket, Porter, 1893 .... 10.00
The Japanese Sandman, Egan, 1920 .... 3.00
The Joke's On Me, Livingston/Evan/Mancini, 1976 .... 8.00
The Jolly Blacksmiths, Paull/Braham, 1905 .... 40.00
The Jolly Yanks, Minkus/Kane, 1943 .... 10.00
The Khaki And the Blue, Trainer, 1917 .... 2.00
The Kinkajou, McCarthy/Tierney, 1926 .... 3.00
The Kiss That Makes You Mine, Elkins, 1915 .... 3.00
The Lad in Khaki, Fadner/Sorensen, 1917 .... 3.00
The Ladder Of Roses, 1915 .... 3.00
The Ladies Who Fought And Won, Lauder, 1916 .... 3.00
The Ladies Man, 1921 .... 10.00
The Lady From 29 Palms, 1947 .... 2.00
The Lambert Of the Irish Emigrant, 1843 .... 15.00
The Lamp Of Memory, 1939 .... 2.00
The Land Of Golden Dreams, Denison, 1912 .... 5.00
The Land Of My Best Girl, 1914 .... 3.00
The Last Call Clear, 1941 .... 2.00
The Last Great Round Up, 1935 .... 3.00
The Last Long Mile, 1917 .... 3.00
The Last Party Of Every Party, 1919 .... 2.00
The Last Rose Of Summer Is the Sweetest Song Of All, 1907 .... 5.00
The Last Round-Up, Hill, 1933 .... 3.00
The Last Time I Saw You, 1945 .... 2.00
The Legend, 1920 .... 2.00
The Letter That Never Came, Howard, 1896 .... 6.00
The Lights On My Home Town, Harris, 1915 .... 3.00
The Lily, Kline, 1896 .... 5.00
The Little Cafe, 1913 .... 3.00

The Little Country School House, Connolly/Magbee, 1912 .... 2.00
The Little Flag On Our House, Manney, 1919 .... 3.00
The Little Ford Rambled Right Along, Foster, 1914 .... 25.00
The Little Girl In Blue, 1907 .... 3.00
The Little Grey Mother, 1915 .... 3.00
The Little Guppy, 1941 .... 2.00
The Little House Upon the Hill, 1914 .... 3.00
The Little Man Who Wasn't There, 1939 .... 2.00
The Little Pig, Dawless, 1941 .... 3.00
The Little Red School House, Wilson/Brennan, 1922 .... 5.00
The Little Stowaway, Smith, 1879 .... 20.00
The Little Things In Life, Berlin, 1930 .... 7.00
The Little Tin Soldier, 1921 .... 2.00
The Little White House, 1926 .... 2.00
The Load Is Heavy, 1929 .... 2.00
The Lock Step Two Step Slide, Golden, 1911 .... 6.00
The Lonely Ones, King/Lewis, 1969 .... 8.00
The Lord Will Understand, 1957 .... 2.00
The Love Boat, 1920 .... 3.00
The Love Nest, 1920 .... 3.00
The Loveliest Night Of the Year, 1951 .... 3.00
The Lovelight In Your Eyes, Yellen, 1917 .... 3.00
The Man Behind, Bryan, 1904 .... 3.00
The Man From Laramie, Washington/Lee, 1955 .... 8.00
The Man From the South, Bloom/Woods, 1930 .... 3.00
The Man I Love, Gershwin, 1924 .... 3.00
The Man That Broke the Bank At Monte Carlo, Gilbert 3.00
The Marines' Hymn, 1942 .... 5.00
The Mascot Of the Troop, Herbert, 1905 .... 5.00
The Memphis Blues, Handy, 1913 .... 3.00
The Messenger Boy, Rooney, 1901 .... 3.00
The Midnight Fire Alarm, Lincoln, 1907 .... 20.00
The Midnight Fire Alarm, Paull, 1900 .... 40.00
The Midnight Flyer, Paull, 1903 .... 40.00
The Midnight Ragtime Ride Of Paul Revere, 1914 .... 15.00
The Midnight Sons, McDonough, 1909 .... 14.00
The Miller, Petrie, 1902 .... 3.00
The Mississippi Dippy Dip, 1911 .... 15.00
The Mississippi Side Step, Berliner, 1899 .... 20.00
The Month of June is a Song of Love, Kahn/Leboy, 1911 .... 7.00
The Moon Is Low, Freed, 1930 .... 3.00
The Moon Of Manakoora, Loesser, 1937 .... 5.00
The Moonlight, The Rose And You, Baer/Schmidt, 1910 .... 3.00
The More I See You, Gordon/Warren, 1945 .... 3.00
The Mother And Her Child Were There, Grossmith 2.00

The Mountain Haze, Hutchison 5.00
The Murmur Of the Shell, Norton 12.00
The Music Stopped, 1943 .... 3.00
The Mystery, Bacon, 1926 .... 7.00
The Narrative, 1929 .... 3.00
The Nasty Way 'E Sez It, Ingle 3.00
The Naughty Lady Of Shady Lane, 1954 .... 2.00
The Navy Goat, Gay, 1921 .... 12.00
The New Moon, Berlin, 1919 .... 12.00
The Newlyweds And Their Baby, Hoffman, 1918 .... 6.00
The Night Has A Thousand Eyes, 1948 .... 3.00
The Night Is Young, 1935 .... 3.00
The Night Of Love, 1927 .... 3.00
The Night Was Made For Love, Kern, 1931 .... 3.00
The Night When Love Was Born, 1932 .... 2.00
The Nightingale's Thrill, 1865 .... 8.00
The Nightingales Of Lincoln's Inn, 1912 .... 3.00
The Object Of My Affection, 1934 .... 2.00
The Ocean Between Us, Cawthorn, 1892 .... 15.00
The Old Brass Rail, 1924 .... 2.00
The Old Covered Bridge, Hill, 1934 .... 6.00
The Old Flag Never Touched the Ground, 1901 .... 10.00
The Old Grey Mare March, Panella, 1915 .... 12.00
The Old Home, 1939 .... 2.00
The Old Mill, Coons, 1879 .... 8.00
The Old Piano Roll Blues, Coben, 1946 .... 3.00
The Old Piano Roll Blues, Coben, 1949 .... 6.00
The Old Plaid Shawl, 1895 .... 3.00
The Old Square Dance, 1942 .... 2.00
The Oyster Rag, Lyle, 1910 .... 15.00
The Pentinent, Van de Water, 1892 .... 3.00
The Perfect Song, Lucas, 1915 .... 15.00
The Phrenologist Coon, Stern, 1901 .... 25.00
The Piccolino, Berlin, 1935 .... 10.00
The Picture Bride, 1931 .... 2.00
The Poor Apache, Rodgers & Hart, 1932 .... 8.00
The Price That I Paid For You, 1915 .... 3.00
The Purple Hills, 1957 .... 3.00
The Quest, Smith, 1885 .... 5.00
The Race Course, E.T. Paull, 1910 .... 20.00
The Raggy Fox Trot, Goffin/Starmer, 1915 .... 15.00
The Ragtime Dream, Goodwin, 1913 .... 15.00
The Ragtime Pipe Of Pan, 1915 .... 3.00
The Ragtime Soldier Man, Berlin, 1912 .... 15.00
The Ragtime Violin, Berlin, 1911 .... 15.00

The Ragtime Volunteers Are Off To War, MacDonald, 1917 .... 8.00
The Rainbow Man, 1929 .... 3.00
The Rainbow Military March, 1918 .... 2.00
The Ranger's Song, 1926 .... 3.00
The Rat Charmer, Neuendorff, 1881 .... 3.00
The Rat Race, 1960 .... 3.00
The Rebekah Song, 1952 .... 2.00
The Red Lantern, Fisher, 1919 .... 3.00
The Red Rose Rag, Madden/Wenrich, 1911 .... 7.00
The Rickety Rickshaw Man, 1943 .... 2.00
The Riff Song, 1926 .... 3.00
The Right Kind Of Man, 1929 .... 4.00
The River Kwai March, 1957 .... 3.00
The Road For You and Me, 1917 .... 3.00
The Rogue Song, Grey, 1929 .... 3.00
The Rose In Her Hair, Warren/Dubin, 1935 .... 5.00
The Rose Of the Mountain Trail, 1914 .... 3.00
The Rovin' Gambler, Manoloff, 1935 .... 3.00
The Rum Tum Tiddle Dance, Schwartz, 1911 .... 8.00
The Runaway Train, Massey/Robinson, 1925 .... 2.00
The Rye Waltzes, Laughlin, 1909 .... 3.00
The Sailor's Dream, Wheeler, 1880 .... 20.00
The Salt Of the Sea For Me, Penn, 1903 .... 20.00
The Secret Of the Violet, 1904 .... 3.00
The Sheik, 1921 .... 3.00
The Shepherd's Soronado, 1929 .... 4.00
The Ship Sails Tonight, Strelezki, 1887 .... 35.00
The Shipwreck, Davenport, 1872 .... 25.00
The Shorter They Wear Em the Longer They Look, 1917 .... 4.00
The Silver Way, 1914 .... 3.00
The Singing River, 1952 .... 2.00
The Skeleton Rag, Madden, 1911 .... 15.00
The Sleepy Hills Of Tennessee, 1923 .... 2.00
The Sleepy Town Express, 1930 .... 2.00
The Sneak, 1922 .... 2.00
The Soldiers Of the Queen, 1898... 12.00
The Song From Moulin Rouge, 1953 .... 3.00
The Song Of the Heart Bowed Down, 1913 .... 3.00
The Song Of the Seabees, 1942 .... 2.00
The Songbird Of Melody Lane, Bryan, 1902.............................. 3.00
The Songs My Mother Liked Best, 1891 .... 3.00
The Soul Of You, 1917 .... 3.00
The Southern Belle, Blandford, 1901 .... 14.00
The Spaniard That Blighted My Life, Jolson, 1911 .... 12.00
The Speed Kings, Losey, 1912 .... 15.00

**Pictured above is a small selection of
Sheet Music Covers that are listed within this book.**

The Spell Of the Blues, 1928 .... 3.00
The Spring Maid, 1909 .... 4.00
The Spring Song, Chaplin, 1957 .... 13.00
The Sunshine of My Heart, Whidden/May, 1929 .... 8.00
The Superman March, Strouse, 1966 .... 10.00
The St. Louis Rag, Turpin, 1903 .... 20.00
The Star Of the East, 1918 .... 3.00
The Star Spangled Banner, Smith 3.00
The Stars And Stripes Forever, Sousa, 1897 .... 20.00
The Stately Homes Of England, 1938 .... 2.00
The Stein Song March, Bullard, 1901 .... 6.00
The Storm King, Paull, 1902 .... 40.00
The Story Of A Soul, Harris, 1916 .... 3.00
The Strawberry Roan, Howard/Fletcher, 1935 .... 13.00
The Sweetest Flower That Blows, Muir, 1916 .... 3.00
The Sweetest Melody Of All, Clarke/Monaco, 1916 .... 3.00
The Tale the Church Bell Told, Young/Lewis, 1918 .... 3.00
The Tempest, Lincoln, 1913 .... 3.00
The Temple Bell, Monckton, 1911 .... 2.00
The Things We Did Last Summer, Cahn/Styne, 1946 .... 2.00
The Thousand Islands Song, 1947 .... 3.00
The Time, The Place, The Girl, 1906 .... 3.00
The Toreador, Caryll, 1901 .... 3.00
The Touch Of Your Lips, Noble, 1936 .... 2.00
The Trail Of the Lonesome Pine, 1913 .... 3.00
The Trailer Song (Roamin' In A Home On Wheels), 1936 .... 10.00
The Train That Never Returned, 1935 .... 3.00
The Triumphant Banner, Paull, 1909 .... 15.00
The Trolley Song, Martin/Blane, 1944 .... 6.00
The Tryst, Cadman, 1904 .... 3.00
The Tune That Never Grew Old, Morse, 1931 .... 3.00
The Twelfth Regiment March, Lincoln, 1908 .... 5.00
The Unforgiven, 1960 .... 5.00
The United Firemen, Snyder, 1914 .... 20.00
The United Nations, Rome, 1942 .... 3.00
The Unknown Soldier's Grave, Lee, 1926 .... 2.00
The Western Flyer, Morton, 1903 .... 30.00
The Whip-Poor-Wills Song, Millard, 1865 .... 15.00
The Whole Town's Wise, Richards, 1914 .... 3.00
The Worst Is Yet To Come, Grant, 1918 .... 8.00
The Wreck, White, 1873 .... 15.00
The Yankee Doodle Boy, Cohan, 1904 .... 17.00
The Yanky Dandy, Kiesling, 1901 .... 14.00
Their Lullaby, Hathaway, 1913 .... 3.00
Theme from a Summer Place, 1959 .... 5.00

Them There Eyes, 1930 .... 2.00
Then Came the Dawn, Dubin/Warren 2.00
Then I Turned And Walked Slowly Away, Fortner/Arnold 2.00
Then I Wouldn't Have To Worry Any More, Bryan/Wells 3.00
Then I'll Come Back To You, Morton, 1917 .... 3.00
Then I'll Stop Loving You, Piantadosi/McCarthy, 1913 .... 3.00
Then You Can Come Back, 1918 .... 2.00
Then You'll Remember Me, 1902 .... 3.00
Then, Winne, 1918 .... 3.00
There Ain't No Maybe In My Baby's Eyes, 1926 .... 2.00
There Are Two Eyes In Dixie, Berlin, 1917 .... 10.00
There Are Two Sides To Every Story, 1926 .... 2.00
There Are Yanks from the Banks of the Wabash, Duke/Dietz, 1943 .. 13.00
There Are Extra Stars Up In The Heavens Tonight, St. John, 1964 ... 13.00
There Is A Tavern In the Town, 1911 .... 3.00
There Is No Breeze, Stone/Dick, 1945 .... 2.00
There Is Somebody Waitin' For Me, Lauder, 1917 .... 3.00
There Must Be A Bright Tomorrow, Wysocki, 1931 .... 2.00
There Never Was A Girl Like You, 1907 .... 3.00
There She Was, Carmichael, 1943 .... 8.00
There Should Be Rules, 1955 .... 2.00
There Was No Bridegroom There, Spaulding, 1895 .... 3.00
There Will Never Be Another You, 1942 .... 3.00
There'll Always Be An England, Parker, 1939 .... 3.00
There'll Be A Hot Time In the Town Of Berlin, 1943 .... 3.00
There'll Come A Day, Boyle, 1917 .... 5.00
There'll Never Be Another You, 1928 .... 3.00
There'll Soon Be A Rainbow, 1943 .... 2.00
There's A Broken Heart For Every Light On Broadway, 1915 .... 3.00
There's A Burma Girl A Calling, 1916 .... 3.00
There's A Cabin In the Pines, Hill/Fisher, 1933 .... 3.00
There's A Cradle In Caroline, 1927 .... 2.00
There's A Dear Spot In Ireland, 1916 .... 3.00
There's A Far Away Look In Your Eye, Taylor/Mizzy, 1938 .... 3.00
There's A Girl In Havana, Coetz/Sloane, 1911 .... 6.00
There's A Girl In the Heart Of Maryland, Carroll, 1913 .... 10.00
There's A Girl In the World For Us All, Davies, 1896 .... 6.00
There's A Girl That's Meant For Me, 1914 .... 3.00
There's A Gold Mine In the Sky, 1937 .... 3.00
There's A Green Hill In Flanders, Flynn, 1917 .... 8.00
There's A Heart Of Gold That's Waiting, Freeman, 1914 .... 3.00
There's A Hole In the Old Oaken Bucket, 1938 .... 3.00
There's A Home In Wyoming, DeRose, 1933 .... 3.00
There's A Light In Your Eyes, 1918 .... 3.00
There's A Little Bit Of Bad In Every Good Little Girl, Fischer 3.00

There's A Little Home In My Land, 1917 .... 3.00
There's A Little Lane Without A Turning On the Way To - - 2.00
There's A Little Road To Heaven, Allen, 1914 .... 5.00
There's A Little Spark Of Love Still Burning, Fischer, 1914 .... 3.00
There's A Long, Long Trail, Elliot, 1915 .... 3.00
There's A Lump Of Sugar Down In Dixie, Jolson, 1918 .... 15.00
There's A Message In the Moon For You, 1919 .... 3.00
There's A Million Reasons Why I Shouldn't Kiss You, 1917 .... 3.00
There's A Mother Always Waiting You At Home Sweet Home 2.00
There's A Mother Old And Gray Who Needs You Now, 1911 .... 2.00
There's A New Moon Over My Shoulder, 1944 .... 3.00
There's A New Star In Heaven Tonight, 1926 .... 10.00
There's A Picture In My Old Kit Bag, Sweet, 1918 .... 3.00
There's A Place In My Heart For You Dear, 1938 .... 2.00
There's A Quaker In Quakertown, 1916 .... 3.00
There's A Rainbow 'Round My Shoulder, Jolson, 1928 .... 12.00
There's A Ranch In the Sky, 1937 .... 3.00
There's A Service Flag Flying At Our House, Hoierr, 1917 .... 10.00
There's A Silver Moon On the Golden Gate, 1936 .... 2.00
There's A Spark Of Love Still Burning In the Embers - - - 2.00
There's A Star In the East, 1916 .... 3.00
There's A Star Spangled Banner Waving Somewhere, 1942 .... 2.00
There's A Typical Tipperary Over Here, 1920 .... 3.00
There's A Wireless Station Down In My Heart, Morgan, 1913 .... 6.00
There's Always A Girl Who Is Waiting, 1913 .... 3.00
There's An Angel Missing From Heaven, Armstrong, 1918.. .... 20.00
There's Egypt In Your Dreamy Eyes, 1917 .... 3.00
There's No Love that's Just Like Your Mother's, 1912 .... 3.00
There's No One But You To Blame, Garton, 1917 .... 3.00
There's No One Too Poor To Be Kind, Rampone, 1898 .... 5.00
There's Nobody Else But You, 1924 .... 2.00
There's Not Another Girlie, Jerome/Schwartz, 1907 .... 3.00
There's Nothing Like A Mother's Love, Lang, 1911 .... 5.00
There's Nothing Sweeter Than A Girl From Dixieland, 1917 .... 3.00
There's One In A Million Like You, Schwartz, 1912 .... 3.00
There's Only One Girl Like You, Allan, 1917 .... 3.00
There's Someone More Lonesome Than You, Klein, 1916 .... 3.00
There's Something In the Name Of Ireland, 1917 .... 4.00
There's Something In the Songs You Sing, 1934 .... 2.00
There's Where My Thoughts Are Tonight, 1899 .... 4.00
There's Yes Yes in Your Eyes, Friend/Santly, 1924 .... 3.00
These Foolish Things, 1935 .... 3.00
They Always Pick On Me, 1911 .... 3.00
They Are Coming Day by Day, Pishion, 1919 .... 3.00
They Call It Dancing, Berlin, 1921 .... 7.00

They Didn't Believe Me Song, Kern, 1916 .... 5.00
They Don't Hesitate Anymore, 1914 .... 3.00
They Gave You A Heart Of Gold, Beam, 1918 .... 3.00
They Go Wild, Simply Wild Over Me, McCarthy/Fisher 6.00
They Got Me Doing It Now, Berlin, 1913.................................... 15.00
They Gotta Quit Kickin' My Dawg Aroun', Perkins, 1912 .... 5.00
They Heeded the Call, Salisbury, 1931 .... 3.00
They Made It Twice As Nice When They Called It Dixieland 12.00
They Met in Rio, Gordon/Warren, 1941 .... 10.00
They Say It's Wonderful, Berlin, 1946 .... 3.00
They Shall Not Pass!, Gonzalez, 1937 .... 13.00
They Start the Victrola, Abrahams, 1914.................................... 8.00
They Took the Stars Out Of Heaven, 1943.................................. 3.00
They Were All Out Of Step But Jim, Berlin, 1918 .... 12.00
They Won't Know Me, 1952 .... 2.00
They'll Be Mighty Proud In Dixie Of Their Old Black Joe 14.00
They're Either Too Young Or Too Old, 1943 .... 3.00
They're On Their Way To Mexico, Berlin, 1914........................... 12.00
They're Wearing Them Higher In Hawaii, 1916 .... 4.00
They've Got Me Doin' It Now Medley, Berlin, 1913 .... 14.00
Think Love Of Me, Grey, 1918... 3.00
Thinking Of You, 1920 .... 2.00
Thirsty For Your Kisses, 1950 .... 2.00
This Can't Be Love, 1938 .... 2.00
This Is the Army Mister Jones, Berlin, 1942 .... 7.00
This Is the Life, Jolson, 1914 .... 12.00
This Is the Moment, Robin, 1948 .... 3.00
This Is the Night, Evans, 1946 .... 2.00
This Is Worth Fighting For, 1942 .... 2.00
This Old House, 1954 .... 2.00
This Year's Kisses, Berlin, 1937 .... 7.00
Tho' the Silver Threads Are 'Mong the Gold, Williams, 1911 .... 10.00
Those Ragtime Melodies, Hodgkins, 1912................................... 15.00
Those Songs My Mother Used To Sing, Smith, 1904 .... 5.00
Those Things Money Can't Buy, 1947 .... 2.00
Those Were the Happy Days Long, Long Ago, 1928 .... 2.00
Thou Shalt Not Steal, Harris/Yellen, 1917.................................. 3.00
Thou Swell, 1927 .... 2.00
Though Rich, I'm No Better Than You, Persley, 1877 .... 5.00
Three Cheers For Old Vermont, Cole, 1908 .... 6.00
Three Coins In the Fountain, 1954... 3.00
Three Fishers Went Sailing, Hullah 2.00
Three Little Words, 1930.. 25.00
Three O'Clock In the Morning, Robledo, 1922 .... 2.00
Three Of Us, 1933 .... 2.00

**Pictured above is a small selection of
Sheet Music Covers that are listed within this book.**

Three Puppet Songs, 1961 .... 2.00
Three Wonderful Letters From Home, Hawley, 1918 .... 12.00
Thrill Me, 1931 .... 2.00
Thrilled, Barris/Greene, 1935 .... 2.00
Through A Long And Sleepless Night, Gordon/Newman 3.00
Through All the World, 1921 .... 2.00
Through the Orange Groves Of Southern California, Wilson 20.00
Through the Years, 1931 .... 2.00
Through These Wonderful Glasses Of Mine, Mahoney, 1916 .... 5.00
Through Twilight Lane, 1917 .... 3.00
Throw Him Down, McCloskey, 1932 .... 2.00
Throw It Out the Window, 1930 .... 2.00
Thumbs Up, Jaffe/O'Brien, 1941 .... 6.00
Thy Voice Is Near, Wrighton, 1881 .... 7.00
Tickle Toes, Spencer, 1910 .... 3.00
Tickled To Death, Hunter, 1899 .... 30.00
Tico Tico, 1943 .... 2.00
Tie A String Around Your Finger, 1924 .... 3.00
Tie Me To Your Apron Strings Again, 1925 .... 3.00
Tiger Rag, De Costa, 1917 .... 5.00
Tiger Rose, 1919 .... 2.00
Till I Met You, Klages/Steel 2.00
Till I Waltz Again With You, 1952 .... 2.00
Till My Luck Comes Rolling Along, Cohan, 1922 .... 6.00
Till the Clouds Roll By, 1917 .... 3.00
Till the Sands Of the Desert Grow Cold, 1911 .... 3.00
Till We Meet Again, Whiting, 1918 .... 10.00
Timber, Hill/Emmerich, 1936 .... 2.00
Time After Time, Cahn/Styne, 1947 .... 3.00
Time On My Hands, 1930 .... 3.00
Time To Cry, Anka, 1958 .... 13.00
Time To Re-Tire, Knight, 1928 .... 15.00
Time Will Tell, 1935 .... 2.00
Ting A Ling the Bells Ring, Berlin, 1926 .... 10.00
Ting, Ling Toy, Earl, 1919 .... 5.00
Tiny Little Fingerprints, 1935 .... 2.00
Tip Toe Through the Tulips With Me, Dubin/Burke, 1929 .... 5.00
Tip-Top Tipperary Mary, MacDonald, 1914 .... 6.00
Tipperary Guards March, Paull, 1915 .... 35.00
Tippie's Love Song, 1947 .... 2.00
Tis But A Lock Of Hair She Left Me, Christie, 1871 .... 10.00
Titantic, Boland, 1912 .... 15.00
Titina, 1922 .... 2.00
To Be Alone, 1953 .... 2.00
To Be Forgotten, Berlin, 1928 .... 3.00

To Each His Own, DeHavilland/Lund, 1946 .... 10.00
To Have, To Hold, To Love, 1913 .... 2.00
To Know You Is To Love You, 1928 .... 6.00
To Lou, 1915 .... 2.00
To Love and Be Loved, Cahn/Van Heusen, 1958 .... 8.00
To Love In Vain, Gay, 1920 .... 2.00
To the End Of the World With You, Ball, 1908 .... 3.00
To the Land Of My Own Romance, Herbert/Smith, 1912 .... 2.00
To the Nightingale, Fessenden, 1879 .... 10.00
To the Pathway Of Love, 1922 .... 2.00
To Think You've Chosen Me, 1950 .... 2.00
To You Roosevelt, Bamber, 1935 .... 35.00
To You Sweetheart Aloha, Owens, 1936 .... 2.00
To You, 1939 .... 2.00
To-Night Or Never, 1931 .... 3.00
Together We Two, Berlin, 1927 .... 3.00
Together Wherever We Go, 1959 .... 2.00
Tomorrow In My Dixie Home Again, Robinson, 1922 .... 3.00
Tomorrow Is Forever, 1945 .... 3.00
Tonight In Dreamland, Palmer, 1916 .... 2.00
Tonight, 1939 .... 2.00
Too Busy, Miller/Cohn, 1928 .... 2.00
Too Fat Polka, 1947 .... 2.00
Too Late Now, Lerner/Lane, 1951 .... 10.00
Too Late To Worry, Dexter, 1942 .... 2.00
Too Many Kisses, 1924 .... 2.00
Too Many Tears, Dubin/Warren, 1932 .... 3.00
Too Tired, Little, 1924 .... 5.00
Too Young To Go Steady, 1955.. 2.00
Tooboogan Rag, Barth, 1912 .... 10.00
Toodle-Oo, 1937 .... 2.00
Toolie Oolie Doolie, Horton, 1946 .... 2.00
Toot Your Horn, Kid, You're In A Fog, Daly, 1910 .... 14.00
Toot, Toot, Tootsie, 1949 .... 3.00
Tormented, Hudson, 1936 .... 2.00
Totem Tom Tom, 1924 .... 2.00
Tour de Noce, Soria, 1903 .... 15.00
Town That Gave Me You, 1911 .... 3.00
Trail Of the Lonesome Pine, 1913 .... 7.00
Train D'Enfer Galop, Ludovic 24.00
Train In the Night, MacGregor, 1931 .... 6.00
Tramping Along, Seeley/Darewski, 1926 .... 15.00
Trans Continental, Rice, 1902 .... 20.00
Travelling Blues, Russell, 1924 .... 6.00
Treasures Gold Can Never Buy, 1899.. 3.00

Tres Moutarde (Too Much Mustard), 1911 .... 3.00
Tripoli, Weill, 1920 .... 3.00
Tripping the Light Fantastic, 1952 .... 2.00
Trouble, Witmark, 1902 .... 12.00
True Blue Lou, Whiting, 1929 .... 3.00
True Blue Sam, 1922 .... 3.00
True Blue, 1929 .... 2.00
True Confession, Coslow, 1937 .... 3.00
True Love, 1956 .... 6.00
Trumpeter March, Ellis, 1924 .... 2.00
Trust In Me, 1936 .... 2.00
Try To Forget, 1931 .... 2.00
Try To Remember, 1960 .... 2.00
Trying, 1925 .... 2.00
Tubbs, Ernes, 1941 .... 5.00
Tuck In Kentucky And Smile, 1926 .... 2.00
Tulip Time, Buck/Stamper, 1919 .... 3.00
Turkey In the Straw, Bonnell, 1904 .... 15.00
Turkish Love Song, 1910 .... 3.00
Turkish Towel, 1926 .... 2.00
Turn Back the Universe, Ball/Brennan, 1916 .... 3.00
Turn On the Charm, 1945 .... 2.00
Turtle Dove Polka, Behr, 1900 .... 5.00
Twas Not So Long Ago, 1929 .... 2.00
Tweedle Dee, 1954 .... 2.00
Twelfth Street Rag, 1919 .... 5.00
Twelve Days Of Christmas, 1949 .... 2.00
Twenty Four Hours A Day, 1935 .... 5.00
Twenty Four Hours In Georgia, 1934 .... 2.00
Twenty Seventh Division, Mizer, 1919 .... 6.00
Twilight Express, Denison/Hager, 1912 .... 10.00
Twilight On the Trail, Alter, 1936 .... 3.00
Twilight, 1908 .... 5.00
Two Apples, Brooks/Ball, 1909 .... 5.00
Two Blue Eyes, Madden/Morse, 1907 .... 5.00
Two Cigarettes In the Dark, 1934 .... 3.00
Two Darkey Songs, Guion, 1918 .... 3.00
Two Dirty Little Hands, Cobb/Edwards, 1906 .... 6.00
Two Dreams Got Together, 1938 .... 2.00
Two Empty Arms, 1932 .... 2.00
Two Hearts, Stolz, 1930 .... 3.00
Two Little Bluebirds, 1925 .... 2.00
Two Little Love Bees, 1909 .... 5.00
Two Little New Little Blue Little Eyes, Friend/Powell 2.00
Two Little Sailor Boys, Madden, 1906 .... 15.00

Two Little Wooden Shoes, 1922 .... 2.00
Two Silhouettes, 1945 .... 10.00
Two Time Dan, 1923 .... 2.00
Ty-Tee (Tahiti), Bibo, 1921 .... 2.00
Tzigani Dances, Bond, 1897 .... 6.00
Ump-Da-De-Ump-Da-De-Aye, Nathan/Leopols, 1915 .... 2.00
Unchained Melody, 1955 .... 2.00
Uncle Jasper's Jubilee, Paull, 1898 .... 30.00
Uncle Remus Said, Lange, 1946 .... 15.00
Uncle Sam's Ships, Erd, 1917 .... 10.00
Uncle Tom's Cabin Rag, 1911 .... 15.00
Under One Flag, Jefford, 1916 .... 6.00
Under the Bamboo Tree, Cole/Johnson, 1902 .... 5.00
Under the Banana Tree, Lamb/O'Connor, 1905 .... 5.00
Under the Blue Skies Of France, Lamb/Solman, 1918 .... 3.00
Under the Double Eagle, Wagner, 1908 .... 7.00
Under the Hebrew Moon, Madden, 1909 .... 5.00
Under the Honeysuckle Vine, 1952 .... 2.00
Under the Matzos Tree, Fischer, 1907 .... 10.00
Under the Mellow Arabian Moon, Nathan/Leopols, 1915 .... 5.00
Under the Rambling Roses, 1916 .... 3.00
Under the Southern Moonlight, Allen, 1910 .... 3.00
Under the Stars, Dailey, 1913 .... 3.00
Under the Yum Yum Tree, Sterling, 1910 .... 5.00
Under Western Skies, 1920 .... 2.00
Undercurrent, Brahms, 1947 .... 8.00
Underneath the Arches, McCarthy/Flanagan, 1932 .... 2.00
Underneath the Cotton Moon, Lewis/Meyer, 1913 .... 3.00
Underneath the Harlem Moon, Gordon/Revel, 1932 .... 2.00
Underneath the Stars, Spencer, 1915 .... 3.00
Unerneath the Mellow Moon, Hall, 1922 .... 2.00
Unrequited, 1900 .... 3.00
Until Tomorrow, 1924 .... 2.00
Until, Sanderson/Teschemacher, 1910 .... 3.00
Up And At 'Em, Stedman, 1918 .... 3.00
Up And Down the Eight Mile Road, Donaldson, 1926 .... 6.00
Up In A Balloon, Leybourne, 1869 .... 30.00
Up In My Flying Machine, Saxby, 1910 .... 20.00
Up In the Air Boys, Brown/Tilzer, 1919 .... 6.00
Up In the Air, Daggett, 1910 .... 10.00
Up In the Clouds, 1921 .... 3.00
Up In Your Old Biplane, Arnold, 1912 .... 20.00
Up Ship And Away, Waring/Dolph, 1944 .... 7.00
Up Went O'Connor On His Wedding Day, Bodine, 1897 .... 30.00
Upon the Trolley Line, Edwards, 1905 .... 15.00

**Pictured above is a small selection of
Sheet Music Covers that are listed within this book.**

Upstairs And Down, Lewis/Donaldson, 1919 .... 3.00
Used To You, Jolson, 1924 .... 10.00
V. V.'s Eyes, Klein, 1915 .... 7.00
Vagabond King Waltz, 1926 .... 3.00
Vale Of Dreams, Baer, 1910 .... 3.00
Valencia, 1925 .... 2.00
Valentine, 1925 .... 2.00
Valley Rose, Branen/Lloyd, 1917 .... 3.00
Valse Annette, Baxter, 1915 .... 2.00
Valse Rose, 1919 .... 3.00
Valse Septembre, Godin, 1909 .... 3.00
Vanity Fair, Mathews, 1907 .... 3.00
Venetia, Sterling, 1906 .... 3.00
Venetian Waters, Daley, 1910 .... 6.00
Venus Waltz, 1914 .... 2.00
Vermont We Love You, Thurber/Bagnall, 1938 .... 3.00
Victorious 26th Yankee Division, 1918 .... 3.00
Victors, Elbel, 1899 .... 5.00
Victory, King, 1918 .... 13.00
Victory Polka, Styne, 1943 .... 2.00
Virginia Lee, Branen, 1915 .... 5.00
Vive La Bacchanal, Leybourne 2.00
Volga Boatman Song, 1938 .... 5.00
Volplane Waltzes, Burnett, 1917 .... 10.00
Wabash Cannon Ball, 1939 .... 3.00
Wagon Wheels, Hill, 1934 .... 3.00
Wait And See, 1919 .... 3.00
Wait Till the Cows Come Home, 1917 .... 5.00
Wait Till the Sun Shines Nellie, VonTilzer/Sterling, 1905 .... 3.00
Wait Till You Get Them Up In the Air Boys, Brown, 1919 .... 15.00
Wait Until We're Married, meyer, 1913 .... 5.00
Wait, Horowitz/Bowers, 1905 .... 6.00
Waiting At the End Of the Road, Berlin, 1929 .... 5.00
Waiting At the Station, Danks, 1866 .... 30.00
Waiting For Nora's Return, Bratton/Ford, 1894 .... 10.00
Waiting For the Robert E. Lee, 1939 .... 5.00
Waiting For the Sun To Come, Gershwin 3.00
Waiting, Cort/Stoddard, 1918 .... 2.00
Wake Up America, Glouga, 1916 .... 10.00
Wake Up Virginia and Prepare, Seifert, 1917 .... 10.00
Walkin' the Dog, Brooks, 1916 .... 5.00
Walking With Susie, Conrad, 1929 .... 3.00
Wallflower Sweet, Fall/Smith, 1911 .... 3.00
Waltz Me Again, 1894 .... 5.00
Waltz Me Around Again Willie, 1906 .... 15.00

Waltz Me Till I'm Dreamy, Howard, 1907 .... 5.00
Waltz Of the Wind, Rose, 1947 .... 2.00
Wander Off Nowhere, Edwards, 1907 .... 3.00
Wander With Me To Loveland, 1919 .... 6.00
Wandering Home, Case, 1920 .... 3.00
Wang-Wang Blues, 1921 .... 5.00
War Babies, Jolson, 1916 .... 15.00
War In Snider's Grocery Store, 1914 .... 6.00
Warmest Baby In the Bunch, Cohan, 1897 .... 20.00
Was It A Dream?, Coslow, 1928 .... 2.00
Washington & Lee Swing, 1920 .... 5.00
Watch Your Step "Show Us How To Do the Fox Trot", 1914 .... 15.00
Watermelon Breezes, Kyro, 1904 .... 20.00
Way Back In Tennessee, 1911 .... 7.00
Way Down East, Burns, 1900 .... 5.00
Way Down In Arkansas, White, 1915 .... 5.00
Way Down In Iowa, Lewis/Meyer, 1916 .... 3.00
Way Down There, Murphy/Tierney, 1917 .... 3.00
We Belong Together, 1932 .... 2.00
We Don't Know Where We're Going But We're On Our Way, 1917   3.00
We Don't Want the Bacon, 1918 .... 5.00
We Have Much To Be Thankful For, Berlin, 1913 .... 15.00
We Just Couldn't Say Goodbye, Woods, 1932 .... 5.00
We Kiss In A Shadow, 1951 .... 2.00
We Knelt Beside Our Baby's Bed, Clements, 1888 .... 8.00
We Loved Each Other In the Long Ago, Madden/Wenrich 3.00
We Met, We Loved, We Parted, Morris/Phillips, 1915 .... 3.00
We Might As Well Forget It, Bond, 1944 .... 2.00
We Must Be Vigilant, Leslie/Burke, 1942 .... 3.00
We Mustn't Say Goodbye, Dubin, 1943 .... 3.00
We Never Miss the Sunshine Till the Storm Holds Sway 2.00
We The Ex-Service Men, Tuccelli, 1939 .... 13.00
We Saw the Sea, Berlin, 1936 .... 7.00
We Will Always Be Sweethearts, Robin, 1932 .... 3.00
We'll Be There Uncle Sam, We'll Be There, Ryan, 1917 .... 6.00
We'll Be Waiting When You Come Back Home, 1918 .... 5.00
We'll Build A Little World Of Our Own, 1930 .... 3.00
We'll Do Our Share, Egan, 1918 .... 10.00
We'll Go Smiling Along, Davies, 1940 .... 8.00
We'll Have A Jubilee In My Old Kentucky Home, Goetz, 1915 ...... 10.00
We'll Hurry To the Church And Then Be Married, 1902 .... 3.00
We'll Make Hay While the Sun Shines, Freed, 1933 .... 5.00
We're Building A Bridge To Berlin, Gordon/Grady, 1918 .... 10.00
We're Coming Uncle Sam to You, Hathway, 1917 .... 3.00
We're Going Over, Longe, 1917 .... 7.00

We're Going To Hang the Kaiser Under the Linden Tree, 1917 ..... 15.00
We're Growing Old Together, Merrill/Dinsmore, 1908 .... 3.00
We're In Love With the Same Sweet Girl, Mohr, 1916 .... 3.00
We're Mighty Glad To See You, Bugbee/Ball, 1921 .... 3.00
We're the Sunday Drivers, Kenny, 1927 .... 12.00
Wearing Of the Green, Werner 2.00
Weary River, 1929 .... 7.00
Wedding Bells, 1947 .... 2.00
Wedding Of the Sunshine And the Rose, Murphy, 1915 .... 5.00
Wee Wee Marie, Bryan/McCarthy, 1918 .... 5.00
Weeping Willow Lane, Frost, 1919 .... 3.00
Weeping Willow Rag, Fischler, 1911 .... 6.00
Weeping Willow, 1914 .... 3.00
Weeping, Sad And Lonely, Tucker, 1863 .... 25.00
Welcome Jack Home, Downey, 1891 .... 6.00
Welcome the Exile Home, Osborne, 1891 .... 5.00
Welcome To My Dream, 1945 .... 3.00
Were You There, Burleigh, 1924 .... 5.00
West Of the Great Divide, Whiting/Ball, 1924 .... 6.00
West Side Story, 1957 .... 3.00
West Wind, 1929 .... 3.00
Westward Ho, Wenrich, 1909 .... 6.00
Wet Yo' Thumb, Cooper/Akst, 1923 .... 15.00
What A Day, 1944 .... 3.00
What A Little Moonlight Can Do, Woods, 1934 .... 5.00
What A Wonderful Mother You'd Be, 1915 .... 3.00
What Am I Gonna Do About You, 1946 .... 3.00
What Are You Going To Do To Help the Boys?, Kahn, 1918 .... 15.00
What cha Gonna Do When There Ain't No Jazz, 1920 .... 10.00
What D'Ya Say?, DeSylva, 1928 .... 2.00
What D'ye Mean You Lost Yer Dog, Allen/Daly, 1913 .... 6.00
What Did I Do, Gordon, 1947 .... 3.00
What Do I Car, 1959 .... 13.00
What Do I Have To Do, 1948 .... 3.00
What Do The Simple Folk Do, Loewe/Lerner, 1961 .... 8.00
What Do You Do Sunday Mary, 1923 .... 2.00
What Do You Think Of That, Rolfe, 1912 .... 2.00
What Do You Want To Make Those Eyes At Me For, 1916 .... 3.00
What Do You Want With Me, 1914 .... 5.00
What Does It Matter, Berlin, 1927 .... 6.00
What Goes On Here In My Heart, Robin/Rainger, 1938 .... 3.00
What Good Will It Do, 1939 .... 2.00
What Have You Done For Me Lately, David/Livingston, 1952 .... 13.00
What Have You Got That Gets Me, Robin/Rainger, 1928 .... 5.00
What Is Life Without Love, 1929 .... 5.00

What Is This Thing Called Love, 1929 .... 3.00
What Might Have Been, Gumble/Clark, 1908 .... 3.00
What the Brass Band Played, 1904 .... 5.00
What the Yankee Boys Can Do, 1917 .... 3.00
What Will I Do Without You, Dubin/Burke, 1929 .... 5.00
What Will Our Great Congress Do In 1901, 1900 .... 7.00
What Will Your Answer Be, Oettinger, 1905 .... 3.00
What Would You Do?, Robin/Whiting, 1932 .... 3.00
What Would You Take For the Baby, 1914 .... 2.00
What Wouldn't I Do For That Man, 1929 .... 3.00
What You Goin' To Do When the Rent Comes 'Round, 1905 ....25.00
What'll I Do, Berlin, 1924 .... 6.00
What'll We Do On A Saturday Night (When the Town Goes Dry ... 6.00
What's Good About Goodbye, Robin/Arlen, 1948 .... 3.00
What's the Good Of Moonlight, 1915 .... 3.00
What's the Matter With Father, Van Alstyne, 1910 .... 5.00
What's the Reason I'm Not Pleasin' You, 1935 .... 3.00
What's the Use Of Dreaming, 1906 .... 5.00
What's the Use Of Going Home, 1915 .... 2.00
What's the Use Of Living Without Love, 1930 .... 3.00
What's the Use Of Loving, 1912 .... 3.00
What's the Use Of Saving Money, Drislane/Meyer, 1910 .... 3.00
What's the Use Of Trying To Forget the One You Love, 1910 .... 3.00
What's the Use Of Wondering, 1945 .... 2.00
Whatever Lola Wants, 1955 .... 2.00
Whatever Will Be, Will Be, 1955 .... 2.00
When A Black Man's Blue, Little, 1930 .... 6.00
When A Boy From Old New Hampshire Loves A Girl - - - 2.00
When A Boy Says, "Will You" And A Girl Says, "Yes", 1908 .... 5.00
When A Dream Is Broken In Two, 1950 .... 2.00
When A Feller Needs A Friend, 1919 .... 5.00
When A Lady Meets A Gentleman Down South, 1936 .... 2.00
When A Little Bit O'Love Creeps In, Kerr, 1911 .... 3.00
When A Woman Loves A Man, Rose/Rainger, 1930 .... 2.00
When Alexander Takes His Ragtime Band To France, 1918 .... 5.00
When All Your Castles Come Tumbling Down, 1922 .... 2.00
When Angels Weep, Harris, 1914 .... 3.00
When Broadway Was A Pasture, 1911 .... 3.00
When Cupid Calls, 1915 .... 3.00
When Cupid Comes A-Tapping, Barrett, 1916 .... 3.00
When Daddy Greets His Son, Panella, 1919 .... 3.00
When Day Is Done, Katscher, 1926 .... 2.00
When Did You Leaven Heaven?, 1936 .... 3.00
When Dreams Come True, Hein/Webb, 1913 .... 5.00
When Evening Shadows Fall, Branen, 1916 .... 3.00

**Pictured above is a small selection of
Sheet Music Covers that are listed within this book.**

When Everything Seems To Go Wrong, 1913 .... 3.00
When First You Told Me That You Cared, Rainville, 1914 .... 2.00
When God Gave Me You, Leslie, 1913 .... 2.00
When Grandma Sings the Songs She Loved At the End - - - 3.00
When Hearts Are Young, 1922 .... 2.00
When His Good Ship Comes Home, Nolan, 1892 .... 10.00
When Hope Has Faded, Solman, 1898 .... 5.00
When I Come Back To Erin, Tice/Callahan, 1916 .... 3.00
When I Come Back To You, Tracey/Stern, 1918 .... 3.00
When I Come Back, 1914 .... 2.00
When I Do Wrong, Clark, 1907 .... 3.00
When I Dream Of Home And Mother Of You, 1911 .... 2.00
When I Dream Of Old Erin, Lee/Friedman, 1912 .... 3.00
When I Dream Of You, 1911 .... 2.00
When I Fell In Love With You, 1917 .... 2.00
When I First Met You, Wilson, 1914 .... 3.00
When I Found You, 1914 .... 2.00
When I Gave My Heart To You, 1901 .... 3.00
When I Get Back From Over There, Morse, 1918 .... 10.00
When I Get Back To Old Virginia, 1915 .... 2.00
When I Get You Alone Tonight, 1912 .... 2.00
When I Go Automobiling, Mack, 1907 .... 18.00
When I Grow Too Old To Dream, 1935 .... 5.00
When I Heard the Song Birds Singing, "Sweet Marie", 1914 .... 5.00
When I Hesitate With You, Epstein, 1914 .... 2.00
When I Leave the World Behind, Berlin, 1915 .... 16.00
When I Look Back And Think Of You, 1916 .... 3.00
When I Look Into Your Eyes, 1905 .... 6.00
When I Lost You, Berlin, 1914 .... 15.00
When I Marry You, Bryan/Gumble, 1908 .... 3.00
When I Met You Last Night In Dreamland, 1911 .... 3.00
When I See My Sugar, 1929 .... 3.00
When I Think Of You, Horwitz/Bowers, 1900 .... 5.00
When I Waltz With You, Bryan/Gumble, 1912 .... 5.00
When I Was A Dreamer, Van Alstyne, 1914 .... 3.00
When I Went To School With You, 1916 .... 5.00
When I'm Looking At You, 1929 .... 3.00
When I'm Sailing On the Nancy Lee, 1914 .... 2.00
When I'm With You, Gordon, 1936 .... 10.00
When Ireland Comes Into Her Own, Stanley, 1919 .... 5.00
When Irish Eyes Are Smiling, Ball, 1912 .... 6.00
When Isabella Green Went Automobiling, Marshall, 1902 .... 30.00
When It's Apple Blossom Time In Normandy, 1912 .... 5.00
When It's Circus Day Back Home, 1917 .... 25.00
When It's Darkness On the Delta, 1932 .... 2.00

When It's Moonlight In Mayo, Mahoney, 1913 .... 5.00
When It's Moonlight In the Garden Of Love, 1915 .... 5.00
When It's Moonlight On the Rio Grande, Nathan/Smith 2.00
When It's Night Time Down In Burgundy, Bryan, 1914 .... 3.00
When It's Night Time Down In Dixieland, Berlin, 1914 .... 16.00
When It's Prayer Meeting Time In the Hollow, 1933 .... 3.00
When It's Twilight In the Mountains, 1940 .... 2.00
When Joanna Loved Me, Wells, 1963 .... 3.00
When June Comes Along With A Song, 1923 .... 2.00
When Kate And I Were Coming Thro' the Rye, 1902 .... 15.00
When Knighthood Was In Flower, Gustin, 1900 .... 10.00
When Love Is Young, 1906 .... 3.00
When Mother Sang Hush A Bye, 1919 .... 3.00
When Mother Was Sixteen, Deagon, 1904 .... 3.00
When My Baby Smiles At Me, Tilzer/Sterling, 1947 .... 5.00
When My Dreams Come True, Berlin, 1929 .... 5.00
When My Golden Hair Has Turned To Silver Gray, 1904 .... 3.00
When My Pa Was Only A Boy, 1883 .... 12.00
When My Ship Comes In, Kahn/Donaldson, 1934 .... 7.00
When Old Bill Bailey Plays the Ukalele, 1915 .... 5.00
When Our Soldier Boys Come Home, Kahn, 1944 .... 2.00
When Taps are Softly Blowing, Watson, 1918 .... 6.00
When That Midnight Choo Choo Leaves For Alabama, 1912 .... 14.00
When the Apple Blossoms Bloom, 1904 .... 3.00
When the Bees Make Honey Down In Sunny Alabam', 1919 .... 12.00
When the Black Sheep Returns To the Fold, Berlin, 1916 .... 15.00
When the Bluebirds Nest Again Sweet Nellie Gray, 1906 .... 6.00
When the Boys Come Marching Home, Friedman, 1916 .... 5.00
When the Cherry Blossoms Fall, 1919 .... 2.00
When the Cherry Trees Are Blooming In Japan, Harris, 1918 ...... 5.00
When the Coons Are On the Move, 1901 .... 45.00
When the Daisies Bloom, Owen, 1909 .... 3.00
When the Dew Is On the Rose, Owen, 1911 .... 5.00
When the Evening Breeze Is Singing Home Sweet Home, 1905 ... 3.00
When the Grown Up Ladies Act Like Babies, Jolson, 1914 .... 20.00
When the Harvest Time Is Over, Taylor, 1916 .... 5.00
When the Light Is Turned Away Down Low, 1896 .... 6.00
When the Lights Go On Again, Seiler, 1942 .... 2.00
When the Little Red Roses Get the Blues For You, 1930 .... 6.00
When the Major Plays Those Minor Keys, 1916 .... 18.00
When the Maple Leaves Were Falling, 1913 .... 3.00
When the Moon Comes Over Madison Square, 1940 .... 3.00
When the Oceans Meet In Panama, 1914 .... 10.00
When the Old Boat Heads For Home, Fuller, 1918 .... 5.00
When the One You Love, 1945 .... 3.00

When the Organ Played At Twilight, Wallace, 1929 .... 7.00
When the Parson Hands the Wedding Band From Me To - - 3.00
When the Rainbow Shines Bright At Morning, 1912 .... 2.00
When the Real Thing Comes Your Way, Spier, 1929 .... 3.00
When the Rest Of the World Don't Want You, Dubin, 1916 .... 3.00
When the Right Girl Comes Along, 1915 .... 3.00
When the Robert Lee Arrives In Tennessee, 1918 .... 5.00
When the Robins Sing In June, Conrad, 1908 .... 3.00
When the Roses Bloom In Avalon, Bryan/Wells, 1914 .... 5.00
When the Roses Bloom In Loveland, Gover, 1916 .... 3.00
When the Shadows Fall, 1918 .... 2.00
When the Sheep Are In the Fold Jennie Dear, 1907 .... 3.00
When the Sun Goes Down In Dixie, McCarron/Tilzer, 1917 .... 3.00
When the Sun Goes Down In Rainbow Land, 1919 .... 2.00
When the Sun Goes Down In Romany, 1916 .... 3.00
When the Sun Sets On My Old Kentucky Home, 1932 .... 2.00
When the Tide Comes In, Millard, 1873 .... 12.00
When the Time To Say Goodnight Comes, Hopper, 1924 .... 2.00
When the Trains Come East From California, 1920 .... 20.00
When the Twilight Comes To Kiss the Rose Goodnight, 1912 .... 3.00
When The Vesper Bells Ring Out Across the Foam, Rowles, 1908 ... 13.00
When the Winds O'er the Sea Blow A Gale, Hyde, 1902 .... 10.00
When the Work's All Done this Fall, 1935 .... 2.00
When the Yankees Go Into Battle, 1917 .... 10.00
When There's Peace on Earth Again, 1917 .... 10.00
When They Christened Brother Johnson's Child, 1914 .... 15.00
When They Play the River Shannon, Ellsworth, 1912 .... 3.00
When Those Sweet Hawaiian Babies Roll Their Eyes, 1917 .... 3.00
When Tomorrow Comes, 1933 .... 3.00
When Tony Goes Over the Top, 1918 .... 3.00
When Two Hearts Discover, 1919 .... 3.00
When Uncle Joe Plays A Rag On His Old Banjo, 1912 .... 18.00
When Verdi Plays the Hurdy Gurdy, 1916 .... 5.00
When Was There Ever A Night Like This, 1912 .... 3.00
When We Meet In the Sweet Bye And Bye, Murphy, 1918 .... 3.00
When We Waltzed In the Dark, 1931 .... 2.00
When We Welcome Our Boys Back Home, Abell, 1918 .... 10.00
When We Were In Sweetheart Land, 1921 .... 2.00
When We Wind Up the Watch On the Rhine, Thompson, 1917 ..... 3.00
When Yankee Doodle Learns, Parlez Francais, Nelson, 1917 .... 10.00
When You And I Were Young, Maggie, Russell, 1906 .... 7.00
When You Are Mine Again, Willey, 1910 .... 2.00
When You Come Back, Cohan, 1918 .... 12.00
When You First Kiss the Last Girl You Love, 1908 .... 3.00
When You Go Back To That Lonesome Town Of Mine, 1917 .... 15.00

When You Hear the Time Signal, Mercer, 1942 .... 5.00
When You Know You're Not Forgotten, Helf, 1906 .... 3.00
When You Play the Game Of Love, 1913 .... 5.00
When You Sang Hush-A-Bye Baby To Me, Logan, 1918 .... 15.00
When You Smile, 1925 .... 2.00
When You Walked Out Someone Else Walked Right In, 1923 .... 5.00
When You Were Queen Of the May, Baer, 1913 .... 5.00
When You Were the Girl On the Scooter, Gordon/Revel, 1933 ...... 12.00
When You Wish Upon A Star, 1940 .... 14.00
When You Wore A Tulip And I Wore A Big Red Rose, 1914 .... 6.00
When You're All Dressed Up And Have No Place To Go, 1912 .... 5.00
When You're Away, Herbert, 1914 .... 5.00
When You're In Love With Someone Who's Not In Love - - - 3.00
When You're In Town, Berlin, 1911 .... 20.00
When Your Mother's Voice Is Calling, 1914 .... 3.00
When Your Old Gray Bonnet Was New, Murphy, 1913 .... 5.00
When Your Sailor Boy In Blue Comes Sailing Home To You 10.00
Whenever I Think Of You, 1917 .... 2.00
Wher the Mocking Bird Sings In the Orange Grove, 1871 .... 10.00
Where Am I?, Warren/Dubin, 1935 .... 3.00
Where Are You?, 1936 .... 3.00
Where Can You Be, 1930 .... 3.00
Where Did Robinson Crusoe Go With Friday On Saturday- - 12.00
Where Did the Night Go, 1952 .... 2.00
Where Did You Get That Girl, Puck, 1913 .... 8.00
Where Did You Get That Girl, Weber/Beck/Frazer, 1913 .... 3.00
Where Did You Leave My Daddy, Rossi, 1919 .... 2.00
Where Do We Go From Here, Wenrich, 1917 .... 7.00
Where I'll Meet Her Bye And Bye, 1902 .... 5.00
Where Is My Mama, Coleman, 1916 .... 2.00
Where Is My Mamma To Night, Losee, 1907 .... 2.00
Where Is My Wandering Boy Tonight, 1914 .... 15.00
Where Is the Song Of Songs For Me, Berlin, 1928 .... 7.00
Where Oh Where, 1950 .... 2.00
Where Or When, 1937 .... 3.00
Where the Bamboo Babies Grow, Brown, 1922 .... 2.00
Where the Black-Eyed Susans Grow, Jolson, 1917 .... 10.00
Where the Edelweiss Is Blooming, Goetz/Sloane, 1911 .... 3.00
Where the Lanterns Glow, 1919 .... 2.00
Where the Lazy River Goes By, 1936 .... 3.00
Where the Mountains Meet the Sky, Williams, 1942 .... 2.00
Where the Red, Red Roses Grow, 1913 .... 5.00
Where the Rippling Waters Flow, Bowers, 1916 .... 3.00
Where the River Shannon Flows, Russell, 1905 .... 6.00
Where the Silver Colorado Winds It's Way, 1901 .... 5.00

**Pictured above is a small selection of
Sheet Music Covers that are listed within this book.**

Where the Suwanee River Winds It's Silv'ry Way, 1904 .... 6.00
Where the Volga Flows, 1922 .... 2.00
Where There's You There's Me, 1935 .... 3.00
Where Was I, Dubin, 1940 .... 3.00
Where'd You Get Those Eyes, Donaldson, 1926 .... 2.00
Where's Elmer, 1933 .... 2.00
Where's My Sweetie Hiding?, Little, 1924 .... 2.00
Which Hazel?, Norworth/Silver, 1921 .... 2.00
While Hearts Are Singing, Grey/Straus, 1931 .... 3.00
While Strolling In the Park One Day, 1939 .... 2.00
While the Dance Goes On, Harris, 1894 .... 6.00
While You're Away, Gilbert, 1918 .... 3.00
Whisper That You Love Me, 1914 .... 6.00
Whisper Your Mother's Name, 1896 .... 5.00
Whisper Sweet, Trent/Johnson, 1935 .... 15.00
Whisper, Stults, 1904 .... 3.00
Whispering Hope, Hawthorne, 1925 .... 3.00
Whispers In the Dark, Robin, 1937 .... 5.00
Whistle It, Herbert, 1906 .... 8.00
Whistle the Blues Away, Coale, 1921 .... 2.00
Whistle While You Work, 1937 .... 25.00
Whistling In the Dark, 1931 .... 2.00
Whistling Rufus, Mills, 1899 .... 20.00
Whistling School Boy, 1910 .... 5.00
White Christmas, Berlin, 1942 .... 5.00
White Crest March, Losey, 1913 .... 12.00
White Cross On Okinawa, 1945 .... 2.00
White Orchids, Tobias, 1945 .... 2.00
White Rose, Whelpley, 1903 .... 3.00
White Wings, 1884 .... 15.00
Who Are We To Say, 1938 .... 3.00
Who Are You With Tonight?, Williams, 1910 .... 15.00
Who Broke the Lock Off the New House Door, 1932 .... 2.00
Who Can Tell, 1919 .... 3.00
Who Cares What People Say, 1947 .... 3.00
Who Cares, Jolson, 1922 .... 10.00
Who Discovered Dixie, 1919 .... 3.00
Who Do You Know In Heaven, 1949 .... 2.00
Who Do You Love, 1918 .... 3.00
Who Paid the Rent For Mrs. Rip Van Winkle?, Jolson, 1914 .... 12.00
Who Tied the Can To the Old Dog's Tail, 1921 .... 3.00
Who Told You That Lie, 1946 .... 2.00
Who Was That Lady, Cahn, Van Heusen, 1959 .... 8.00
Who Will Be With You When I Go Away, Farrell, 1913 .... 20.00
Who Wouldn't Be Blue, 1928 .... 2.00

Who Wouldn't Be Jealous Of You, 1928 .... 2.00
Who Wouldn't, Kahn/Donaldson, 1926 .... 3.00
Who'd Be Blue, Woods, 1926 .... 2.00
Who's Afraid Of the Big Bad Wolf, 1933 .... 15.00
Who's Little Heart Are You Breaking, Berlin, 1917 .... 15.00
Who's Loony Now?, Selden, 1919 .... 5.00
Who's That Knockin' At My Door, Kahn, 1927 .... 2.00
Who, Harbach, 1925 .... 2.00
Who-oo? You-oo That's Who, Ager, 1927 .... 2.00
Whoop'er, Wood, 1911 .... 3.00
Whose Little Heart Are You Breaking Now, Berlin, 1917 .... 8.00
Why Can't This Night Go On Forever, Newman/Jones 2.00
Why Can't You, Jolson, 1929 .... 6.00
Why Did It Have To Be, 1947 .... 2.00
Why Did You Make Me Care, Solomon/Maguire, 1912 .... 3.00
Why Didn't You Leave Me Years Ago, 1920 .... 2.00
Why Do I Always Remember, 1926 .... 2.00
Why Do I Dream Those Dreams, Dubin/Warren, 1934 .... 3.00
Why Do I Love You, Kern, 1927 .... 5.00
Why Do Summer Roses Fade, Carpenter/Barker 3.00
Why Do They All Take the Night Boat To Albany, 1918 .... 15.00
Why Doesn't Santa Claus Go Next Door, McCree, 1908 .... 3.00
Why Don't We Say We're Sorry, 1947 .... 2.00
Why Don't You Be My Sweet Man, Trent/Donaldson, 1924 .... 15.00
Why Don't You Do Right, 1942 .... 2.00
Why Don't You Haul Off And Love Me, 1949 .... 2.00
Why Don't You Practice What You Preach, Hoffman, 1934 .... 2.00
Why Don't You Smile, 1912 .... 3.00
Why Don't You Try, Williams, 1905 .... 15.00
Why Dream, Robin/Whiting, 1935 .... 3.00
Why Is the Ocean So Near the Shore, 1913 .... 3.00
Why Not Say "Yes" Love, Turney, 1883 .... 5.00
Why Should I Build Castles In the Air, 1919 .... 2.00
Why Stars Come Out At Night, Noble, 1935 .... 6.00
Why Was I Born, Kern, 1929 .... 3.00
Why, Pyper, 1926 .... 2.00
Wigglin' Dance, 1917 .... 3.00
Wild Cherries Rag, Berlin, 1908 .... 20.00
Wild Flower, 1923 .... 2.00
Wild Flowers We Gathered, 1914 .... 2.00
Wild Is the Wind, 1957 .... 3.00
Wild Rose, Kern, 1920 .... 3.00
Will She Come From the East, Berlin, 1922 .... 12.00
Will the Angels Let Me Play, 1905 .... 5.00
Will the Angels Play Their Harps For Me, 1928 .... 3.00

Will the Roses Bloom In Heaven, Harris, 1911 .... 5.00
Will Ya Huh, 1926 .... 2.00
Will You Be Sorry, Kahn, 1928 .... 2.00
Will You Forgive If I Forget, 1909 .... 3.00
Will You Love Me Then As Now, 1914 .... 2.00
Will You Really Promise Me, 1910 .... 2.00
Will You Remember Tonight Tomorrow, 1938 .... 2.00
Will You Remember, 1917 .... 6.00
Will You Take A Little Walk, Fleming, 1909 .... 3.00
William Tell, 1902 .... 3.00
Willie Had A Motor Boat (putt, putt, putt, putt) 1914 .... 15.00
Willow Weep For Me, Ronell, 1932 .... 2.00
Wine Song, 1934 .... 3.00
Wings Of the Morning, 1919 .... 7.00
Wings Over The Navy, Mercer/Warren, 1938 .... 13.00
Winning Ways, Dodd, 1921 .... 2.00
Winter Nights, Clarke, 1914 .... 5.00
Winter Wonderland, 1934 .... 2.00
Winter, Bryan/Gumble, 1910 .... 3.00
Wish You Were Here, 1952 .... 2.00
Wishing And Waiting For Love, 1929 .... 3.00
Wishing Will Make It So, 1939 .... 3.00
Wishing, 1939 .... 3.00
Wishing, Waiting And Longing, 1951 .... 2.00
Witching Hour, Kummer, 1908 .... 3.00
With A Love Like Mine, Barron, 1918 .... 5.00
With A Song In My Heart, 1929 .... 2.00
With All My Heart, Kahn, 1935 .... 2.00
With Every Breath I Take, Robin/Rainger, 1934 .... 3.00
With My Eyes Wide Open I'm Dreaming, Gordon/Revel, 1934 ...... 5.00
With My Guitar And You, 1930 .... 5.00
With My Head In the Clouds, Berlin, 1942 .... 7.00
With Plenty Of Money And You, Warren/Dubin, 1936 .... 3.00
With Tears In My Eyes, 1943 .... 3.00
With the Wind And the Rain In Your Hair, 1930 .... 2.00
With these Hands, 1950 .... 2.00
With You, Berlin, 1929 .... 7.00
With You, Clay/Johnson, 1913 .... 3.00
With You, Dear, Brown/Scott, 1904 .... 5.00
Without A Song, Rose, 1929 .... 15.00
Without A Word Of Warning, Gordon/Revel, 1935 .... 3.00
Without Love, 1930 .... 3.00
Without My Gal, 1930 .... 2.00
Without That Certain Thing, Nesbitt, 1933 .... 2.00
Without You, 1945 .... 3.00

Wives And Lovers, 1963 .... 3.00
Won't You Be My Husband, 1908 .... 3.00
Won't You Be My Sweetheart, Verner, 1893 .... 5.00
Won't You Be My Sweet Man, Trent/Donaldson, 1924 .... 12.00
Won't You Come And Waltz With Me, 1914 .... 2.00
Won't You Let Me Be Your Chum, Skilling, 1916 .... 2.00
Won't You Let Me Take You Home, Doerr, 1912 .... 7.00
Won't You Play A Simple Melody, Berlin, 1914 .... 14.00
Wonder When My Baby's Coming Home, 1942 .... 2.00
Wonder Why, 1951 .... 3.00
Wonderful Copenhagen, Loesser, 1951 .... 3.00
Wonderful Dad, 1923 .... 3.00
Wonderful Pal, Tracey, 1919 .... 2.00
Wondering, 1952 .... 2.00
Woodland Echoes, Wyman, 1908 .... 3.00
Woody Woodpecker, 1948 .... 10.00
Would You Be A Sailor's Wife, Bennett 15.00
Would You Believe Me, 1947 .... 3.00
Would You Care?, Harris, 1905 .... 8.00
Would You Leave Your Happy Home For Me, Sterling, 1906 .... 12.00
Would You Like To Take A Walk, 1930 .... 2.00
Would You Miss Me, 1907 .... 5.00
Would You Rather Be A Colonel With An Eagle On Your- - 2.00
Would You Take Me Back Again, 1913 .... 5.00
Would You, Freed, 1936 .... 7.00
Would You, Sterling, 1920 .... 2.00
Wouldn't It Be Nice, 1945 .... 3.00
Wouldn't It Be Wonderful, Clarke, 1929 .... 3.00
Wreck Of the Titantic, Baltzell, 1912 .... 20.00
Wreck On the Southern Old 97, Whittier, 1924 .... 10.00
Write A Loving Letter To Your Mother, Adams, 1886 .... 10.00
Write Me A Letter From Home, Hays, 1866 .... 12.00
Write To Me Often Darling, 1878 .... 3.00
Wunderbar, Porter, 1948 .... 2.00
Wy-lets, Johnson/Russell, 1927 .... 2.00
Wyoming, 1946 .... 2.00
Yaaka Hula Hickey Dula, Jolson, 1916 .... 10.00
Yacht Club, Barker, 1895 .... 20.00
Yaddie Kaddie Kiddie Kaddie Koo, 1916 .... 6.00
Yale Blues, 1927 .... 2.00
Yam, Berlin, 1943 .... 5.00
Yankee Bird March And 2 Step, Johnson, 1910 .... 15.00
Yankee Dewey, Stevens, 1899 .... 12.00
Yankee Doodle Blues, Gershwin, 1922 .... 6.00
Yankee Doodle Dandy, Cohan, 1932 .... 6.00

Yankee Doodle, Schackburg, 1942 .... 5.00
Yankee Hustler March, Schmitz, 1902 .... 30.00
Ye Barn Dance, Shannon, 1908 .... 5.00
Ye Ho Mt. Lads Ye Ho, Shields, 1911 .... 8.00
Yearning, Carter/Moret, 1918 .... 3.00
Years, Years Ago, Kahn/Friedman, 1911 .... 3.00
Years, Years, Years, Havez/Hirsch, 1908 .... 3.00
Yes Sir! That's My Baby, Kahn/Donaldson, 1920 .... 2.00
Yes, Grattan 3.00
Yes, My Heart, Merrill, 1961 .... 8.00
Yes, My Love, 1904 .... 5.00
Yesterday, Wilhite, 1926 .... 3.00
Yip I Addy I Ay, Cobb/Flynn, 1908 .... 3.00
Yoo Hoo, 1921 .... 3.00
You 'Ad Better Beat It, Banks, 1911 .... 6.00
You Alone, 1906 .... 3.00
You And I, 1941 .... 2.00
You And the Night And the Music, 1934 .... 2.00
You And the Waltz And I, 1942 .... 3.00
You And Your Beautiful Eyes, 1950 .... 3.00
You Are Beautiful, 1958 .... 2.00
You Are Just Like A Rose To Me, Jones, 1913 .... 3.00
You Are Love, 1928 .... 2.00
You Are My Lucky Star, Freed/Brown, 1935............................. 5.00
You Are My Rain Beau, 1922 .... 2.00
You Are My Sunshine, 1940 .... 2.00
You Are the Ideal Of My Dreams, 1910 .... 5.00
You Are the Image Of Mother, 1916.. 3.00
You Are the Rose Of My Heart, Allison/Kendis, 1914 .... 3.00
You Are There, 1967 .... 3.00
You Belong To My Heart, 1943 .... 5.00
You Broke My Heart To Pass the Time Away, 1913 .... 5.00
You Broke the Heart That Loved You, 1915 .... 2.00
You Broke the Only Heart That Ever Loved You, 1946 .... 2.00
You Brought Ireland Right Over To Me, 1917 .... 3.00
You Call It Madness, But I Call It Love, Conrad, 1931 .... 2.00
You Can Always Tell A Yank, Lane/Harburg, 1944 .... 10.00
You Can Have Every Light On Broadway, 1922 .... 2.00
You Can't Afford To Marry If You Can't Afford A Ford 20.00
You Can't Beat American Love, 1910....................................... 5.00
You Can't Brush Me Off, Berlin, 1940 .... 3.00
You Can't Expect Kisses From Me, 1911 .... 3.00
You Can't Get Away From It, 1913 .... 3.00
You Can't Give Your Heart To Somebody Else, 1906 .... 3.00
You Can't Have Everything, Gordon/Revel, 1937 .... 5.00

You Can't Make A Fool Out Of Me, Cunningham, 1923 .... 5.00
You Can't Make Me Stop Loving You, Mills/Leslie, 1910 .... 2.00
You Can't Pull the Wool Over My Eyes, Ager, 1936 .... 2.00
You Can't Run Away From Love, Dubin/Warren, 1937 .... 5.00
You Can't See the Sun When You're Crying, 1946 .... 2.00
You Can't Stop Me From Loving You, Marshall, 1913 .... 6.00
You Can't Take Me Away From Dixie, Rose, 1923 .... 5.00
You Can't Walk Back From An Aeroplate, 1927 .... 25.00
You Cannot Shake That "Shimmie" Here, Wells, 1919 .... 15.00
You Could Make Me Smile Again, 1951 .... 2.00
You Could Hear A Pin Drop, Newman/Pollack, 1943 .... 8.00
You Couldn't Be Cuter, Kern, 1938 .... 3.00
You Dear, Nathan, 1911 .... 2.00
You Did That, West, 1893 .... 5.00
You Did, Gilbert, 1913 .... 3.00
You Didn't Want Me When You Had Me, 1919 .... 2.00
You Do Something To Me, Porter, 1929 .... 3.00
You Do the Darndest Things, 1936 .... 3.00
You Do, Gordon, 1947 .... 5.00
You Don't Have To Know the Language, Burke/Van Heusen 3.00
You Don't Remind Me, 1950 .... 2.00
You Fell Out Of A Star, 1947 .... 2.00
You Flew Over, Harrison/Verges, 1927 .... 6.00
You For Me-Me For You, Meyer, 1922 .... 2.00
You Gave Me Your Heart, Wheeler, 1922 .... 6.00
You Go Your Way, I'll Go Mine, Clay, 1915 .... 3.00
You Gotta Be A Football Hero, 1933 .... 2.00
You Have A Wonderful Way, Donaldson, 1918 .... 2.00
You Have Got Me Guessing, 1911 .... 2.00
You Have Taken My Heart, Mercer, 1933 .... 2.00
You Hit the Spot, Gordon/Revel, 1935 .... 5.00
You Keep Coming Back Like A Song, Berlin, 1943 .... 6.00
You Know What I Mean, Dubin, 1919 .... 3.00
You Leave Me Breathless, Freed/Hollander, 1938 .... 3.00
You Left Me Out In the Rain, 1924 .... 2.00
You Made Me Love You, McCarthy/Monaco, 1913 .... 5.00
You Make Me Feel So Young, Gordon, 1946 .... 3.00
You May Belong To Somebody Else But Your Heart - - - 6.00
You May Bury Me In De Eas, Burleigh, 1917 .... 5.00
You Missed the Boat, 1950 .... 2.00
You Must Have Been A Beautiful Baby, Warren/Mercer, 1938 ..... 5.00
You Mustn't Be Gone Too Long, 1906 .... 3.00
You Need Someone To Love, 1926 .... 2.00
You Never Can Be Sure About the Girls, Brown, 1917 .... 3.00
You Never Can Tell, 1916 .... 3.00

You Never Knew About Me, 1917..5.00
You Never Know, 1938 ....2.00
You Ought To See Her Now, 1919 ....3.00
You Oughta Be In Pictures, 1934 ....3.00
You Promised To Write Me A Letter, Wilson, 1877 ....12.00
You Remind Me Of My Mother, Cohan, 1922 ....5.00
You Remind Me So Much Of My Mother, Dubin, 1915 ....3.00
You Rhyme With Everything That's Beautiful, 1943.....................2.00
You Said Something When You Said Dixie, 1923 ....2.00
You Said Something, Kern, 1916..3.00
You Seem To Be Forgetting Me, 1916 ....3.00
You Should Have Thought Of That Before, 1943 ....2.00
You Sing That Song To Somebody Else, 1927 ....2.00
You Stingy Baby, Tracey, 1917 ....3.00
You Stole My Heart, 1946 ....2.00
You Tell 'em, 1920 ....2.00
You Tell Her I S-t-u-t-t-e-r, Rose/Friend, 1922 ....3.00
You Tell It, Or Jitney-Bus Joy, Hendon, 1915...........................20.00
You Tell Me Your Dream I'll Tell You Mine, 1939.........................2.00
You Till the Judgement Day, Sterling, 1914 ....3.00
You Took All I Had, 1916 ....5.00
You Took the Sweet From Sweetheart, 1919 ....2.00
You Took the Words Right Out Of My Heart, Robin/Rainger 5.00
You Used To, Young/Roellinger 2.00
You Want Lovin', Coslow, 1929 ....2.00
You Were Meant For Me, Freed/Brown, 1929 ....5.00
You Will Remember Vienna, 1930 ....3.00
You Won't Be Satisfied, 1945 ....2.00
You Wouldn't Know the Old Place Now, 1912.............................2.00
You'd Be So Nice To Come Home To, Porter, 1942 ....3.00
You'd Be Surprised, Berlin, 1919 ....10.00
You'd Never Know That Old Town Of Mine, 1915 ....2.00
You'll Always Be the Same Sweet Baby, Brown, 1911 ....3.00
You'll Always Be the Same Sweet Girl, Sterling/Tilzer 5.00
You'll Be Mine In Apple Blossom Time, 1931 ....2.00
You'll Be Sorry, 1939 ....2.00
You'll Be Too Late When You Knock On My Gate, After 'While 5.00
You'll Do the Same Thing Over Again, Bryan/Gumble, 1911 ....3.00
You'll Find Your Answer In My Eyes, 1929 ....3.00
You'll Have To Get Off And Walk, Reed, 1907 ....20.00
You'll Have To Put Him To Sleep With the Marseillaise................5.00
You'll Miss Me Someday, Howard, 1916 ....3.00
You'll Never Get UpTo Heaven That Way, Lerner, 1933 ....2.00
You'll Never Go To Heaven, Bryan, 1937.................................2.00
You'll Never Know, Faye/Payne, 1943 ....10.00

You'll Never Know, Gordon/Warren, 1943 .... 3.00
You'll Never Know, Harris, 1891 .... 5.00
You'll Never Walk Alone, 1945 .... 2.00
You're A Beautiful Brown Eyed Burglar, Whiting, 1914 .... 3.00
You're A Dangerous Girl, Jolson, 1916 .... 15.00
You're A Grand Old Flag, Cohan, 1906 .... 20.00
You're A Great Big Blue-Eyed Baby, Brown, 1913 .... 5.00
You're A Great Big Lonesome Baby, Kahn, 1917 .... 3.00
You're A Heavenly Thing, Young, 1935 .... 2.00
You're A Naughty Baby, Vincent, 1917 .... 3.00
You're A Real Sweetheart, Friend, 1928 .... 2.00
You're A Sweet Little Headache, Robin/Rainger, 1938 .... 3.00
You're A Sweetheart, 1937 .... 3.00
You're Absolutely Wonderful, McCarthy, 1918 .... 3.00
You're All I Need, Kahn, 1935 .... 3.00
You're All the World To Me, Lamb/Jones 2.00
You're An Old Smoothie, 1932 .... 3.00
You're As Dear To Me As "Dixie" Was To Lee, 1917 .... 5.00
You're Breaking Mother's Heart, Dresser, 1890 .... 3.00
You're Driving Me Crazy, Donaldson, 1930 .... 2.00
You're Easy To Dance With, Berlin, 1942 .... 15.00
You're Getting To Be Habit With Me, Dubin/Warren, 1932 .... 5.00
You're Here, And I'm Here, Kern, 1914 .... 3.00
You're In My Arms, Carr/Popplewell, 1941 .... 8.00
You're In Style When You're Wearing A Smile, Brown, 1918 .... 3.00
You're Irish And You're Beautiful, Tobias, 1943 .... 2.00
You're Just A Flower From An Old Bouquet, 1924 .... 5.00
You're Just Homesick That's All, 1915 .... 3.00
You're Just In Love, Berlin, 1950 .... 3.00
You're Just Like A Rose, 1920 .... 2.00
You're Laughing At Me, Berlin, 1937 .... 10.00
You're Lonely, I'm Lonely, Berlin, 1940 .... 5.00
You're Making A Miser Of Me, Dubin/Ball, 1919 .... 5.00
You're More Than the World To Me, Branen/Solman 3.00
You're My Baby, Brown/Ayer, 1912 .... 5.00
You're My Past, Present And Future, Gordon/Revel, 1933 .... 5.00
You're Nobody Til Somebody Loves You, 1944 .... 3.00
You're Simply Delish, Freed/Meyer, 1930 .... 5.00
You're So Understanding, Raleigh/Wayne 2.00
You're Such A Comfort To Me, Gordon/Revel, 1933 .... 5.00
You're the Best Little Mother Of All, Friedman, 1914 .... 5.00
You're the Cream In My Coffee, 1928 .... 5.00
You're the Dawn Of A Wonderful Day, Williams, 1915 .... 3.00
You're the Girl I've Been Longing For, Shannon, 1913 .... 3.00
You're the Haven Of My Heart, O'Conner/Morse, 1913 .... 3.00

You're the Most Wonderful Girl, Abrams, 1913 .... 5.00
You're the Nicest Little Girl I Ever Knew, Coleman, 1916 .... 3.00
You're the Only Star, Autry, 1938 .... 5.00
You're the Rainbow, Robin/Rainger, 1943 .... 3.00
You're the Top, Porter, 1934 .... 3.00
You're Too Dangerous Cherie, 1947 .... 3.00
You've Got Everything, Donaldson, 1934 .... 2.00
You've Got Me Crying Again, Jones, 1933 .... 2.00
You've Got Me In the Palm Of Your Hands, 1932 .... 2.00
You've Got Me This Way, Mercer, 1940 .... 3.00
You've Got Something There, Whiting/Mercer, 1937 .... 3.00
You've Got To Go In Or Go Under, 1918 .... 3.00
You've Got To See Mamma Every Night, Rose, 1923 .... 5.00
You've Got What It Takes, 1937 .... 2.00
You've Got Your Mother's Big Blue Eyes, Berlin, 1913 .... 15.00
You, Adamson/Donaldson, 1936 .... 5.00
You, None But You, Armstrong, 1899 .... 3.00
You, Robyn, 1891 .... 7.00
Young And Foolish, 1954 .... 2.00
Young And Healthy, Dubin/Warren, 1932 .... 5.00
Younger Than Springtime, 1949 .... 2.00
Your Cheatin' Heart, Williams, 1952 .... 3.00
Your Daddy Did the Same Thing 50 Years Ago, 1912 .... 10.00
Your Eyes, 1928 .... 2.00
Your Flag And My Flag, Ryder, 1916 .... 5.00
Your Head On My Shoulder, 1934 .... 3.00
Your Heart, 1911 .... 3.00
Your Lips Are No Man's Land But Mine, 1918 .... 5.00
Your Love Is My Love, 1956 .... 15.00
Your Mother And Mine, Goodwin/Edwards, 1929 .... 5.00
Your Mother Is Your Best Friend After All, Coleman, 1916 .... 3.00
Your Picture Says Remember, Henry/Lamb, 1908 .... 3.00
Your Picture, Cow, 1944 .... 2.00
Your Prayer And Mine, Jones, 1918 .... 3.00
Yours And Mine, Freed/Brown, 1937 .... 6.00
Yours is Not the Only Aching Heart, Whitson/Quigley, 1907 .... 8.00
Ypsilanti, Bryan, 1915 .... 3.00
Yvonne, Cherubini, 1921 .... 5.00
Zigeuner, 1929 .... 2.00
Zin! Went the Strings Of My Heart, 1935 .... 5.00
Zing A Little Zong, Robin/Warren, 1952 .... 5.00
Zion, Hugh, 1906 .... 2.00
Zip-A-Dee-Doo-Dah, 1946 .... 15.00